P9-CAB-737

To the memory of Herb Score,
the voice of the Tribe for so many of us.
To my jail ministry teammates:
Gloria Williams, Mark Matthews,
Frank Williams, Steve Haley
and Roberta Pluto.
—Terry Pluto

To my family: Wendy, Nick, Kelsey, Bradley and Katie.
Thanks for letting me live out my dream of
broadcasting Major League Baseball.
To the memory of Herb Score and Mike Hegan.
They were incredible broadcast partners and teachers.
And to the Cleveland Indians organization
and fans of the Indians everywhere:
You have never made this feel like a job.
I'm the lucky one.
—Tom Hamilton

Also by Terry Pluto

On Sports:

Joe Tait: It's Been a Real Ball (with Joe Tait)
Things I've Learned from Watching the Browns
LeBron James: The Making of an MVP (with Brian Windhorst)
The Franchise (with Brian Windhorst)
Dealing: The Cleveland Indians' New Ballgame
False Start: How the New Browns Were Set Up to Fail
The View from Pluto
Unguarded (with Lenny Wilkens)
Our Tribe
Browns Town 1964
Burying the Curse
The Curse of Rocky Colavito
Falling from Grace
Tall Tales
Loose Balls
Bull Session (with Johnny Kerr)
Tark (with Jerry Tarkanian)
Forty-Eight Minutes, a Night in the Life of the NBA (with Bob Ryan)
Sixty-One (with Tony Kubek)
You Could Argue But You'd Be Wrong (with Pete Franklin)
Weaver on Strategy (with Earl Weaver)
The Earl of Baltimore
Super Joe (with Joe Charboneau and Burt Graeff)
The Greatest Summer

On Faith and Other Topics:

Faith and You
Everyday Faith
Champions for Life: The Power of a Father's Blessing (with Bill Glass)
Crime: Our Second Vietnam (with Bill Glass)

GLORY DAYS IN Tribe Town

TERRY PLUTO · TOM HAMILTON

GLORY DAYS IN Tribe Town

THE CLEVELAND INDIANS AND JACOBS FIELD, 1994–1997

GRAY & COMPANY, PUBLISHERS
CLEVELAND

© 2014 Terry Pluto and Tom Hamilton

All rights reserved. No part of this book may be reproduced or transmitted in any form or by any means, electronic or mechanical, including photocopying, recording, or by any information storage or retrieval system, without written permission of the publisher.

Gray & Company, Publishers
www.grayco.com

ISBN: 978-1-938441-35-6
Printed in the United States
2

Contents

About this Book

When I approached Tom Hamilton with the idea for a book about the Tribe in the 1990s, it was because his voice was the soundtrack of those baseball glory years for many of us.

Tom insisted that his voice be only one of many in the book, and that is the case. This is not a book about him, it's about the team and the fans. But so often, Tom told stories that set up chapter after chapter.

Tom also quickly mentioned that Herb Score was the lead broadcaster, and how much he appreciated Herb's kindness. He said the same thing that Joe Tait and Nev Chandler had told me: you learned so much baseball sitting next to Herb each night in the radio booth.

The book also is a combination of recent interviews and interviews done many years ago.

For example, the chapters on Eddie Murray and Dennis Martinez were easy for me to write because I first covered them in 1979 when I was an Orioles beat writer for the old Baltimore Evening Sun. I had notes of interviews with them (and men such as Orioles Manager Earl Weaver) dating back decades, and that helped add color to their stories.

Over the years, I wrote in-depth stories about different trades. John Hart loved to tell his war stories about the baseball winter meetings, and many of those are recounted in this book. I covered the Tribe dating back to when I was a Tribe beat writer for The Plain Dealer (1980–84), and later as a columnist with The Plain Dealer and Akron Beacon Journal. When the book says, "In an interview done in 1995 . . ." that interview was with me—unless otherwise noted.

Dick Jacobs died in 2009. I interviewed the former Tribe owner several times, and parts of those interviews are in this book. Some other interviews are with people who have since died. The first person that Patrick O'Neill called after selling the team to Jacobs was me, because we both had a connection with Benedictine High School. That newspaper story helped give an inside account of how Jacobs approached buying the team.

This book ends after the 1997 season. The Indians were contenders for four more years, but never again came close to reaching the World Series.

I recall former General Manager John Hart telling me that the build-up to the new ballpark and the early years at Jacobs Field were the most fun. After 1997, the Indians found themselves selling much of their future to try to reach the World Series one more time.

There were still great teams and great players after 1997. It's a shame that Travis Fryman and Robbie Alomar never played in a World Series with the Tribe. They missed it by one year or two. But the teams that most Tribe fans love are those from the early 1990s through 1997.

This book is not meant as a year-by-year history of that era.

It's more like an impressionistic painting. It's what happens when fans sit around and start talking about the Tribe from the 1990s. They talk about special moments. They talk about favorite players. They talk about the new ballpark.

They talk about how it *felt* to be a Tribe fan in those years.

That's what this book is about—the time, the people and the feeling.

There are many inside stories about how the team came together, trades that were made and the men behind the team that was on the field.

But most of all, this is a book about a time when Cleveland really was a Tribe Town, and the people who made that happen.

—Terry Pluto

GLORY DAYS IN Tribe Town

When Cleveland Really Was a Tribe Town

It's been a while, almost 20 years, since Cleveland was a baseball town.

Close your eyes and think back to the middle 1990s. Those weren't baseball seasons, they were year-long celebrations. It was the end of baseball's darkest decades in Cleveland. It was Jacobs Field packed with fans wearing Wahoo red, white and blue. It was horns blaring from the cars on East 9th Street and Ontario Avenue. It was a late-night symphony of toots after yet another Indians victory.

It was Tom Hamilton screaming one word that said so much—BALLGAME!

The Tribe radio voice uttered that word on the final out of every Tribe victory.

BALLGAME!

"I'd never seen anything like it," said Orel Hershiser, who had an outstanding career pitching for the Dodgers before signing with the Indians prior to the 1995 season.

"You'd walk on to the field for batting practice and so many fans were already there—hours before the game," he said. "Then they'd watch our laser show from our hitters in B.P. Oh my Lord, what a lineup! We had Paul Sorrento batting eighth, and he hit 25 homers that year. There was an energy in the park from the fans as they watched our hitters taking B.P."

There's more.

"After B.P., we'd go into the locker room," said Hershiser. "Maybe guys would work out in the weight room. Or maybe relax a bit. Then we'd come out for the game . . . walking down the tunnel to the dugout . . . and there it was . . . *sellout!*"

Yes, it was a sellout every night.

"Remember that energy I talked about during batting practice," said Hershiser. "Now, it had turned to bedlam. You could feel that something special was going to happen."

The Tribe played only 144 games that season (because of labor problems), and they won 100 games.

Final record: 100-44.

And the Tribe won 27 of those in their final at-bat—18 at Jacobs Field.

You didn't want to leave early, because with this team the game really never was over until the last out.

"It was a show every day," recalled Omar Vizquel.

Think about the names, the lineup:

- Kenny Lofton, CF.
- Omar Vizquel, SS.
- Carlos Baerga, 2B.
- Albert Belle, LF.
- Eddie Murray, DH.
- Jim Thome, 3B.
- Manny Ramirez, RF.
- Sandy Alomar, C.
- Paul Sorrento, 1B.

Over and over, Hamilton would bellow . . . "There's a drive . . . deep left . . . A-WAY BACK . . . GONE! It's halfway up the bleachers!"

Then Hamilton would pause before yelling the name of the home run hero: "Manny Ramirez, on a 2-2 pitch off Dennis Eckersley, has won it!"

That was the game when Eckersley walked off the mound and said *"Wow!"* as he saw where that ball landed.

Wow was the perfect word for that Tribe team.

Wow was a leadoff hitter such as Kenny Lofton, who won a Gold Glove in center, won a stolen-base title, batted .310 and played the game with utter disdain for opposing pitchers. He didn't think any of them should get him out.

Wow was Vizquel being a maestro at shortstop, sometimes making better plays with his bare hand on ground balls than many infielders did with their gloves.

Wow was Baerga hitting above .310 for his fourth consecutive season.

Wow was Belle . . . 50 homers . . . 50 doubles . . . the first and only player ever to do that in the same season.

Wow was Murray, batting .323 and collecting his 3,000th big-league hit that season.

Wow was Thome just learning that he was "country strong," as batting coach Charlie Manuel called him. Some of his homers were so high that they appeared on the radar screen at Cleveland Hopkins Airport—or at least, it seemed so.

Wow was Alomar being the team leader and anchor behind the plate.

Wow was Sorrento, a journeyman first baseman who Hamilton believes was "the unsung hero" of that team.

"Other teams hated the way we played," said Vizquel. "On home runs, some of our guys would just flip their bats up in the air. Other teams thought we were showing them up. They hated us."

And Vizquel loved it.

So did the rest of the Tribe.

"One of my favorite pictures was in the playoff game against Boston when Albert hit that homer [in Game 1] and Boston asked to check his bat [for cork]," said Hamilton. "Albert stood up in the dugout, made a muscle with his arm and pointed to his bicep. He just glared at them."

It was as if Belle was telling the world: *Take that!*

"Holy smoke, our lineup was like Murderer's Row back then," said Hershiser.

Several players remember Baerga in the dugout before a game screaming "WE'RE GOING TO KILL YOU!" at Roger Clemens as he warmed up to start a playoff game for Boston against the Tribe.

"I did yell that," said Baerga. "Clemens looked at us like 'Wow . . . those young guys are crazy!' We were living the dream. We were so cocky, but we also were so good. And we beat Clemens that day."

Baerga paused for a moment, thinking back to when he was young, when the Indians were headed to the World Series for the first time in 41 years.

"It didn't matter who pitched," he said. "It didn't matter how many runs we were down, or what was the inning. We were sure we were coming back to beat you."

"You should have seen Carlos," said Lofton. "He'd swing at everything. The pitch wouldn't even be close to the plate. He didn't care. See it, swing at it—that was Carlos."

In 1994–95, Baerga walked only 45 times in 999 official at-bats. That didn't make him the ideal "Moneyball" player, where the accent is on reaching base and drawing walks, but Baerga was money on this team as he batted .361 with runners in scoring position.

"Our swagger wasn't intentional," said Lofton. "It was just us being us. People used to nit-pick about how we dressed or how we played—that's because they couldn't beat us on the field."

The Indians won the Central Division by 30 games. At the time, that was the largest margin for a division or league champion since 1901.

"That team was never satisfied," said Hamilton. "They wanted to win every game."

And in some games, it was as if they wanted to bludgeon the other team.

"A lot of teams would play us and they'd think, 'We better be ready to rock because we know those guys are going to score a lot of runs,' " said Vizquel. "They knew we'd wear out their pitchers. You could feel it. We intimidated people."

"Omar was never afraid," said Baerga. "Never afraid to steal a base. Never afraid to field a ball with his bare hand. Never afraid to be Omar."

That Tribe team led the league in everything from batting average to runs scored to home runs to stolen bases. Forgotten because of the bombing bats was that the 1995 Indians also had the best earned-run average (3.83) in the American League. Next came Baltimore (4.31), so the Tribe's pitchers were far superior to the rest in this era of shattered home-run records.

"What a fascinating mix of personalities on that team," said Mark Shapiro, who was the Tribe's minor-league director in 1995. "We had Omar and Carlos, where everything was fun. There were eccentrics like Albert and Manny. We had some humble guys like Jim Thome and Charlie Nagy. We had some great veterans like Eddie Murray and Orel Hershiser. The common link was how they came together to dominate other teams."

Shapiro paused.

"When I think of a baseball team dominating, I think of that 1995 team," he said. "We had guys driven to be great that year."

There was a game when the Indians were behind 8-0 to Toronto, and came back to win on a Paul Sorrento home run.

There was a game when Belle belted a 420-foot homer into the center-field picnic area. It turned a 5-3 loss into a walk-off 7-5 victory. Yes, it was the ultimate grand slam—the kind that ends a game and sends fans almost floating to their cars.

There were so many great games.

"The fans first came to see the new stadium," said Charles Nagy. "Then they came to see us. Sellouts night in, night out."

Nagy remembers talking to pitchers on the other teams, and "how they were glad when they missed us in the rotation. For a few years, no one wanted to play us—especially at home. The crowd would get going. Kenny would play center field and steal bases like a maniac. Carlos hit every pitch they threw up there. Jimmy [Thome] and Albert, they crushed the ball."

But Vizquel was the heartbeat.

"Omar taught the city how to be cool," said Hershiser, laughing at the memory. "Off the field, he's an artist. On the field, he was an artist with how he played shortstop. Omar drove a yellow Porsche. We used to joke about how only Omar could really interpret what Manny Ramirez was saying, and how Manny was the one who could understand what Julian Tavarez was talking about. The thing about Omar was how he got along with everyone. He cut across every racial and class line. He was 'cool,' but the conservatives loved him. The senior citizens loved him. Everyone loved Omar."

And everyone in Northeast Ohio loved just about everyone in a Tribe uniform in the middle 1990s.

"It was magic," said Lofton.

Hershiser still remembers the feeling of driving to the ballpark.

"The city was going through such a turnaround," he said. "They were restoring buildings, putting up new buildings . . . and in the middle of it was Jacobs Field. There was such a community feel, so much pride in what was happening to the city and the team. People had Wahoo signs in their front yards. There were posters of the players in about every restaurant. It was like being in a college town, and you were the star quarterback. Not just me—but all the players felt like that."

Then Hershiser remembered what it was like to walk into the ballpark.

"I'd park my car and head into the tunnel," he said. "The security guard wanted a high five. So did the lady by the elevator. I'd see the concessions people checking in for the jobs, and we'd high-five and talk about the game the night before. The ballplayers were the privileged few, and the rest of these people were working so hard just to make a living. It was like we came from two separate societies, but that 1995 season turned us into one big community."

Hershiser says the best team that he ever played for was the 1995 Cleveland Indians.

"And the three best baseball years of my life . . . I mean three in a row . . . was being with the Indians from 1995 to 1997," said Hershiser. "I had great years with the Dodgers. I love the Dodgers. I'm now one of their broadcasters. I loved pitching for them. My favorite year was 1988 with the Dodgers [when he won the Cy Young Award and the World Series]. But I never had three years in a row like those with Cleveland. When I'm in town, people recognize me and thank me. I thank them for how they treated all of us back then."

On the night the Indians clinched the Central Division title, Mike Hargrove thought about meeting a fan in 1992.

"He was a young father," said Hargrove. "We were on the team's winter caravan, making a stop somewhere. The man said he had been a Tribe fan forever, that his father had taken him to games—and he'd never forgotten those games with his dad. He had a boy with him and said it was his son, who was 5 years old."

Then the man told Hargrove, "I want to be able to take my son to games and watch the Indians when they are really good, so that he will become a lifelong fan like me. I want him to cherish the moments at games with me like I do the games that I went to with my dad."

It was three years later, and Hargrove said, "As Jimmy [Thome] caught that ball for the last out to give us the title, I thought about that man and his son as I ran on to the field. I hoped that man and his son were at the game."

The Indians beat Baltimore 3-2 on that night of September 8, 1995.

Two nights before, Baltimore's Cal Ripken broke Lou Gehrig's consecutive game streak of 2,130. Two months earlier, Eddie Murray recorded his 3,000th career hit. The two former Baltimore teammates talked on the field before the Sept. 8 game. Fans watched two future first-ballot Hall of Famers. Then Murray knocked in two runs during the game.

The game was saved by Jose Mesa—SEÑOR SLAM! screamed the scoreboard as he took the mound. Mesa was 46-of-48 in save conversions that season. He had more saves than any other big-league team in 1995. He had more saves than any Tribe pitcher in any season—ever. He had a ridiculous 1.13 ERA.

That final out was a pop up caught by Thome at third base. The sellout crowd stomped and screamed and clapped and . . . yes, many of them also wept. The scoreboard blinked one huge word . . . CLINCH!

The players returned to the field wearing caps and shirts proclaiming A.L. CENTRAL CHAMPS. They assembled in center field to help raise a championship banner. Remember, this team had not won anything since 1954—41 years before.

As the banner went up, the sound system played "The Dance" by Garth Brooks. It was the favorite song of Steve Olin, the Tribe reliever who died in a boating accident in the spring of 1993.

Sandy Alomar helped raise the banner with tears dripping down his face. Fireworks painted the sky red, white and blue. Fans wanted to stay and party all night.

Hargrove seemed stunned to actually be a part of this, having played on so many bad Tribe teams from 1979 to 1985, then worked his way up through the farm system as a manager to take over the team in the middle of the 1991 season.

"I kept thinking about 40 years," he said. "Forty years of frustration for the fans. Forty years and now this . . . something fans would always remember."

The team sold shirts reading: "September 8, 1995 . . . I was here to see THE CLINCH."

They printed about 20,000 and fans quickly paid $28 each. Just like game tickets, the shirts were a quick sellout. The Indians sold about $120,000 in merchandise that night. Bruce Springsteen's "Glory Days" later blared over the sound system.

Kenny Lofton addressed the crowd with a hand-held microphone and proclaimed: "THANK YOU CLEVELAND, YOU AIN'T SEEN NOTHIN' YET!"

Nearly 20 years later, Lofton said, "I had played in the old Stadium. I had a sense of history, and what that night meant to the fans. It had real meaning to me, too."

Baerga was like one of the Tribe fans when he saw the team bring in veterans such as Dennis Martinez, Eddie Murray and Hershiser.

"And Omar, too," said Baerga. "We got those players and I started thinking we could beat anyone . . . the Yankees, Boston, the White Sox . . . we could beat them all."

That was one of the messages that Hargrove delivered in his first meeting of spring training in 1995.

"I felt a real sense of purpose from the moment they arrived in Winter Haven," said Hargrove. "Every year, a manager gives that first speech with the lay of the land . . . you know, the house-keeping things about how we'd handle spring training."

But then Hargrove began to speak directly from his heart. He talked about "the chance to make history." He talked about how long it had been since the Indians had won anything, all the way back to 1954. He talked about "writing our own chapter" by getting to the playoffs.

"I looked around the room and while the players always listen to that first talk, this time, they were really listening," said Hargrove. "They knew this was their chance to do something very special, very meaningful—something that would always be remembered."

WHERE IT CAME FROM

In the Booth With Herb

Two weeks after Tom Hamilton was hired to do the Tribe radio broadcasts, he met Herb Score.

It was late January. Hamilton was still working at his Columbus radio station. The Tribe was on its winter media tour. Hamilton went to Mansfield, where he introduced himself to Score.

Score had been through several partners before Hamilton:

1. Bob Neal (1968–72).
2. Joe Tait (1973–79).
3. Nev Chandler (1980–84).
4. Steve Lamar (1985–87).
5. Paul Olden (1988–89).

It's hard to know exactly what Score thought about Hamilton's hiring, other than that he wasn't consulted. He never was consulted. The radio station hired a broadcaster, and the team approved it. Score didn't seem to worry much about who'd be sitting next to him. His view was, "You do your job and I'll do mine."

During their first meeting, Score was friendly, but didn't have any interest when Hamilton suggested they do a trial run together before spring training.

Score simply said, "I don't think that's going to happen."

Hamilton said that was OK, whatever Score thought was best.

He told Hamilton three things:

1. "Never ask about my family on the air. I don't talk about my family."

2. "Never say, 'Isn't that right, Herb?' That's because I may not agree

with you and I don't want to say something on the air and embarrass you by saying that I didn't think that was the case."

3. "Have fun with the games."

Hamilton found Score to be gracious. "He really was telling me things to help me."

At this point, Score could have said, "Hey, I'm the senior broadcaster. You've never done a big-league game. Here's what we do, so keep quiet and listen."

But Score never treated any of his partners like that. Nor did he have any significant personality conflicts with the men working next to him.

In early March, Hamilton arrived in Tucson for the Tribe's spring training.

"This was going to be my first game, we were playing the Giants in Scottsdale," said Hamilton. "I really didn't know Herb. He invited me to ride up to the game with him, and I thought that the two-hour drive would be a good chance for us to get to know each other."

The moment Score pulled out of the parking lot, Hamilton started talking.

And talking.

And talking.

Score didn't say much. He did have his Frank Sinatra tape playing.

But Hamilton talked and talked and talked some more.

"I'm Chatty Cathy and about halfway there, I bet Herb wanted to throw me in the trunk," said Hamilton. "I was just so nervous . . ."

He wanted Score to like him.

He wanted Score to give him advice.

He wanted to talk because this was his first game and part of him feared that if he messed up, he'd never survive spring training. Score wasn't thrilled with the babble, but kept his mouth shut. He seemed far more tuned into Sinatra than his new partner.

When they finally arrived at Scottsdale for the game, Giants broadcaster Hank Greenwald came up to Hamilton and introduced himself. As he talked to Hamilton, he said: "Welcome to the big leagues, I know you're going to do a great job."

Greenwald was, in Hamilton's words, "a legendary Giants broadcaster. I couldn't even believe he knew my name."

Hamilton doesn't remember much about the actual broadcast, other than being a bit jittery at times.

In Columbus, Wendy Hamilton and their son Nicholas were driving around town, trying to listen to the game on the car radio.

"This was long before the internet," said Hamilton. "It was on WWWE [now WTAM] and the signal kept fading in and out."

The game ended, and Hamilton remembers it "being about 95 degrees. I'm from Wisconsin, and I'm really hot. I'm thinking how I'd love to have a beer, but I wasn't going to say anything to Herb. But I was thinking how good a beer would taste before getting back in that car with Herb before two more hours of Frank Sinatra. But I don't really know Herb. I don't know if he even drinks beer."

As they were leaving the park, Score said, "You know what? You did a good job today. How about you take the stuff back to the car and I get us some beer? Then we'll just sit here by the picnic table, we'll each have a beer. Then we'll get back into the car and drive to Tucson."

Hamilton was in awe of how Score seemed to read his mind and said exactly what a rookie broadcaster needed to hear at that point.

Hamilton went to the car and waited for Score. He came back empty-handed from the store nearby.

"Herb, were they out of beer?" asked Hamilton.

"Yep, all they had was Miller Lite," said Score.

As Hamilton recalled years later, "To Herb, Miller Lite wasn't beer . . . and I love Miller Lite. But if Herb can't have a Heineken, he doesn't want a beer."

They climbed back into the car. Herb plugged in the Sinatra tape. Hamilton sort of leaned back and kept quiet.

"I figured out that Herb just didn't like to talk much," he said. "It wasn't personal. It was just Herb. He was happy to have me there with him as Sinatra sang."

Hamilton laughed and said, "I think if I had started talking again on the way back, he would have duct-taped my mouth shut for the next trip."

As they returned to Tucson, Hamilton felt a tremendous sense of gratitude toward his new partner, because Score treated him as a partner.

"He treated me as an equal when there was no reason to do so," said Hamilton. "I wasn't his equal. He had pitched in the big leagues. At that point, he had been broadcasting for a long time [four years on television, followed by 22 on the radio]. He knew everyone in baseball, and they all knew him. But he worked hard at making me feel relaxed."

During those long spring drives in Arizona, Hamilton developed a love/hate relationship with Frank Sinatra music.

"That was about all Herb would listen to," he said. "Frank Sinatra, Frank Sinatra. By the end of all those spring drives, I knew those songs better than Sinatra."

Then Hamilton laughed.

By the middle of that 1990 spring training, Score did give Hamilton a lesson in reality.

The Indians also had a rookie public relations director, John Maroon. He joined Hamilton and Score (and Sinatra) for those long rides from Tucson to the Phoenix area for preseason games.

"John and I were very excited about the season, thinking this was going to be the year the Indians made the playoffs," said Hamilton.

The 1989 Indians were 73-89. The franchise had not played a post-season game since being swept in the 1954 World Series. The Tribe had not been true contenders since 1959.

Remember, this was 1990 . . . decades since the last team really worth talking about, a team that had a pitcher named Herb Score.

The 1990 Tribe's opening day lineup was this:

- Mitch Webster CF
- Jerry Browne 2B
- Candy Maldonado LF
- Cory Snyder RF
- Keith Hernandez 1B
- Chris James DH
- Brook Jacoby 3B
- Sandy Alomar C
- Rafael Santana SS
- Bud Black P

"Herb was listening to these two idiots [Hamilton and Maroon] going on and on, and finally, he couldn't take it anymore," said Hamilton.

"We stink," Score said. "This is NOT a good team. There is no way we're going to be a contender or in the playoffs. We're terrible."

Joe Tait often said, "No one has seen more bad baseball than Herb Score."

The point being that Score knew a bad team when he saw one.

Score then realized that he had to make a point to Hamilton.

Slowly, he said this: "But it doesn't matter. You treat every game like it's a playoff game because someone is listening to that game. They looked forward all day to that game. It may be the highlight of their day. You owe them your best effort, no matter the record. Because when the game starts, our record doesn't mean anything. The record or strength of the team can never impact your broadcast."

Hamilton said it was perhaps the best bit of advice that he ever received in broadcasting.

"All those years of doing horrific baseball, yet it never changed his broadcast," said Hamilton.

During that first season, Score had other advice for Hamilton.

One day, he told Hamilton that he didn't believe in second-guessing the manager. Score had a great relationship with the managers and coaches. He didn't see second-guessing as part of his job. Score also believed that sometimes other factors may be behind the managerial decisions, things not known by the public. Often, Score did know, but he was told it in confidence.

"If you told Herb something and asked him to keep it quiet, he kept quiet," said Hamilton.

Joe Tait said you couldn't get Herb to betray a confidence even if you tore off his fingernails. It was a point of honor.

Score also stayed away from criticism of a player who seemed to be not hustling.

"Sometimes, a guy is hurt and he can't run hard," said Score. "We just don't know about the injury."

Hamilton never saw Herb Score pitch, but he knew Score was "a great, great pitcher."

At least, until he got hurt.

Score never talked much about his career on the air, other than to joke about being a lousy hitter—which was the case.

But he could have been the next Bob Feller for the Tribe. He was Sandy Koufax or Steve Carlton before anyone ever heard of Sandy Koufax or Steve Carlton.

Score was a phenom of a high-school pitcher. Larry Brown was a Tribe shortstop in the 1960s. His brother Dick Brown was Score's catcher at Lake Worth High in Florida.

"I remember seeing games where players made bets on who would hit the first foul ball off Herb," said Larry Brown in a 1993 interview. "He not only was the fastest pitcher any of us had ever seen, he was wildest. He also had a great curve."

This was before the major-league amateur draft, when any high school senior was eligible to be signed by any team. It was a bidding war.

"Every team but Washington made an offer," said Score, also in a 1993 interview. "A few teams knew I wanted to sign with Cleveland because of Cy Slapnicka, and they told me, 'Whatever Cleveland offers you, we'll beat it.' But Cy Slapnicka had watched every game that I pitched in my last three years of high school. He became part of our family. He really did camp on our doorstep."

Slapnicka was the legendary scout who had signed Bob Feller, Jim Hegan and other Tribe stars.

"Cy had a lot of friends in Lake Worth," said Score. "He had them taking me to dinner, telling me that I should sign with Cleveland because they knew how to develop pitchers."

The year was 1952. The Tribe had a starting rotation of Bob Lemon, Early Wynn, Mike Garcia and Feller. In those days the Tribe battled the Yankees nearly every year for the American League pennant.

"Cy did a great job recruiting me," said Score. "He told me about scouting Feller, and that impressed me. I could have signed for $100,000 with some teams, but I wanted to play for Cleveland."

On June 7, 1952, Score signed for $60,000 with the Tribe.

It was his 19th birthday.

"In most seven-inning games, I'd strike out 17-18," said Score. "I threw some no-hitters. Of course, I walked more than a few, too."

Score opened up about his career when interviewed for the book, "The Curse of Rocky Colavito." He did it because he knew the focus of the book was Colavito, his best friend in baseball. And he wanted to help with the project.

"Herb was a very private person," said Hamilton. "He just wouldn't talk about his career, about how he felt about it—or anything. He talked about his family. He loved to talk about other players, but not himself. I just know that [former Yankee shortstop] Tony Kubek told me that Herb was harder to hit than Sandy Koufax. If you look at Herb's stats, the first two years are as good as anyone in baseball."

Hamilton paused.

"I'd tell Herb that and he'd say . . . 'eh' . . . and change the subject," said Hamilton.

The radio executives asked Hamilton to entice Score to talk more about his time pitching for the Tribe.

"They wanted his stories," said Hamilton. "I wanted to hear them, too. But Herb just wouldn't do it. The one guy he liked to talk about was Ted Williams. But Herb didn't think it was right to talk about his own career."

Score climbed through the Tribe farm system. In 1954, Score was 22-5 with a 2.62 ERA at Class AAA—and wasn't even promoted to Cleveland. That's because the Tribe won the American League pennant with a 111-43 record. Now understand this: The Indians played 154 games, and the pitching staff completed 77 games. That's right, half of the starts were complete games! They also led the league with a 2.78 ERA. Feller was 13-3 with a 3.09 ERA as the fifth starter. So Score was a 22-game winner in the minors (completing 21 of 32 starts) with nowhere to go.

The next season, he was promoted to Cleveland. In 1955 and 1956, he had a combined record of 36-19 with a 2.68 ERA, leading the league in strikeouts both seasons. All of that by the age of 23.

"I remember games where it seemed no one hit the ball to the outfield off Herb," said Rocky Colavito. "Ted Williams told me that Herb was the best pitcher he ever faced. Sandy Koufax never won 20 games until he was 27. Herb did it at 23. Herb never complained. Think about all he had been through. He never had an excuse for anything that happened, never was a 'Woe is me' guy."

In 1957, Score had completed three of his first four starts and had a 2-1 record with a 2.04 ERA. He appeared on his way to another 20-win season when he took the mound at old Cleveland Stadium against the Yankees on May 7.

Gil McDougald was the second batter of the game for Yankees. The count was two balls, two strikes. Score fired a fastball on the outside corner, and McDougald drilled it right up the middle.

"When Herb threw a fastball, he came straight over the top," said Jimmy Dudley, the Tribe's radio broadcaster for that game. "He almost touched the ground with his fingers when he followed through. He just couldn't get his glove up in time to stop that line drive. He went down, and I thought he may have been killed. The ball had hit him in the face. The crowd was total silence, like a funeral parlor when the priest shows up."

Til Ferdenzi covered the game for the New York Journal American. He wrote: "I heard the crack of the bat and the sickening thud as the blur of the baseball struck Herb Score. Score went down as if he had been shot . . . Blood poured from his right eye. His mouth was ajar . . . Was the Cleveland pitcher alive or dead? If he was alive, would he ever see through that eye again?"

The ball was hit so hard, it was fielded on a single bounce by third baseman Al Smith, who threw out McDougald at first. But the Yankee just stared at Score, bleeding as he lay in the dirt of the pitcher's mound. He never ran to first base.

Score was taken to the hospital. Later that night, McDougald and Yankee outfielder Hank Bauer visited Score in the hospital. His face was bandaged and he was in no condition to talk.

"I'll quit this game if he loses his eye," McDougald told Bauer. "The hell with it, I'm not playing anymore."

At the hospital, Score asked to see Hal Lebovitz, his close friend and a Plain Dealer columnist. He wanted Lebovitz to call his mother in Lake Worth to say he'd be OK. The next day, doctors said Score would not lose an eye . . . but they weren't sure about his vision.

"I had a tear in the retina of my right eye," said Score. "I had surgery. I could see after the surgery. I was in the hospital for three weeks, and I missed the rest of the season. Gil McDougald talked to me. He felt terrible. I told him not to worry. I never blamed him. What about pitchers who bean hitters [in the head]? They didn't mean it, it just happened. This was the same type of thing."

At the time, Score had a career record of 38-20 with a 2.63 ERA. After being hit in the eye, he was 17-26 with a 4.43 ERA.

"Everyone says it was the eye injury," said Score. "The eye was never a problem. After the surgery, my vision was fine. I went to spring training [in 1958] early and I was throwing the ball well. At the end of spring training, I sprained an ankle. When the season opened, I had the flu. But there was nothing wrong with my arm."

Score started the home opener, but left after three innings, allowing three runs.

"I didn't throw well, but I still had the flu," he said. "But a few weeks later, I pitched a game against the White Sox and I was my old self."

That was on April 23, 1958. It was the last time that baseball would ever see the same Herb Score who looked headed to Cooperstown in his first two seasons. In that game against the White Sox, Score threw a nine-inning shutout, allowing three hits and striking out 13.

His next start was seven days later. In between, one of his games was rained out.

"It was a cold, wet night and I got through the first few innings just fine," said Score. "About the fourth inning, my forearm felt sore. It was a 2-1 game, and I wanted to stay in there. I figured it would loosen up. By the seventh inning, my arm was really hurting. I threw a pitch that bounced about 10 feet in front of the plate. I tried another pitch, and the same thing happened. I left the game. The Washington team doctor examined my arm and said he thought I'd damaged a tendon in my elbow. He told me to wait a few days and see how it felt. That night, my arm hurt so bad, I couldn't get my arm through the sleeve of my sport coat."

Score tried to throw a week later, but his arm still hurt. He went to a specialist in Baltimore, who also told Score that he had damaged an elbow . . . a torn tendon.

"I rested for a month, tried to throw and it felt pretty good," he said. "They decided to try me in relief, test the arm. I came into a game in Washington . . . same place I got hurt. I struck out five of the first eight guys that I faced. There were two outs in the ninth inning, I wound up and it felt like someone was stabbing me in the arm. The batter popped up to end the game."

Score said he rested his arm, "and the crazy thing was that my arm only hurt when I threw my fastball. It was fine on my breaking pitches, so I threw a lot of curves. But I was never the same pitcher after that. It was my arm, not the eye that ended my career."

Score admitted that he changed his motion over the years, "But that was because of my arm injury, not being hit in the eye."

Score had no regrets about the eye injury. But he knew that if his elbow injury happened in the 1980s, he could have had reconstructive elbow surgery. It's known as "Tommy John surgery," and it has saved the careers of hundreds of major-league pitchers.

"But medical science was different then," he said. "There was really nothing they could do."

Herb Score never wanted to be a broadcaster.

"In high school, I couldn't stand in front of a group and put three words together," he said. "I was president of the Letterman's Club, but I made the vice president stand up and give the speeches. In my first few years as a player, if I had to make a speech somewhere, it seemed I couldn't sleep for a week. After a while, I gradually got over the fear."

In 1963, Herb Score was pitching for Class AAA Indianapolis. He was 30 years old. His record for the Chicago White Sox farm team was 0-6 with a 7.66 ERA. Score sometimes said that he pitched until "they tore the uniform off my back. If you want to play, you keep playing. If you quit too early and then want to come back, they may not want you."

By 1963, no one wanted Score the pitcher. It was seven years since he was 20-9 with a 2.53 ERA, leading the American League in strikeouts. What followed was seven years of injuries and frustration, of a few good games that mostly were a cruel tease followed by months of a once great pitcher struggling to be mediocre.

After the 1963 season, Score said, White Sox General Manager Ed Short told him that Tribe President Gabe Paul wanted to talk to him about broadcasting. "I never had thought about broadcasting. But I was still living in Cleveland. I was working for an office furniture company in the off-season. I was at the end of my career, so I figured it was worth talking to Gabe."

Paul arranged a meeting with Score. He explained that Tribe television broadcaster Ken Coleman had to do some Browns games. Paul wanted to know if Score was willing to do three Tribe games in September.

"Let's see how you like it, and we'll see how we like you," said Paul.

Score really had nothing to lose. He knew his pitching career was over.

"After those games, he asked me if I'd like to do the TV games in 1964," said Score. "I thought it was a great opportunity."

He was paired with Bob Neal, whom Score credits with developing him as a broadcaster.

"He was a true professional and could have had a lot of resentment toward me because I was an ex-athlete put in the booth with him," said Score. "I have seen it happen where a professional broadcaster didn't like an ex-athlete, and he made it hard for him—ruined his career. But Bob Neal accepted me and taught me a lot."

The best piece of advice?

"You're a broadcaster now," Neal told Score. "Don't live on what you did as a player. No one cares. Don't say, 'When I played . . .' You are a broadcaster, act like it."

That's what Score did, and it was part of the reason that he was so reluctant to discuss his career.

Joe Tait said Score would have been "a great general manager. He knew talent and he really knew the game."

But Score wanted no part of the front office. He knew there was far more stability in the broadcast booth. General managers and managers came and went during his time with the Tribe (late 1963–1997), but Score stayed.

"There were times when I knew about trades and things in advance," said Score. "But it was not for me to say anything. I'd just wait until the front office made the announcement."

In fact, Score was sometimes consulted about player moves, especially when Paul ran the Tribe. He was a valued friend of various managers and general managers, because they knew Score always kept his word to keep their conversations private.

On the air, his view was, "The broadcaster should not be the story; the game is the story."

He didn't believe in saying what a manager should do during his broadcasts.

"Of course I had ideas of what I'd do," said Score. "But I also knew that somewhere out there was a father and his kid listening to the game. And the father would say, 'Son, this is a good time to bunt.' Why take that away from the father? I've had people say I wasn't critical enough of someone who made an error or a mistake on the field. If a guy makes an error, you mark down 'error' on the scorecard. You tell people that he made an error. If a guy drops a pop up or strikes out with the bases loaded, he knows he messed up. The fans know he messed up. You tell people what happened, but there is no reason to dwell on it."

Score did television for four years, then switched to radio along with Neal in 1968.

It's fascinating that Score was close to Neal, who had few friends in the Cleveland media. He didn't talk to partner Jimmy Dudley on or off the air for the last few years they did games on radio. Tait worked with Neal at some radio stations in the news and sports departments, and found him to be "a negative, bitter guy."

It's hard to know if Neal embraced Score because Neal knew that Score was loved by the Tribe front office (and the Indians did approve the broadcasters), or because Neal simply liked Score and wanted to help him.

"Bob Neal is why I had a career in broadcasting," said Score. "He made it easy for me."

Over the years, Score was known for his mistakes on the air:

"Swing and a miss, called strike three!"

"The Indians have just walked the bases loaded on 10 straight pitches!"

"There's a two-hopper to Duane Kuiper, who catches it on the first bounce."

On long trips, Score would become confused about where the Tribe was playing . . . sometimes having the team in the wrong city or facing the wrong team. Most fans didn't care. They had their favorite Score stories, and he came off as likable and sincere.

"My broadcasting style was conversational," said Score. "Just two guys talking baseball in the booth. It doesn't have to be formal. It's not the White House or the opera."

Score never listened to tapes of his broadcasts.

"I heard that crap going out, why hear it again coming back in?" he said, laughing. "When I make a mistake, I know it right away. I correct it. But once it's out of my mouth, it's gone. Just don't cover up your mistakes. You are on the air for three hours saying who knows how many words. You're human. You'll make mistakes. Nothing you can do about it but correct them."

One of Score's greatest attributes was accepting reality. You can't rewrite history.

Score always dressed impeccably. He seemed to have just stepped out of a barber shop. Every hair was in place. His suits fit perfectly. Even in a polo shirt, he looked immaculate.

He credited his wife, Nancy, for picking out his clothes.

"Herb and Nancy were a special couple," said Hamilton. "Nancy laid out all his clothes for him. She shopped for him. No one dressed better than Herb, but Herb never picked out his own clothes. He left that to Nancy. He always wore a coat and tie to road games. Didn't matter if it was 100 degrees, coat and tie on the road. At home, it was a nice polo shirt. I'd never wear a coat and tie unless it was a travel day and we were flying out after the game. I stayed with dress pants and a nice shirt. He never told me how to dress."

Score wanted to portray a classy image, a throwback to the time when people dressed up to go to baseball games.

He had a nasal, Long Island accent that could be a bit disconcerting unless you grew up listening to it. He loved to talk about the weather. He'd tell most of us more than we needed to know about how the clouds looked and how the wind blew as a storm formed over Lake Erie just beyond the bleachers.

If the Indians were playing in a dome, then Score would give the weather conditions both outside and in.

"I don't have any pet phrases," Score said. "Why say `Going, going, gone,' on a home run when the guy hits the ball out like a bullet? Then I just say, 'That ball is gone,' because it is."

"A true gentleman" is how most of his friends characterized Score.

"What do I have to complain about?" Score asked. "I have the best job in baseball. I get to go to all the games, but I'm under none of the pressure. When the game is over, I can forget it and go home to my family."

Hamilton said, "I could never have had a better partner breaking into the business. Herb was always gracious. He treated me as an equal from Day One, and I learned so much from him. Part of the reason for my lasting in Cleveland and being accepted by the fans is how Herb accepted and treated me. I'll always be grateful to him."

Hank Peters, the Moses of Tribe Baseball

When Dick Jacobs bought the Indians in 1986, John Hart was managing in Rochester, the Class AAA team for the Baltimore Orioles.

Most people think Hart was the architect of the Tribe's 1990s revival. There is a lot of truth to that.

But it's not the whole truth.

"The best decision that Dick Jacobs made after buying the Indians was to bring in Hank Peters as team president," said Tom Hamilton. "Hank has never received the credit that he is due. It's Hank Peters who made that Joe Carter trade, bringing in Sandy Alomar and Carlos Baerga. It's Hank who hired John Hart and Danny O'Dowd. It's Hank who had the vision of how to build up the farm system, and he knew how to do it because he was [general manager] in Baltimore when the Orioles had a great farm system. It was Hank who took all the shots from the media when the Indians were slowly building the teams that would be so good in the 1990s. The fact that Dick Jacobs knew enough to hire Hank Peters was the first sign that Dick Jacobs was a very smart man when it came to owning a baseball team."

You also can add giving Mike Hargrove a chance to manage the Tribe as one of the best moves by Peters.

So when you look at the 1995 Indians, you see that the two top front-office people, Hart and O'Dowd, were hired by Peters. The manager, Hargrove, was promoted through the minors and eventually put in charge of the major-league team by Peters.

Peters had spent the previous 12 years as president and general manager of the Baltimore Orioles. He was 62 and basically pushed out of the job by former Orioles owner Edward Bennett Williams. He was quickly hired by Jacobs on November 3, 1987.

Nearly as fast, Peters convinced Jacobs to double the budget for the farm system and for the scouting staff.

For those who know some inside baseball about the Tribe front office, consider that Peters quit as the Indians' minor league director in 1971.

The reason?

"They were cutting our farm system budget in half," said Peters. "I told them that that was like committing suicide for a franchise."

The Indians were in financial quicksand. The team was for sale. An easy place to slash the budget is at the minor-league level, because it takes a few years before anyone sees that the price was steep and damaging. Baseball teams need to scout and draft correctly, or the talent stops flowing to the major-league level.

In the middle 1980s, you would go to the minor-league camp in spring training and see players wearing old Tribe uniforms from the 1970s. Some were 10 years old, and had the outline of names of former players such as GAMBLE and POWELL on the back.

So Peters fixed at least two of the Tribe's problems—the minor-league and scouting budgets.

And the franchise that slashed his budget by 50 percent in 1971 had its budget doubled by Peters in 1987.

In the five years that Peters ran the Tribe, the team's first-round picks were Mark Lewis, Charles Nagy, Calvin Murray, Tim Costo and Manny Ramirez. Peters didn't actually make those picks—but the men hired by him did.

Ramirez and Nagy were products of his farm system. Nagy was the team's most consistent starter in the 1990s, and Ramirez was an elite hitter.

When you dig deeper into the drafts in the Peters era, you find Jim Thome (13th round, 1989), Brian Giles (17th round, 1989), Herbert Perry (2nd round, 1991) and Chad Ogea (3rd round, 1991).

The investment urged by Peters and bankrolled by Jacobs paid off for the Tribe. The minor-league director from 1988 to 1992 was O'Dowd, who was hired by Peters.

But in the late 1980s, the products of those drafts had yet to reach Cleveland.

"I was hired right after the Joe Carter deal [of December 6, 1989]," said Hamilton. "I arrived in town to see Hank Peters being killed by the media. You know how it goes—the Indians traded another star for a bunch of minor-leaguers. Very few people really knew what the Indians had gotten back in Sandy [Alomar], Carlos [Baerga] and Chris James."

Hamilton had been working in Columbus, where the Class AAA Clippers were a Yankee minor-league team. He paid attention to the Indians and Reds, "because back then, Columbus was divided in terms of what team they followed."

But Hamilton had never been exposed to the drumbeat of doubt that was the soundtrack surrounding the Tribe for decades until he was hired to be Herb Score's radio partner for the 1990 season.

Over and over, Tribe fans told him, "This is what they always do, the Indians always trade their good players. They're always rebuilding—and it never changes."

Peters tutored the young broadcaster in how baseball (especially the front office) works.

"Hank had a plan, and he had a good plan," said Hamilton. "But back then, no one wanted to hear it."

Peters had his strikeouts.

He signed Keith Hernandez to a two-year, $3.5-million contract. That was supposed to cover the 1990 and 1991 seasons. But Hernandez was coming off a knee injury. He was 36, his body was breaking down. He batted only .200 for the Tribe in 43 games, and spent most of the 1990 season in the trainer's room. The Tribe cut him, and that was the end of his career.

The signing also didn't fit with Peters' plan of adding prospects in trades and in the draft. It was just a bad idea.

But it also served as a warning to the Tribe front office, especially to Hart and O'Dowd. When they were considering an aging player while still building the team in the early 1990s, they wanted to avoid "another Keith Hernandez."

While Jacobs was working quietly with local politicians to make a new baseball stadium a reality, he left the building of the team to Peters. He also wanted Peters to train a front office to take over.

At the end of the 1989 season, Peters was 65. He brought in John Hart as the general manager in waiting.

The obvious question was, "Why John Hart?"

Little in his background seemed suited for the front office.

In fact, Hart's goal at that point was to be another Earl Weaver, the next great manager of the Baltimore Orioles. Peters hired Hart right off the coaching staff of the Orioles. Hart had spent the previous seven years on the staff at every level of the Baltimore organization (six seasons as a minor-league manager, then as a third-base coach for the Orioles). Virtually all of his experience had been on the field. Yes, he worked with prospects, but his main job was not talent evaluation.

He was a manager, a teacher, a motivator of players.

One of Hart's favorite lines is, "I like power arms and power bats. I never would have signed a player like me."

Hart played three years in the Montreal farm system. At the age of 22, he had advanced to Class AA. He was a catcher who batted .221 with one homer and 18 RBI in 271 at-bats in 1971. Even more alarming, he had 13 errors and 21 passed balls in 81 games, according to Baseball-Reference.com.

That was the end of his pro career, with a lifetime .223 average and two homers in 758 at-bats.

Hart then spent the next 10 years owning a health club, coaching high school sports and managing a summer baseball school. He had a mind that understood business. His father had worked his way up from being a guy who unloaded food trucks to being president of the Associated Grocers of Florida. Hart talked about how his father had only a high school education, but a Harvard MBA in terms of practical experience.

"He went toe-to-toe with [former Teamsters president] Jimmy Hoffa and guys like that, negotiating contracts," said Hart.

The story of Hart's father is important, because it had an impact on the man who helped drive one of baseball's most remarkable revivals.

From his father, Hart learned to create his own opportunities. And that failure is not final.

Hart also loves the action—the winning and losing.

That's why he coached on the side while also running businesses.

It's also why he grabbed the chance to be a minor-league manager for the Orioles. It wasn't just starting at the ground floor, it was the baseball basement. Hart was hired to manage Bluefield in the Appalachian League. It was summer rookie ball, where players began their pro careers. Hart was hired just for the summer. Hart said there was no contract, just a handshake and a $4,000 salary.

He was hired by Tom Giordano, the Orioles minor-league director. Giordano's memory is different, Hart having a contract and a two-year commitment. One of the fun things about seasoned baseball guys talking about the old days (especially in the low minors) is how they often have different stories, even clashing memories. But the point is that Hart can thank Tom Giordano for changing his life. And Tribe fans also can thank Giordano for discovering Hart. Giordano was a key contact. He had spotted Hart leading Boone High in Orlando to a Florida state title. He liked the young coach, and knew Hart had played pro ball. Giordano was close to Peters, the Orioles' general manager. That meant Peters began paying extra attention to this young minor-league manager.

While Hart knew he was there to teach the young players what it means to be a pro and enhance their skills, he also was out to win.

And win big.

The most notable player on that team was named Ripken—but it was Billy Ripken, the younger brother of Cal Ripken.

Others who played in the majors were Ken Gerhart, Jim Traber, Eric Bell and John Habyan.

It was not a Dream Team for those who believe Baseball America is the Bible of Prospects. But Hart managed them to a 47-22 record. He has stories of being on the team bus after a loss, walking up and down the aisles at 2 a.m. and talking to players about the game and their performance. He was 33 years old, and acted as if every nine innings was a life-and-death wrestling match.

To Hart, it felt like it. He was married, had a daughter and, as he said, "No one [in baseball] really knew my name."

So he held 9 a.m. special workouts after night games at home.

While he never said it, looming over him was his own frustrating playing career. It was over so quickly. At 33, he had another shot at pro baseball. This time, he had to make it work.

He spent six years managing in the minors for the Orioles. He became friends with Peters. Hart was relentless. He operated on about four hours of sleep. He tended to pace when he talked. He'd look you in the eye when making a major point, and it was tempting to believe that he was speaking about something that he knew . . . ABSOLUTELY . . . POSITIVELY . . . KNEW . . . was the THE TRUTH.

He was the 1986 Class AAA International League Manager of the Year at Rochester.

By 1988, he was the Orioles third-base coach for Frank Robinson in Baltimore.

That's when Peters called and said, "Come to Cleveland" for the 1989 season.

The job was "special assignment scout." Many in the Cleveland media assumed Hart would be the next Tribe manager, if Doc Edwards faltered.

That happened, as it did to virtually every Tribe manager from 1960 to 1991—or until the hiring of Mike Hargrove.

The closet any manager came to surviving four full seasons (648 games) with the Tribe in that span was Pat Corrales. He made it 635 games between 1983 and 1987.

Hart came down from the front office to manage the final 19 games of 1989, replacing Edwards. The record was 8-11. Hart tended to approach every night as if it were a football game. He made countless changes, and you could see the pressure on his face.

What Hart didn't know was that Peters was teaching him a lesson that went something like this: "Son, you don't want to be in the dugout. The front office is a better place to be."

Peters was developing his own farm system in Cleveland, and not just on the field.

It was also in the front office.

In 1990, Hart became the top assistant to Peters, and it was clear that he was being groomed to take over when Peters retired.

Peters also had hired O'Dowd, who began in the marketing and broadcasting department with the Orioles. He later moved to the baseball side in the minor-league department. In 1988, Peters hired O'Dowd in Cleveland.

O'Dowd was only 28.

Peters wasn't bothered by O'Dowd's limited front-office baseball background. Peters remembered how he began in baseball, working in the public relations department of the old St. Louis Browns.

What Peters saw in O'Dowd and Hart were two young guys with zero sense of entitlement, almost obsessed with proving they could build a winner in Cleveland. They didn't come from any of baseball's royal families, such as the Bavasi clan. Peter Bavasi was the Tribe's team president before Peters.

Nor had O'Dowd and Hart worked for several teams, which was a plus in one very major respect. They didn't say things such as, "When I was with the Yankees, we always had money for . . ."

In 1983, the Indians hired Mike Ferraro as manager. He came from the Yankees, where he was the third-base coach. He also had played with New York. He was shocked and overwhelmed by the depressed circumstances that he found in Cleveland. He told stories about George Steinbrenner, Yogi Berra, Bob Lemon and Billy Martin. A wonderful man who also battled kidney cancer in the 1983 season, Ferraro felt helpless and hopeless trying to manage the Tribe. He was mercifully fired after 100 games (a 40-60 record). He went on to have a solid career as a big-league coach with the Royals and he later returned to the Yankees.

O'Dowd's baseball experience was at Rollins College, not in pro ball.

But like Hart, he knew that his moment was *now* in terms of making a mark in the front office.

O'Dowd also was a quick study, a man who adopted many of the new statistical measures that were in their infancy in baseball.

Peters was the steady hand, the man who seemed to never be angry or frustrated. He was the perfect baseball front-office Godfather. Criticism didn't bother him much. He understood that it would take years . . . yes, *years* . . . to turn around the Indians.

In a sense, he was like Moses to Cleveland baseball. Peters knew the Promised Land was out there. Late at night, he could picture a new ballpark with seats filled, fans screaming, a young team winning.

But he also knew that he probably would not be there to see it—at least not running the team.

Just as Moses had trained Caleb and Joshua to lead the people to the Promised Land, Peters had trained Hart and O'Dowd.

He also made one last hire before he retired after the 1991 season—Mark Shapiro.

Shapiro also had a Baltimore connection. His father is Ron Shapiro, a top baseball agent. When Peters was general manager of the Orioles, there were seasons when about 10 players were represented by Ron Shapiro. Peters knew the Shapiro family very well, and brought in Mark as a front-office intern. Twenty years later, Mark Shapiro was team president, the same job held by Peters when Shapiro was hired.

Sandy Alomar: The Tribe's Underappreciated Star

"It was snowing."

That's what Sandy Alomar remembers about his first game with the Indians.

"A breeze was blowing right in my face," he said. "It was so cold, so windy. I felt like I was going to freeze to death when I stood at home plate."

The year was 1990. John McNamara managed the Indians, and they played at old Cleveland Municipal Stadium on the shore of Lake Erie. The Indians were supposed to play a three-game series against the Yankees. One game was lost to rain, another to snow. They played the third game, and the "crowd" was announced at 6,000.

"In one of those postponed games, Cory Snyder hit a homer," Alomar recalled. "He was so bitter when they called [off] the game."

Alomar is from Puerto Rico, but talks about the Indians like someone who grew up in Parma or Garfield Heights. He talks about bad weather, empty stadiums and losing teams—at least, that's how it was early in his Cleveland career.

"There were games at the old Stadium when the wind was whipping and the snow was flying," Alomar said. "I'd look at those people in the stands and wonder, *What are they doing here?* And that stadium always smelled sort of musty and old."

Municipal Stadium had two dressing rooms for Tribe players. Most were on the main floor, but "if you were on the disabled list, or maybe a rookie, you were in this little room upstairs," Alomar said. "It's like you were in limbo."

The trainers' room was more like a walk-in closet. There was no real weight room.

"Breezy," Alomar said. "That wind was blowing every game, and it always seemed to be blowing right in my face."

Tom Hamilton came to Cleveland in 1990, the same year as Alomar. "I first met Sandy in 1989, but he doesn't remember it," said Hamilton. "It was at the Class AAA All-Star Game in Columbus, back when I was doing the Clippers games on radio. He was the two-time Class AAA Player of the Year, but the Padres kept him in the minors because they had Benito Santiago as their catcher. I remember him hitting an absolute bomb in that All-Star Game at Cooper Stadium."

After that 1989 season, Alomar was traded by San Diego, along with Carlos Baerga and Chris James, for Joe Carter.

"That's when the real building of the Indians of the 1990s began," said Hamilton. "Joe Carter was a great player, but he wasn't going to re-sign here when he became a free agent. Hank Peters made that trade, getting Sandy and Carlos. Two future All-Stars, two young players the Indians could have for a long time. This trade changed the course of the franchise."

In 1988, Alomar was named the MVP of the Class AAA Pacific Coast League, but he was sent back to the minors in 1989 by the Padres. In 1989, he was the MVP again and was named Minor League Player of the Year by Baseball America.

"I didn't know much about the Indians, I just knew it was the major leagues," he said. "I don't remember having seen their games on TV. Someone told me that they played in a huge stadium. That was about it."

But Alomar was thrilled by the trade.

"This was my chance," he said.

Alomar was the 1990 American League Rookie of the Year and was the first rookie catcher to start an All-Star Game.

"Sandy wasn't just the first of the new stars that we had coming," said Hamilton. "He was the first one to sign a long-term contract. He was represented by Scott Boras, who never wants a player to sign an extension with his current team. He always wants to take them out on the free-agent market. But Sandy appreciated the fact that the Indians allowed him to get his big-league career going."

When Alomar sat down with General Manager John Hart and

Assistant General Manager Dan O'Dowd, he listened to their vision of building a team with young players who sign long-term contracts years before becoming free agents. The idea was to keep the likes of Jim Thome, Albert Belle, Charles Nagy, Baerga and Alomar together for several years and have that team ready to win when the Tribe moved into the new stadium in 1994.

"Sandy defied Scott Boras when Boras wouldn't negotiate an extension," said Hamilton. "No one does that to Scott Boras. I remember Sandy telling me, 'Scott Boras works for me, I don't work for him. He doesn't understand that.'"

Hamilton was stunned.

Boras is baseball's most powerful agent. He has a way of making players see the world through his bottom-line, grab-the-last-dollar eyes.

"Nobody does to Scott Boras what Sandy did," said Hamilton. "But that's always been Sandy. He's his own man. I have tremendous respect for that."

Actually, it was Alomar and Carlos Baerga who combined to sign first, and both were represented by Boras.

"I argued with Scott every day for a month about signing the extension," said Baerga. "But I talked to my father. I wanted to stay. What if I got hurt? Why wait? Sandy felt the same way."

They did it together.

In 1993, they were the first significant Tribe players to sign long-term contracts.

"I was told to wait [for free agency]," Alomar recalled. "All I ever did was wait to get to the big leagues. I was comfortable in Cleveland. I felt good here, so I signed."

Hamilton recalled a story that showed what Alomar meant to the Tribe in the early 1990s.

"We were on a chartered plane, stuck on the runway in Detroit," he said. "There was this incredible lightning and thunderstorm, and they were making us wait to take off. Rich Dauer was one of our coaches. He got on the P.A. system and said, 'We just got a call from Hank Peters. He said for Sandy to get off, and the rest of us should just take off and see if we can make it through the storm.'"

The point of the joke?

"Sandy was the one guy in those early years that we couldn't afford to lose," said Hamilton. "And we all knew it."

* * *

Alomar comes from Salinas, Puerto Rico. During a 1996 visit to his home town, Alomar gave two reporters a tour.

His father was a major-league infielder, but his little-league field was mostly dirt, rocks and a few clumps of grass—and only a catcher's throw to second base from the Caribbean Sea. There was a small, chicken-wire backstop seemingly one good gust of wind from being blown away.

"I played there when I was 8 and 9 years old," he said. "Every day, I played here. Fields like this are why there are so many good Latino infielders. They learn to play with bad hops. They are not afraid to stick their noses in there."

The batter's box where Alomar squatted in the area behind home plate was mostly a hole. "We used to raise money for our own uniforms," he said. "We had caps and T-shirts with team names. We wore jeans and spikes or tennis shoes. We didn't expect to have a new full uniform like kids today."

The park where he played is still lined with coconut trees. Often, rusty pickups drive by with megaphones on the roof. The voices from the passing vehicles join the never-ceasing salsa music to form the soundtrack of this country.

"Those guys in trucks sell fruit," he said.

Automation has replaced the wagon and donkey for the street peddlers from Alomar's youth. Some of these businessmen set up shop on the side of the road, selling brown juice in plastic jugs.

"Don't drink that stuff," Alomar said. "It's like stool softener."

During the tour, Alomar stared at the Caribbean Sea and talked about the seafood.

"We have grilled grouper . . . broiled grouper . . . fried grouper."

Lots of grouper.

When Alomar played on this little diamond, the name of his team was the Flying Fish.

"Even though we played pickup games every day, we only had one official game a week, every Saturday," he said. "The team we played here was called the Beach Team. When it would rain and we couldn't play, we cried."

The Alomars are a royal baseball family in Puerto Rico. His father, Sandy Sr., was a big-league infielder for 15 years. Brother Robbie is a member of the Hall of Fame who played 17 seasons. Sandy played

20 seasons, including 11 with Cleveland, where he made all six of his All-Star teams. The Alomars lived on B Street, which should be called Alomar Boulevard. His house was there. So was a home belonging to his parents. And his sister. And his brother.

"We own three of the houses, all in a row," he said.

The narrow streets were built for burros. The pavement sometimes buckles from the heat and is awash during heavy rains. Some houses are painted pink, avocado, turquoise, orange and other eye-popping colors. They are right on top of the sidewalks, only five feet from the street. The Alomars are the royal family of Salinas, but their homes are stylish, not pretentious.

In the middle 1990s, when the Indians were dominating the American League, Baerga was more popular in Puerto Rico than Alomar. Sandy didn't have any local television commercials, but the Puerto Rican airwaves were filled with his brother Robbie and Baerga. Robbie was the spokesman for Labatt beer and Mennen Speed Stick, which he pronounces "Speed-A-Stick" in the commercial. Baerga was selling "Bimbo Cookies," a vanilla creme. He shared the spotlight, eating cookies with his daughter, Carla. In another commercial, Baerga said you should trust your money to Banco Popular. Yet another commercial featured Baerga and his mother, Baldry, sitting in some empty bleachers. Carlos said that his mother was enrolled in a certain medical plan—and if he trusted them to cover his mother, you can trust them, too.

During the 1990s, Alomar was an All-Star, but not the best catcher on the island. That was Ivan Rodriguez, who was more popular than Sandy.

"If I had a different last name, I probably would be better known," he said. "People meet me and say, 'You're Sandy. You are Roberto's brother.' A lot of Puerto Ricans know my name, but not my face. I think you have to be an MVP to get any respect around here."

He laughed about that.

But with the Indians of the 1990s, the most respected player in the clubhouse was Alomar.

"Sandy would have been a Hall of Famer, except for the injuries," said Hamilton. "In my 25 years in baseball, I've never seen anyone who cared as much about the art of catching and being a good teammate as Sandy. He called a great game, knew his pitchers. He is one of the toughest people mentally and physically. He played with so many injuries, never making excuses. No one has any idea how much pain that he played with."

Hamilton paused.

"Sandy had microfracture knee surgery before anyone even heard of it," he said. "No one ever knew the pain he endured to play."

Only four times in his 11-year Tribe career did Alomar play 100 games in a season.

"I had 10 different knee surgeries," he said. "I had a microfracture surgery [in 1995] before I really knew what it was . . . That's where they drill holes [in the kneecap] to create bleeding [and hopefully, grow cartilage]. I came back in three months and played."

In 1993, he had back surgery to repair a ruptured disk.

He had seven surgeries on his left knee, three on his right.

He had bone spurs.

"I had to keep changing my stance at the plate so I could stride," Alomar said. "I played most of my career on one leg. I came back and played two months after back surgery. I don't even know how many times I broke my fingers, because I just played with those injuries."

During his prime, Alomar was 6-foot-5, 220 pounds. That's tall for a catcher. Perhaps all the squatting of that big body led to the knee problems. But what was he supposed to do? Shrink? He could have played another position, but he was such a great catcher.

And he loved calling the pitches, leading his team.

"Sandy had some great years, but that 1997 season is the best year that I've ever seen any Tribe player have," said Hamilton. "He showed what he could do if he had a year where he was healthy."

Alomar caught 119 games in 1997, batting .324 with 21 homers and 83 RBI. He had a 30-game hitting streak. He homered in the 1997 All-Star Game, played in Cleveland, and was the first Indian ever to win MVP of an All-Star Game.

He played all 18 post-season games, driving in 19 runs and hitting five homers.

"It seemed every time we needed a big hit that year, Sandy got it," said Hamilton.

"In the first round of the playoffs, we were facing elimination by the Yankees . . . and Sandy homered off Mariano Rivera. No one hit homers off Rivera in big games like that back then, but Sandy Alomar did."

"I never heard a crowd louder than our fans were in that series," Alomar said. "Never. Not even in a domed stadium, which is always louder. Our fans were great."

He paused, thinking about that homer off Rivera.

"I actually hit him pretty good in my career," he said. "Not sure why. I sorta closed my eyes and swung!"

Looking back, there is a certain degree of frustration for Alomar about the 1997 season. The team came within one out of a World Series title. Alomar showed what he could do if finally healthy—the 451 at-bats were the most in any of his 20 major-league seasons.

"Sandy often is the fifth or sixth player mentioned when people talk about the Indians of the 1990s," said Hamilton. "He should be right at the top of the list because of his leadership and commitment."

Hamilton recalled a year when Omar Vizquel was unhappy with his contract and wanted to renegotiate. The star shortstop took his case to the media, which bothered Alomar.

"I remember Sandy saying, 'You signed it, you live up to it,' " said Hamilton. "Sandy had no problem standing up to guys, even someone who was as respected as Omar. Sandy helped calm down that situation. Even Albert Belle didn't mess with Sandy. Everyone knew he was the leader. Sandy is Puerto Rican, but he's comfortable in Cleveland. He can talk to anyone from anywhere—black, white, Latino."

Alomar loves being part of this special era of Tribe history. He still marvels at Progressive Field, which opened in 1994.

"To this day, it's a beautiful park," Alomar said. "When we first moved in there, I couldn't believe it. And the teams we had, what great players! I played with some of the best ever."

Alomar said that to fully appreciate Vizquel's talent at shortstop, "You had to see it on the field."

As a catcher, Alomar said he could watch the ball leave the bat and think, "No way anyone will get that."

Then Alomar laughed.

"Not if they hit it to Omar," he said. "Good hops, bad hops . . . he got them all. His reactions were ridiculous. Then we had Robbie [Alomar] at second base. It was the same thing. I don't think anyone was like Robbie and Omar [at second and short] playing together."

A Gold Glove winner as a catcher, Alomar loves defense.

He praised the play of Matt Williams and Travis Fryman at third.

"I had no idea how good those guys were until I played with them," he said. "Great reactions. Amazing."

Alomar said the names almost with reverence: Albert Belle . . . Jim Thome . . . Charlie Nagy . . . Kenny Lofton . . . Manny Ramirez . . . Vizquel . . . Robbie Alomar.

"And then there was Carlos [Baerga]," Alomar said. "No one could throw a fastball past that little guy. Man, could he hit it."

He laughed.

"I knew those guys were good," he said. "But at the time, I had no idea how really good all of them were. I have a sense of pride of playing with guys who will be Hall of Famers."

Alomar sounds like a Tribe fan who sat in the bleachers during the glory years. That's part of what makes Alomar so important to the franchise. He sees the teams through the eyes of a player . . . and the fans. He was there, shivering at the old stadium with John Adams' drum echoing over nearly 80,000 mostly empty seats. And he was there when the new ballpark was jammed with fans wearing Wahoo red, white and blue.

"The feeling of being on those championship teams," he said. "I want our fans and the players to feel that again."

After leaving the Tribe following the 2000 season, Alomar played with five different teams from 2001 to '07, mostly as a backup catcher.

"I felt very bad when the Indians let Sandy go," said Hamilton. "They had Einar Diaz and thought he was ready to be the regular catcher. The offer they made Sandy was an insult, just a token. The message was clear, they wanted him to leave. I thought it was wrong, because Sandy had left a lot of money on the table over the years to stay in Cleveland."

At this point, Alomar was 34. His body was beaten up. He had still played in 97 games, batting .289 with seven homers. But General Manager John Hart thought Alomar was a backup catcher and wanted to pay him like it.

"I think John regrets how he handled that with Sandy," said Hamilton.

Alomar was hurt by it, and signed with the Chicago White Sox. He batted .245 in 70 games.

But Alomar refused to dwell on it.

Cleveland has always been the home of his heart.

After retiring in 2007, Alomar was a coach with the New York Mets in 2008–09 and wondered if he would ever have a chance to return to Cleveland. Before the 2010 season, former Tribe Manager Manny Acta called and offered him a chance to be the first-base coach.

"I jumped at it," Alomar said. "For me, it was coming home. No place in baseball means as much to me as Cleveland."

He wanted to leave New York for Cleveland?

"Absolutely," he said.

Did some people say he was crazy to do that?

"Sure," he said.

But he'd heard that before, every time he signed an extension to keep playing for the Tribe.

Alomar seems destined to be a major-league manager. He has interviewed for a few jobs and was the Tribe's interim manager for the final six games of 2012 after Acta was fired.

"I never sat in [Acta's] chair or at his desk in the six days I had the job," Alomar said. "He treated me with great respect, and I did the same for him. I wasn't the manager. I was just the interim."

Hamilton said, "Sandy said it wasn't his job, he didn't want to disrespect Manny Acta by sitting at the desk."

Alomar seemed destined to be the manager in 2013 until Terry Francona's name surfaced as a candidate.

"I knew they'd hire him if he wanted the job," Alomar said. "I don't blame them. I understand. He has won two World Series. He's a heckuva guy."

Alomar was under contract for 2013, and Francona immediately asked him to join the new staff as bench coach.

"I could have gone elsewhere [as a coach], but why?" he asked. "I'm not worrying about managing right now. If it happens, it happens. I wish I could have gotten the job, but I'm a realist. This is a very good situation for me. Tito treats me well and with respect."

"Sandy handled Terry Francona coming with incredible class," said

Hamilton. "A few days before the end of the [2012] season, Terry Francona's name had surfaced as a candidate for being the next manager. Sandy told me that he wasn't going to get the job. No one told him, but he knew. Terry had the background. They had played together in winter ball, and they got along. He said he still wanted to manage, but was willing to wait and learn. Sandy always had to wait for good things to happen. Most guys don't have his loyalty. Their egos get in the way. But he loves Cleveland. He's told me a few times how he may be somewhere where they win a World Series, but it would never mean as much to him as if he can be with the Indians when it happens here."

The Stadium: Finally, Out With the Old

Tom Hamilton's first trip to the old Stadium was in 1987.

He was working for WBNS in Columbus, doing sports in the morning, talking about Ohio State and Columbus Clippers games.

"The Clippers were the Class AAA team of the Yankees, and there were nights when we were out-drawing the Indians," he said. "When I walked into Cleveland Stadium, I was overwhelmed. It was just . . . so . . . HUGE! It was hard to comprehend how BIG that old Stadium was . . . but there was something else . . . it was so EMPTY. It was still a great park because it was a major-league park, but here was this huge ballpark where they were playing a major-league game and it seemed like no one was in it."

Something else occurred to Hamilton that night in 1987.

"Why would anyone sit in the bleachers? They were so far away. The game is barely a rumor if you're sitting out there," he wondered.

He also looked at the fences, and then well beyond them to the grandstand. He wondered why they built a stadium that was so . . . so . . . enormous.

"I worked in Milwaukee and old County Stadium was somewhat like Cleveland Stadium," said Hamilton. "In some ways, it looked so much like it. That's why they filmed the 'Major League' movies in Milwaukee—even though they were about the Indians and it was supposed to be set in Cleveland. But County Stadium had about 53,000 seats. The fans in Milwaukee really were on top of the action. The old Cleveland Stadium had about 80,000 seats, some of them behind huge pillars. Others were so far away from the game . . ."

Hamilton paused to talk about the old press box. To reach it from the grandstand, you walked across narrow catwalks suspended from the upper deck. There was a sense that if they shook a bit in the wind, and that perhaps one day—well, they just might give out and you'd fall perhaps 100 feet into the chairs below.

"You'd be going into the press box on those catwalks and fans could see you and they'd be screaming at you," said Hamilton. "The view from the press box was outstanding. You were right behind the plate, not very high up. You could see straight out over the center-field bleachers, and there would be Lake Erie. On a nice afternoon, you'd see the sailboats on the lake as you were doing the game. And in the spring, I swear there were days when I saw chunks of ice bobbing on the water."

Hamilton's first visit to the Stadium in 1987 was during a season where the Tribe finished 61-101. They barely drew 1 million fans.

"I never imagined that three years later, I'd be doing the Indians games," he said. "Never in a million years. When that happened, Cleveland Stadium became to me what old County Stadium was when I went to the Braves games as a child. I understood how Cleveland fans had an attachment to the place and to all the great players who they had watched there. It was the same for me in Milwaukee with Hank Aaron, Eddie Mathews, Warren Spahn and all those guys. Milwaukee was where I saw my first major-league game. We came in from our farm in Wisconsin every year for one game—a doubleheader. We sat in the right-field bleachers. My favorite player was Hank Aaron, and he played right field. So that's where we sat. It was a big deal to me, being in a big-league ballpark. As a kid, I thought it was heaven."

Then Hamilton began to laugh.

"Before I did the Indians games, I'd sometimes listen to the Tribe [radio broadcast]," he said. "I'd hear that guy screaming: 'WHO . . . LEE . . . OOO' for Julio Franco. He'd do it over and over: 'WHO . . . LEE . . . OOO!' It was irritating. Then I'd hear the guy with the drum in the bleachers. Remember, I hadn't been to Cleveland at this point in my life. I didn't know John Adams. I'd just hear this guy pounding away all game during the radio broadcast. I wondered, *Is that drum the size of Rhode Island or what?* But Cleveland Stadium will always be special to me just as it is to many fans—because it's where I first got my chance to do major-league games."

* * *

IT'S PERFECT!

That was the banner headline in The Plain Dealer the day Jacobs Field opened in 1994.

IT'S PERFECT!

That was said about another stadium. A stadium in Cleveland.

The year was 1932 and that's what Judge Kenesaw Mountain Landis had to say about Cleveland Stadium when it opened on July 31, 1932.

The baseball commissioner just gushed to reporters: "It's the only park that I know where spectators can clearly see from any seat. Look at those people in center field, they can see every play."

Maybe if they were using telescopes, because the people in center field sat in the bleachers . . . and the bleachers were nearly 500 feet from home plate. There was no center-field fence when the park opened, so you needed to hit a ball 470 feet to reach the center-field bleachers.

Judge Landis added: "Not a barrier to block one's view. Comfortable chairs. This is perfection."

Landis was introduced by former Tribe player-turned-public address announcer Jack Graney as "the man who never made a mistake."

Not sure about that. Yes, it's the job of the commissioner in any age to sell baseball and the parks where the major-league games are played, but the judge could have been taken to court and charged with perjury when he insisted, "Not a barrier to block one's view . . ."

Guess he didn't see all those poles scattered in the upper and lower decks.

For those of us who remember what we now call "The old Stadium," this was a time when it was new. It was when the infield had the greenest grass, when the dirt seemed perfect, when the diamond really sparkled. It was when a public-address system was a marvel, when the idea of watching baseball on the shores of Lake Erie sounded like a day at the beach.

It was special.

It opened in the darkest days of the Depression, and in some ways, it was a symbol of hope. If Cleveland could build such a huge stadium at a time when it seemed as if nothing good was happening in the country, there was a reason to celebrate.

The Indians began the 1932 season at League Park, located on East

66th Street and Lexington Avenue. It was a neighborhood ballpark, close to the two streetcar lines. Shoeless Joe Jackson lived only a few blocks away near Lexington Avenue. He walked to and from the park for games. The Tribe was owned by the Robison family, and they also owned the streetcar lines. That's why the park ended up on East 66th and Lexington.

Cleveland Stadium was a shock to players and fans, because League Park had only 22,500 seats. It was a wooden structure with a rightfield wall that was a mere 270 feet from home plate. OK, it was listed at 290 feet. And there was a 40-foot-high wall, higher than Boston's 37-foot-high Green Monster. But those who played there swore it was much closer than the alleged 290 feet.

When the new Cleveland Stadium opened in 1932, it was 320 feet down both foul lines. But it was 463 feet in the power alleys! Remember, no fence.

"I loved it," said pitcher Willis Hudlin in a 1992 interview. "But our hitters were almost beat [by the size of the Stadium] before the first game. They'd hit the ball 420 feet and it would be caught, and they'd come back to the bench talking to themselves."

Fans were excited by the new public-address system. At League Park, lineups and other announcements were made through a megaphone.

That first game of July 31, 1932 drew 80,248 fans. By far, it was the largest crowd ever to watch a major-league baseball game.

"When I stepped on the field that day, it was hard to believe that there were so many people in one place," said Mel Harder in a 1992 interview. "It was the most awesome thing that I've ever seen."

Ticket prices: $1.40 for box seats, $1.10 for lower reserved, 85 cents for unreserved in the outfield and 55 cents for the bleachers. Those were close to the same prices at League Park.

The Plain Dealer also reported a traffic jam of more than 25,000 cars and 1,000 taxi cabs and buses bringing people to the Stadium. Former stars Nap Lajoie, Cy Young, Tris Speaker, Elmer Flick, Bill Wambsganss and about 20 other retired players were at the game to watch Lefty Grove pitch the Philadelphia A's to a 1-0 victory over Mel Harder and the home team. Batters complained about all the fans in the center-field bleachers wearing white shirts. It seemed the ball wasn't coming out of the pitcher's hand—but from the white shirts.

The Cleveland Press insisted that all "but 17 fans" in the bleachers were wearing white shirts. For accuracy's sake, it must be mentioned that this was an estimate, but the point was made.

According to the Cleveland Press, "Nine innings later when Eddie Morgan drove out on a long fly ball to right to end the game, 80,164 persons sat still for 60 seconds. There was no immediate rush for the exits as seemed to be the case at League Park."

But when they did leave, there were problems in the parking lot—nothing more than a patch of dirt, where it cost 25 cents to leave your car.

"When the last auto moved away, a cloud of dust hung over the lakefront," wrote the Cleveland Press. "Something must be done about it . . . the city should spend $5,000 for oil [to combat the dust]."

After watching a few games at the Stadium, J.G. Taylor Spink wrote in the Sporting News: "I never thought I'd see the day when we'd have a park like Municipal Stadium. I guess you could put the Polo Grounds in this place and never see it . . . I sit out in the Stadium and the breeze blows off Lake Erie and some of the bugs they call 'Canadian Soldiers' blow in with those breezes. But I'm having the time of my life."

Obviously, it was summer when Mr. Spink stopped by the Stadium, or he would not have been too pleased to be in the wind.

After one day, crowd control ceased to be an issue at the Stadium. The Indians drew only 21,128 for the second game. Only 6,996 paid for tickets. The rest were free passes to students and others. Once again, the Indians lost, 1-0, to the Philadelphia A's.

As the Stadium was opening, several city officials claimed the Tribe would average an extra 10,000 per game above League Park because fans could walk to the Stadium from their workplaces downtown. Furthermore, lakefront real estate would increase in value and there would be massive development.

But the Depression hit. Unemployment was above 20 percent. Few of those who did work had extra cash for baseball or anything else.

The story behind the Stadium is important because the lease was an issue when it opened—and when the Indians worked so hard to move out into what became Jacobs Field.

Cleveland Stadium was one of the very first publicly financed sports facilities. Voters approved $2.5 million in bonds for construction of the venue. That was in 1928. There are conflicting reports about the purpose of the Stadium. Some insisted it was to help Cleveland attract the 1932 Olympics. Others said that was never a goal. But the point is voters agreed to pay $2.5 million—and the final cost was about $3 million. It opened in 1931 with the Tribe still playing at League Park as owner Alva Bradley was fighting with the city about terms of the lease.

The first sporting event at the Stadium wasn't a baseball game. It was a heavyweight title fight between Max Schmeling and Young Stribling. Schmeling won.

It was nearly 13 months later that the first baseball game was played.

And it didn't last for long.

In an attempt to get out of his lease with the city, Bradley submitted data showing that the Tribe averaged 5,817 fans (gate receipts of $3,716) per game for 91 dates in 1932 and 1933. In games played at League Park during that span, Bradley claimed the Tribe averaged 6,690 fans ($5,200) per game. In 1934, the Indians were back at League Park, playing at the Stadium only on weekends and holidays. In 1939, they played some night games at the Stadium, but the team remained mostly at League Park.

The final year of Bradley's ownership was 1945, when the Tribe drew 558,182 fans. Bill Veeck bought the Tribe in 1946 and moved all the games to the Stadium by 1947. He also installed portable fences to help the hitters. It was 320 feet down both foul lines, 408 feet to dead center field.

Fans packed the place. Under Veeck, attendance kept soaring: 1 million, 1.5 million, 2.6 million (in 1948, the all-time Municipal Stadium record), 2.2 million.

The Tribe drew at least 1 million fans every year from 1946 to 1955, and this was when 1 million was considered excellent.

But from 1956 to 1978, the Tribe broke 1 million only twice in 23 years.

Mike Hargrove arrived with the Tribe in 1979, and may be the only player in baseball history to be thrilled when he was traded from San Diego to Cleveland.

That's because Hargrove spent his first five years in the majors with Texas, batting .293 (.809 OPS). He also was from Texas, so it was home. He was traded to San Diego after the 1978 season. And he was miserable, batting .192 with no homers and eight RBI for the Padres in 52 games. That's when former Tribe General Manager Phil Seghi traded Paul Dade to the Padres for Hargrove.

Hargrove batted .325 for the Tribe for the rest of 1979. He played in Cleveland through 1985, and his Tribe career average was .292 (.778 OPS). While fans remember all his nervous twitches and hitches before each pitch, the man called "The Human Rain Delay" was a terrific hitter. His tendency to draw walks made him a "Moneyball" player before that baseball gospel became popular. He was in the top 10 in on-base percentage for most of his big-league seasons.

"Every time I walked into the old Stadium, I sensed the history," said Hargrove. "I knew all the great players who had played there. And I knew how so many fans loved it, because it was where they watched baseball while growing up."

Hargrove paused, then added: "But every time I walked into the clubhouse, I felt like I needed to take a shower. It was a dark, damp and mildewy, greasy-looking place."

Here's something that the news reports on the 1932 opening of the Stadium didn't discuss—it was built over a land fill. Yes, that part of the lakefront was a dump.

"One day, I was playing first base," said Hargrove. "I was standing there, and I sensed something behind me. I looked over my left shoulder and suddenly, there was a hole. It was maybe a foot deep. It was about two feet in diameter, about 15 feet behind me."

It was Cleveland's version of a sink hole.

As Hargrove departed from the field, he pointed to the hole and told the first baseman for the other team, "See that, be careful."

Hargrove and others said the infield "wasn't too bad until football season."

Remember, the Browns also played at the Stadium. And by August, you could see the yard markers on the field. On some fly balls, former Tribe center fielder Rick Manning would wave his arm as if he were signaling for a fair catch of a punt as the fly ball settled into his glove.

"The day after a Browns game, Phil Seghi would walk into his office and find a puddle on his desk, courtesy of the ladies room upstairs," said former Tribe President Gabe Paul in a 1989 interview.

In the early 1980s, the infield was voted the "worst in baseball" in a survey conducted by Sports Illustrated.

"During football season, the turf was all torn up," said Hargrove. "Then they started painting the grass so it would look green for baseball."

There was more.

"Ten years ago, they went down 18 inches and found nothing but a landfill," said Paul in the 1989 interview. "I'm not kidding, there were stove tops and parts of kitchen sinks under there."

Paul also went on a rant about "rug worms" that were invading the infield.

Hargrove said nothing about worms, "But I found a stake in the ground by first base," he said. "There were a couple of them. I pulled them up."

By 1974, Browns owner Art Modell had taken over the Stadium from the city, paying a dollar a year in rent. Modell was then responsible for the upkeep of the facility.

Almost from that moment, it seemed the Tribe and Browns were at war with the Stadium as a battleground. They often sued each other during those years.

The Tribe was paying 8 percent in gross revenues as rent. They received only 20 percent of all food concessions, 27 percent of other revenues. The rest went to Modell.

Paul insisted in the early 1980s that about 50,000 of the chairs dated back to 1932.

"They should be museum pieces," he said.

Dick Jacobs bought the team in 1986. He already knew the situation with the Stadium was a loser for baseball. Fans never had to buy tickets in advance—especially before the season. There were always tickets available because there were so many seats.

"Two men can't share one lunchbox," Jacobs often said, meaning football and baseball franchises have much different needs.

A stadium with close to 80,000 seats was ideal for the Browns of the 1980s, when Brian Sipe and later Bernie Kosar quarterbacked winning teams that were embraced by the city.

But 10,000 fans could be considered a decent crowd for most Tribe games in that decade.

"I remember when we traded for Mark Whiten and Glenallen Hill [in 1991]," said Hamilton. "They had come from Toronto, where the Blue Jays were drawing close to 4 million a year. They acted as if Satan himself had made the deal that brought them to Cleveland. They were not happy. We had some good guys like John Farrell, Bud Black and Tom Candiotti who loved Cleveland. Grover was always like that. But in the days of the old Stadium, most guys wanted no part of coming here."

Nev Chandler sat in Tom Hamilton's chair next to Herb Score long before Hamilton. From 1980 to 1984, he did the Tribe games on radio before switching to the Browns in 1985. He died of cancer in 1994 at the age of 47.

"People used to say the Indians needed to make the Stadium into a home-field advantage," said Chandler in a 1993 interview. "What home-field advantage? The Indians didn't want to play there, either. For most games, it was cold, gray and demoralizing. A little rain turned the field into a quagmire. I grew up watching games there. But I can tell you that it went from a field of dreams to a nightmare by the 1980s."

Mark Shapiro's main memory of the old Stadium was from early in the 1992 season.

He had been hired by the Indians to an entry-level position in the front office.

"I was just happy to be in the big leagues, so I didn't care where it was," said Shapiro. "I just wanted to work in baseball."

But over and over, he heard words like this from friends—those who worked in baseball and casual fans: "Going to Cleveland, just what are you thinking?"

He ignored the noise, went to work.

But in the month of May, his father visited Cleveland. A veteran agent based in Baltimore, Ron Shapiro sat with his son at a Tribe game.

"We're in this cavernous ballpark," said Shapiro. "We were already in last place. The Cavs had a good team [they were in the Eastern Conference Finals in 1992]. We were still in the AL East back then, really a hopeless situation. There were about 500 people in the stands."

For a while, the Shapiros—father and son—didn't say much. Ron Shapiro was based in Baltimore, where Mark Shapiro grew up.

"The Orioles had just opened Camden Yards," said Shapiro. "And we were waiting to see if the vote would pass for our new park to be built."

Finally, Ron Shapiro said to his son, "Are you sure you know what you are doing?' "

For some of us, the Stadium will bring back memories. Walking down the West Third Street Bridge, you'd run into an old man with a dancing monkey and a German Shepherd. He had a hat on the ground, hoping his humble animal show would convince fans to drop in a few coins.

In the 1960s, a dime bought you a scorecard and a thumb-sized golf pencil. Yes, people kept score back then. And above the Stadium was the Chief Wahoo sign, the Chief standing on one leg, holding a bat, slowly spinning around. Walking into the Stadium, you could smell hot dogs on the grill. And Stadium mustard. And cotton candy for a quarter. Walking up the ramps, you'd encounter the greenest grass that you've ever seen. That's especially true for us of a certain age when only about 20 Tribe games a year were televised, and it was in black and white. That made the field look gray.

Beyond the bleachers was Lake Erie. The sailboats. The freighters. The endless blue water heading into the horizon.

Of course, this is a romanticized version for those who watched the Tribe in the 1940s through the 1960s.

But even the most nostalgic fans knew the team needed a new park by the 1970s. Lots of maneuvering led to the Tribe finally moving into Jacobs Field in 1994. There is no need to re-heat all the old political hash of the final years of the Tribe playing at the old Stadium. But the fact is, no Jacobs Field, no one would even be talking about the Indians now. They would have moved decades ago.

"The Stadium will always mean a lot to me," said Hamilton. "When you would fill that place up for opening day or the Fourth of July, there was nowhere else like it."

He paused.

"It may have been a dump—but to some people like me, it's special because it was our dump!" said Hamilton.

Carlos Baerga: The Heartbeat of the Tribe

Years later, Carlos Baerga is amazed that it happened to him.

"I batted third in that lineup," he said. "People always ask me how that could happen, me hitting third with all those great players."

Then Baerga lists the names: Eddie Murray, Albert Belle, Jim Thome, Kenny Lofton, Manny Ramirez, Sandy Alomar, Omar Vizquel.

Batting third for the Tribe on opening day from 1992 to 1996 was Carlos Baerga.

"That's because Carlos could hit," said John Hart. "I mean, he could really hit. The whole lineup could hit. One year [1994], we batted Thome seventh, and Manny hit eighth a lot of the time."

In 1995, the No. 8 batter was often Paul Sorrento, a first baseman who hit 25 homers.

From 1992 to 1995, Baerga's average season was hitting .315 with 19 homers and 97 RBI. He became the first second baseman since Rogers Hornsby in the early 1920s to have consecutive seasons of 200 hits, 20 homers and 100 RBI.

In the middle 1990s, Baerga heard himself mentioned with Hornsby.

"I looked it up," Baerga said. "He's the one with 200 hits, .300 batting average, 20 homers and 100 RBI. He did it two years in a row."

That was back in 1921 and 1922. Hornsby was the last second baseman to do that back-to-back . . . until Baerga in 1992 and 1993. And Baerga might have made it three years in a row, but the 1994 season was cut short by the baseball strike. He batted .314 that year with 15 homers and 90 RBI in 135 games.

In 1993, Baerga was the first switch-hitter to homer twice in an inning, once from the left side and once from the right. He did it against the New York Yankees. His 114 RBI that 1993 season were the most by any American League second baseman since 1950.

Heading into the 1996 season, Baerga was 27. He was a three-time All-Star, a lifetime .305 hitter.

As that season began, General Manager John Hart said, "Because we have so much talent, many people just don't realize that Carlos is a great player. Look at his numbers. He will get his 1,000th career hit this year. If he stays healthy the next 10 years and keeps putting up the kind of numbers he has so far, I think you have to talk about Carlos and the Hall of Fame."

Hall of Fame? Hornsby & Baerga?

"Why not?" Hart asked. "Take a good look at what Carlos has done already."

Hart made those comments in a 1996 spring training interview.

"Looking back, Carlos had some amazing years," said Hart. "I do remember making the Hornsby comparison, and I wasn't the only one. In his first four years in the big leagues, he was an extremely productive player."

Yes, once upon a time, he was that good.

Not .358 good, which was Hornsby's lifetime average.

But very, very good.

"When I was younger, it came easy for me," said Baerga. "When I went to the plate, I knew I could hit. I just knew it."

His father taught Baerga to switch hit. He also managed his son in youth leagues.

"He made me play against older kids," said Baerga. "When I was 8, I played in a league for 10-12 year olds. When I was 15, I was in the top league in Puerto Rico, playing against guys between 18 and 40. Some had been in the minors. My father told me that to get better, I had to play against the best."

When Baerga was 17 in 1985, he signed with the San Diego Padres for $75,000. The Padres liked Baerga, but weren't sure where to play him. His body was a bit squat, his movement about as fluid as a fish flopping on a deck when Baerga pursued a ground ball.

In 1987, Baerga made 29 errors at second base while batting .305 with seven homers in Class A.

In 1988, Baerga made 27 errors at shortstop, batting .273 with 12 homers in Class AA.

In 1989, Baerga made 32 errors at third base, batting .275 with 10 homers in Class AAA.

So the Padres tried him at second, short and third base. None of the positions seemed like a good fit. The Padres also had All-Stars Robbie Alomar at second and Garry Templeton at short. Yes, they needed a third baseman. But was Baerga a third baseman? Was he even an infielder? The Padres weren't sure.

Tribe General Manager Hank Peters was talking about a franchise-changing trade before the 1990 season. San Diego wanted Joe Carter, who was heading to free agency after hitting 35 homers. Peters targeted Sandy Alomar, the two-time Minor League Player of the Year.

"The debate was over the third player," said Hart, who was Peters' assistant. "They wanted us to take either Gerald Clark or Thomas Howard."

At the 1989 Winter Meetings, Hank Peters had gout. He walked with a limp. Every moment seemed to hurt. It was hard to concentrate.

"We had no young players of note," Peters said in a 1998 interview. "Our best player was Joe Carter, and he was a year away from free agency. We offered him a lot of money to stay, but Joe said he planned to go on the market after the [1990] season. I couldn't let that happen. We had to make a deal that would turn this franchise in the right direction."

Usually, Peters would be in the hotel lobby, the coffee shop and everywhere else to mingle at Winter Meetings. But his leg was aching. He assigned Dan O'Dowd and Hart to work the different rooms, stirring up interest in Carter. O'Dowd and Hart had worked with Peters in Baltimore, and now were young executives with the Tribe.

"The Cardinals wanted Carter," said Peters. "They offered us Vince Coleman and Willie McGee. Both outfielders, both with big contracts, both veterans."

The Tribe wanted young and cheap talent.

Peters wanted a catcher, and he loved Sandy Alomar, who was in the San Diego farm system. Hart had scouted Alomar several times in Class AAA, and was absolutely sold. The Tribe's catcher in 1989 was Andy Allanson, and that wasn't working. Alomar was their prime target.

But the Tribe also wanted the Padres to know other teams were interested, so they could drive up the price for Carter.

"I kept telling John and Danny O'Dowd to say we had 12 teams interested in Carter," said Peters.

But the Tribe was interested in only one team—San Diego.

The Angels offered outfielder Devon White and Jeff Manto, who were their prized prospects.

Just think for a moment if the Indians had accepted Coleman and McGee for Carter.

Or Manto (who ended up with the Indians, usually playing in Class AAA) and White.

The Padres' general manager was Jack McKeon, known as "Trader Jack."

Peters limped into McKeon's suite, along with Hart and O'Dowd. It really was a smoke-filled room, as McKeon loved cigars.

The deal began with Carter and Alomar.

Next, Peters asked for Chris James, a journeyman outfielder.

That was fine with Trader Jack.

"We need a third player, a prospect," said Peters.

Trader Jack and his scouts went to another part of the hotel suite, talked for a while, and returned with a list.

"Where's Baerga's name?" asked Peters.

"Not available," said Trader Jack.

Peters wanted Baerga. Hart had scouted him and loved the infielder. Mike Hargrove was the Tribe's Class AAA manager, and he raved about Baerga because he had seen Carlos in the minors.

"Look," said Peters. "We have a dozen teams interested in Carter."

Trader Jack said, "No way."

Peters said, "Then no deal."

He mentioned the dozen teams, once again.

But he didn't move. More names were mentioned. More cigars were smoked. And yes, more pain came from gout.

"I wanted Carlos," said Hart. "I scouted [Class AAA] Las Vegas at least seven times, and I kept seeing Carlos hit. He really didn't look like a player physically, at least not a second baseman. But you just knew here was a hitter, a natural-born hitter."

Peters sat there and kept talking to Trader Jack. He knew the man with the cigar. He knew Trader Jack loved to make trades. And he knew Trader Jack really wanted Carter.

Finally, Trader Jack said, "I'm not going to let a prospect hold up this deal."

And it was done.

At the time of the trade, Baerga was optimistically listed at 5-foot-11, 165 pounds. He probably wasn't that tall, and certainly not that light. He was a bowling ball of a ballplayer. He batted .275 with 10 homers and 74 RBI at Las Vegas, but those numbers were compiled by a 20-year-old.

"Did I know Carlos would hit like he did for us? No," admitted Hart. "But I knew he'd hit."

When it came to his fielding, Hart didn't really care. He believed Baerga would drive in more runs than he let in, and he'd be only 21 when joining the Indians in 1990. That was young enough to improve with the glove.

Nor was Hart concerned with Baerga's refusal to walk. He drew only 30 bases on balls in 562 plate appearances in 1989 for Las Vegas. Hart was not as consumed with finding hitters with high on-base percentages as many executives are today. He just wanted hitters, period.

"Part of the reason [San Diego traded Baerga] was his style as a hitter," Hart said. "You'd watch him up there, and he'll swing at two pitches in a row that were over his head. You say, 'Carlos, what are you doing?' Then the next pitch is a foot outside and almost in the dirt—and he'd line it down the right-field line for a double."

Baerga didn't subscribe to the Ted Williams school of patient hitting. He didn't step to the plate thinking about what kind of pitch he'd see and where that pitch would be thrown. He never came close to being a league leader in walks, as Hornsby did three times. In fact, Baerga seemed as if he'd rather take a bath in battery acid than give up a chance to get a hit by taking four pitches.

His approach was, "See the ball, hit the ball."

Even in his best seasons, it seemed he never walked. And he swung at terrible pitches. Too often, he was behind in the count. But in 1995, Baerga batted .343 when he had two strikes on him. That's right, .343 when he was on the edge of striking out. No other American League batter could make that claim. In fact, no other AL hitter batted better than .310 with two strikes.

"I know some people didn't think I was any good because I didn't look like a ballplayer," he said. "I'm not real tall, but I am the tallest one in my family. My father is only 5-foot-5. I knew if they ever let me play, I could play."

Tom Hamilton said the Tribe front office told him that "Carlos was the gem" in the deal. They were convinced Alomar would become a terrific big-league catcher. "But as they told me, when you trade Joe Carter, you have to get more than one guy who can play in return."

Hamilton mentioned another factor in the deal.

"Sandy and Carlos are both from Puerto Rico," he said. "The Padres were known for their scouting in Puerto Rico. They seemed to get some of the best players from there."

When Baerga was traded to the Tribe, he had never been to Cleveland before. He knew very little about the Indians.

"I didn't care if the team was any good," he said. "I just wanted a chance to play in the big leagues. After the 1989 season, I was the MVP of the Puerto Rican winter league. I was playing second and third base. When the Indians traded for me, I wasn't sure where I'd play."

In 1990, the third baseman was Brook Jacoby, the second baseman was Jerry Browne.

"They were going to send me to the minors, but [Manager] John McNamara brought me to Cleveland as a utility man," said Baerga. "I thought of myself as a second baseman, but I didn't care where I played. I just wanted to play."

Hamilton remembered when they played Baerga at third for a few games, "And I thought, 'Oh, my, this is trouble.' At first he didn't play that well. I remember thinking, 'Well, at least we got Sandy,' because you could tell that Sandy was a future All-Star."

Baerga actually was sent to the minors for 12 games in late July, where he batted .380 at Class AAA Colorado Springs. Overall, he was a .260 hitter with seven homers with the Tribe. No hint of what was to come.

In 1991, he was voted the Tribe's Man of the Year when he batted .288 with 11 homers and 69 RBI. Second base belonged to him.

Consider these batting averages: .312, .321, .314 and .314.

That was Carlos Baerga from 1992 to 1995.

"You know when I really felt like I was a major-leaguer—the 1992 All-Star Game," said Baerga. "I walked into that clubhouse and there were Wade Boggs, Kirby Puckett, Roger Clemens and guys like that, guys I had watched on TV. And there I was, with them. I was like, 'Man, what am I doing here?' But I was an All-Star, too."

Hart said Baerga's love of the game was exactly what the Tribe needed in the early 1990s. The old Stadium was often a place where you saw more seagulls and pigeons than fans. When Baerga was the 1991 team MVP, the Tribe had a 57-105 record and baseball seemed hopeless.

"Carlos was so much more than great hitter," said Hart. "He and Sandy were our leaders. Carlos was the happiest guy in the clubhouse."

Hamilton says Baerga had "one of the biggest smiles that you've ever seen in your life. He was the vocal leader on the team, the guy in the clubhouse who'd rally the other players. He was so upbeat and positive, you felt good just being around him. He was a cheerleader for Albert Belle. He really could pick up Kenny Lofton."

Hamilton still smiles when he talks about Baerga.

"He wasn't from this country and English was his second language, yet he never let the language barrier be a problem," said Hamilton. "Sandy was the same way. They worked at learning English. Think about it. Sandy and Carlos were two of our early leaders, and they both were from Puerto Rico. But they related to whites, blacks, Latinos . . . everyone. They are special people."

When Hart and Assistant General Manager Dan O'Dowd came up with the plan to sign young players to long-term deals even though they were years away from free agency, they targeted Alomar and Baerga—two of the players who came from San Diego in that trade. Both were represented by Scott Boras, the super-agent who didn't want his clients to postpone free agency with the contracts planned by the Tribe.

"I wanted to sign," said Baerga. "I fought with Scott for more than a month. The Indians gave me my chance. I loved playing for them. Scott kept telling me not to do it. But I talked to my wife. I talked to my father. I came from a poor family. It was the spring of 1992, and Scott wanted me to wait another year. But what if I got hurt?"

Baerga signed a three-year, $8 million deal in the spring of 1992. Alomar also signed a long-term contract with the Tribe. He also was a Boras client, and he signed with the Tribe against the advice of his agent. Boras' approach was for his players to become free agents as soon as possible, so they could make the most on the open market with teams bidding on them. Baerga and Alomar were both postponing free agency for a year by signing extensions with the Tribe.

"Both Sandy and Carlos went against the [agent's] wishes, and it helped build the franchise," said Hart. "If they don't sign, not sure if the others do. That's what I mean by certain guys being more than just good players. They were leaders."

Baerga was "infectious" because of his passion for the game and his teammates, according to Hart.

"Then Sandy and I went to Albert [Belle], Kenny [Lofton] and Charlie [Nagy] and convinced them to sign, too," said Baerga. "And they did."

In the spring of 1993, when the Tribe was devastated by a boating accident in which pitchers Steve Olin and Tim Crews were killed and Bob Ojeda was seriously injured, none of the players wanted to face the media. They were so distraught. But it was Baerga who agreed to speak. After all, he was the team captain.

Baerga spoke through tears: "What happened yesterday is kind of hard for our team. We lost two of our teammates. We have to keep going. The team is real down right now. The first thing we have to think about is their families."

Remember that at this point, Baerga was 24 years old. English was his second language. Yet, he was the one who stepped in front of the microphones when so many other players couldn't do it.

Later that day, Baerga met Belle at the spring training complex. The ballpark was empty. They played catch on the field, saying very little. It was Baerga's way of comforting Belle, who seemed in shock.

"In those years, Carlos was the heart and soul of our team," said Hart.

Hamilton said Baerga "was a great player in those days, but swallowed his ego and didn't care that others got more credit. But that made everyone in the clubhouse love Carlos."

By 1994, collecting young players and keeping them together for a few years worked. The Tribe added veteran free agents Eddie Murray and Dennis Martinez. And they were playing in a new ballpark.

"Jacobs Field was like a new life to us," recalled Baerga. "I loved playing so much for Cleveland. Every time we stepped on the field, we thought we would win. That feeling in Cleveland in those days, I never had to pay for a meal. Everywhere you went, people were great."

Baerga did improve enough at second base to be OK.

"Carlos had a great arm and was absolutely fearless on the double play," said Hart. "I mean fearless. He'd stand right in there with that runner bearing down on him. His bat gave us an enormous plus at second base. What other second baseman would have hit enough to bat third in a lineup like ours? Think of all our great hitters, and think about the guy Mike [Hargrove] picked to hit in front of Albert Belle. That tells you something."

By 1994, Baerga was listed at 5-foot-11 and 200 pounds. At the time of the deal, his weight was listed at 165. He ran like a penguin—his arms going one way, his legs another.

"But at the plate, everything came together," said Hamilton. "He was a line-drive machine, a double machine. He was never going to hit tape-measure home runs, but my gosh, those line drives . . . he hit the ball so hard. When he was batting .300 and getting 200 hits a year, the only one not surprised by that was Carlos. He had tremendous confidence in himself."

Late that season, the Indians began to be concerned about Baerga's weight. Hart talked about Baerga sometimes "losing his concentration." He mentioned Baerga "needing to say no to people. He was appearing before almost every group that wanted him."

And all those groups had free food and drinks for one of the Tribe's most popular players. His weight soared to 228 in the spring of 1994, and was down to 220 by the end of the season. But he batted .314 with 19 homers and 80 RBI in 103 games before the players' strike ended the season in August.

In the spring of 1994, Baerga signed another contract extension—this time, $21 million for four years.

And he kept hitting.

In 1995, the Tribe won 100 games. Baerga was an All-Star, batting .314 for second year in a row. He batted .361 with runners in scoring position and led the league with a .343 average with two strikes.

He still was Carlos, still hitting, still in the middle of most of the Tribe rallies.

"I'd never believe that a year later, I'd be traded," said Baerga. "Never. People forget that I hurt my ankle in the 1995 [playoffs]. I took shots just to play. I used to play winter ball to stay in shape, but that year I couldn't do it. When the next season began, my ankle still wasn't right."

In the spring of 1996, Baerga was heavy once again and his bat seemed slower. He seemed stuck in the mud trying to play second base. His attitude had slipped a bit, because for the first time since he established himself as a big-leaguer, playing the game was work. Real work. And not much fun. In 1996, Baerga was only 27, but he looked 35. He admitted he came to training camp heavy "because I wasn't able to play winter ball."

His ankle wasn't 100 percent when the 1996 season opened. He seemed to have lost range in the field, and some pitchers were concerned that his fielding was having a negative impact on the team.

He arrived in training camp in 1996 at 230 pounds. To his credit, he lost 25 pounds by May.

But he also seemed to lose something else in terms of performance.

Not long after the trade, Hart said, "For the last three years, Carlos showed up in training camp 20-25 pounds overweight. We warned him there would be problems, that it would hurt his performance."

If he could still hit over .300 and drive in 90 runs, the Indians never would have traded Baerga.

But suddenly, his bat slowed down. One hundred games into the season, he was batting .267 with 10 homers and 55 RBI. Not bad, but not Carlos. And his fielding was more suspect than ever. The Indians noticed that he was breaking a lot of bats—a sign that his bat speed had slowed. Those inside pitches that he once pulled down the line were now being hit on the thin handle of the bat, and the bat shattered.

"I just couldn't get healthy," he said. "I hurt my groin . . . my hamstring . . . my wrist."

Now, many years after the trade, Hart doesn't want to go into any detail on the reports that Baerga had too many long nights, too many parties.

"We all know that Carlos could have taken better care of himself during those days, and he knows it, too," said Hart. "It's just a shame. It really hurt to trade him, but I felt I had to do it."

Hamilton said the key players on the Tribe of the 1990s "were treated like a bunch of rock stars." Everyone wanted players such as Baerga at their restaurants, clubs and parties.

"Not long before he was traded, I heard from people in the organization that it could happen," said Hamilton. "That was not something you talked about on the air. But they were concerned about his conditioning and they were afraid that he could lose 'it,' quickly."

The "it" was the quick bat, the reflexes that made Baerga a great hitter from 1992 to 1995. And they were right. He never was the same after 1995.

"This was probably the most painful trade that I ever made with the Indians," said Hart. "But we knew we had to make a deal before the bottom fell out. The talent just wasn't there anymore for Carlos."

The Tribe received Jose Vizcaino and Jeff Kent from the Mets for Baerga and Álvaro Espinoza.

"The trade broke my heart because I thought we'd go back to the World Series," said Baerga. "I really thought I'd pull myself together if they just gave me more time."

The day after the trade, an airplane flew over Jacobs Field with this banner: TRADE HART, KEEP BAERGA.

But Baerga batted only .193 for the Mets after the deal. His defense was so bad, they used him at first and third base, rather than second. He continued to have muscle pulls and other nagging injuries. That sometimes happens when a player keeps gaining and losing weight. The Mets were amazed at how many bats were broken by Baerga, who no longer was able to get around on inside fastballs. He used to pull those pitches down the line for doubles. Now, they were in on his hands, shattering the bat. Just a half-second of reaction time made a huge difference.

Not long after the deal, Baerga told New York Daily News columnist Mike Lupica: "I'm 28 years old. I'm not hurt. I'm working hard every day. And I can't put my bat on a ball down the middle of the plate anymore."

Baerga did pull himself together to an extent. In 306 games with the Mets, he was a .267 hitter with only 18 homers. He never quite had the same bat speed. While with the Mets, he realized that his lifestyle had to change. He recommitted himself to Christianity, and at least found a way to remain a viable big-leaguer.

He now says his faith "saved my life."

But he was never the Carlos Baerga of 1990–95 again. His last great season was at the age of 27.

"You know what meant a lot to me?" he said. "When I came back [for 22 games] in 1999. I loved playing in Cleveland. Looking back, I'm not mad at John for trading me. I believe God has a purpose for everything, and I learned a lot from that about not taking anything for granted."

Baerga batted only .228 in 63 plate appearances for the Tribe in 1999. But then, he was a utility infielder. Tribe fans gave him huge ovations every time he came to the plate.

"This is my house, where I started," Baerga said after his first game back, and he spoke as tears rolled down his face.

Baerga dropped a lot of weight and played through 2005 for a variety of teams, mostly as a backup after leaving the Indians. After retiring, he became a broadcaster for ESPN's baseball telecasts in Spanish.

"I talk to players now about taking advantage of every opportunity and not taking anything for granted," said Baerga. "I just lost concentration. You need to always prepare to play and be responsible."

And when Baerga did all the right things a few years after the trade, "the game was just harder for me. It never was as easy or as good as when I played for the Indians."

Hamilton loves seeing Baerga, as they cross paths a few times each season when Baerga is doing games for ESPN.

"He's still the same Carlos, the guy who makes you want to be around him," said Hamilton. "And no one loved being a Cleveland Indian more than Carlos."

John Hart's Greatest Sales Job

When the 1991 Tribe season began, Hank Peters knew it would be his last as president of the team.

He was preparing John Hart to take over. He would let Hart make most of the major decisions in 1991, and they were going to be the kind of moves that inspire the fans and media to loathe the front office.

Hart and O'Dowd talked to Peters about dumping virtually every significant veteran and starting over with young players—players from their own farm system, players acquired from elsewhere.

In 1990, the Tribe was 77-85. The top three starters were Greg Swindell, Tom Candiotti and Bud Black.

By the start of the 1992 season, all three were gone. So were most of the other Tribe veterans.

"Hank knew there would be a lot of criticism, but he took the hit," said Hamilton.

That allowed Hart and O'Dowd to begin to put into place what became known in the front office as "The Plan."

Hamilton learned of it right after being hired in 1990. That season, voters approved the Gateway project that included building a new baseball stadium to open in 1994. The goal was to have a contender in 1994.

Not 1991.

Not 1992.

Not 1993.

It would begin in 1994. That's when all the young players would have a few years of big-league experience and be ready to contend.

And when fans had any hint of that timetable, they moaned.

In Cleveland, the joke was that the Indians were always in the first year of a new four-year plan.

Or maybe it was the second year.

But then no one ever saw the result of the four-year plan, because it changed every few years.

"John was the one who articulated the plan the best," said Mark Shapiro.

The first time Shapiro heard it, he was sitting in Hart's office at the old Cleveland Stadium. He had just joined the team after the 1991 season, when the Indians had stripped the roster and finished with a 57-105 record.

"I was sitting in his office, looking at the missing tiles in the ceiling," said Shapiro. "There was this sad plastic plant in the corner. He had a space heater going by his desk."

Hart's office looked as pathetic as the 1991 team did on the field. That team had 53 different players wearing Cleveland uniforms that season, including 23 rookies.

It looked chaotic . . . manic . . . and hopeless.

"But when he talked about how it would all come together in the new ballpark, I could see it," said Shapiro. "That's because John really believed it. He was so passionate, you found yourself buying into what he was saying."

Hamilton didn't know exactly what to think when Peters retired at the end of 1991, turning the team over to Hart.

"But I had confidence in John and Danny [O'Dowd] because Hank had picked them and trained them," said Hamilton. "Hank had a track record of building winners in Baltimore. John and Danny had no track record, good or bad. They had never run a team before. But I had a feeling that it would work out because those guys were so smart and worked so hard. They were so determined that I thought they just might be able to do it."

It was one thing to convince Hamilton and Shapiro about the vision. And it was understandable that Peters would buy into the building process, because Peters knew it was the only way the Tribe would ever have success.

But the Indians had to do more than find a way to acquire and develop young players. They also had to keep those players around (and the payroll under control) in the age of free agency and arbitration.

One day, Hart and O'Dowd were talking about how a middle-sized market such as Cleveland could compete with the teams in New York and Boston in a sport with no salary cap. They were talking about another middle-market franchise, the Pittsburgh Pirates. They won 98 games and made the playoffs in 1991, but it was easy to see that team would soon lose its stars.

Bobby Bonilla and Barry Bonds were headed to free agency, and no one expected the Pirates to be able to afford them. Bonilla signed with the Mets after 1991, Bonds with the Giants following the 1992 season.

"Arbitration also was a killer," said Hart.

He talked about how the Indians had taken Swindell to arbitration, and lost. The Indians offered $1.4 million. The arbitrator accepted the $2 million bid of Swindell's agents.

Both sides hated it, because the Indians had to knock their own player to prove their demand was fair. They also had to do it in front of the player, who was present at the hearing.

"I never want to go through that again," said Hart.

Hart and O'Dowd were talking about teams such as the Pirates losing their stars. And how arbitration could be "a real bloodbath," as Hart called it. And how all of this conspired to undercut the Tribe's plan of having a contending team ready for 1994.

It's unclear exactly who came up with the concept of signing young players to long-term deals long before they were eligible for free agency and arbitration. That's how it often worked with Hart and O'Dowd. They brainstormed. They offered ideas. They took notes. They came up with more ideas.

"John tended to be more big-picture, Danny knew how to make the details work," said Hamilton. "They were a great combination."

Over and over, they talked about how "the system makes no sense." Hart was especially livid about how an arbitrator ["not even a baseball guy"] was determining the salaries of baseball players at the hearings.

The $2 million doesn't sound like much now, but it put Swindell among the top 10 percent of salaries paid to pitchers in 1991. He finished with a 9-16 record and 3.48 ERA.

Suddenly, one of them said, "Why wait?"

That was "why wait" for arbitration to come?
Why wait for free agency to tempt players?
Why wait for things to happen?
Why not sign the key players to multi-year deals right now?

Before spring training of 1992, Hart and O'Dowd set up a meeting with owner Dick Jacobs.

Hart was jittery, even more so than normal. He barely slept. He woke up several times in the previous few nights, making lists of points that he wanted to make to Jacobs. This was the game of his professional baseball life, or at least he felt like it was. The more he discussed the state of baseball in the early 1990s with O'Dowd, they more they believed this was the ONLY way the Indians really could compete.

They had to sign young players quickly—long before the players could even imagine the golden dreams of free agency.

In spring 1992, Jacobs was about to turn 67. He knew the new ballpark was still two seasons away. His team had lost 105 games. He had agreed with Peters that Hart was the right guy to be the next general manager, but Peters had never proposed an idea like this.

As Hart said, "No team has ever done this before. I was asking Dick to go way out on a limb—into the great unknown."

Hart began to talk about the evils of arbitration and free agency, at least to owners and team front offices. He discussed how "so many unknowns" made it hard to control payroll costs.

It was unique. It was risky.

But it was something else . . . it was the kind of idea that made Jacobs millions in his other business ventures.

It also hung on one key point: that Hart and O'Dowd would identify the right players to sign to long-term deals. And luck would be part of it, because those players had to stay healthy.

"John had his honor on the line, I had my checkbook," Jacobs said in a 1995 interview.

They talked some more—and Jacobs said to go for it.

Hart did.

But he also knew something else: If it failed, he'd never be a general manager again. Both he and O'Dowd knew most of baseball would think they had lost their minds once the contracts were announced.

* * *

Hart and O'Dowd identified 12 players that they wanted to sign long-term. They signed 11. Most of these contracts also contained team options for an additional year. So a guaranteed three-year deal was really a four-year deal in terms of keeping a player under control of the team.

Here's a list, and it's fun to look at the names with the guaranteed portion of the contracts:

- Sandy Alomar, $7.3 million for three years
- Carlos Baerga, $6.9 million for three years
- Charles Nagy, $4 million for three years
- Mark Whiten, $3.5 million for three years
- Jack Armstrong, $2.9 million for two years
- Scott Scudder, $2.7 million for two years
- Glenallen Hill, $2.6 million for two years
- Dennis Cook, $2.2 million for two years
- Steve Olin, $2.2 million for two years
- Dave Otto, $2 million for two years
- Alex Cole, $1.2 million for two years

Remember the team had an extra year at the end—an option at their discretion.

Their only miss in the spring of 1992 was Albert Belle, who turned them down.

Now, when you hear about "The Plan" to sign young players to multi-year deals that was pioneered by the Indians, the assumption is they got most of it right. They did not.

They nailed the top three on their list: Alomar, Baerga and Nagy.

None of the others were with the Tribe when they moved into the new stadium in 1994.

Alomar, Nagy and Baerga had two or fewer years of major-league experience.

"We could miss on some of the guys with lesser contracts, but not those at the top of the list," said Hart. "Once we had Sandy and Carlos, they were recruiting other guys to commit and stay."

The Indians were able to trade Dave Otto (granted free agency after 1993), Hill, Whiten and most of the others.

"I remember when Pittsburgh claimed Otto on waivers at the

Winter Meetings," said Hart. "We had a celebration in our suite. We got out of $500,000."

Give Jacobs credit for not dwelling on misses (Otto, Scudder, Cole, etc.) and continuing to support his young front office in their plan.

Hart said that one of the first calls he received after the first wave of extensions was announced came from Dodgers General Manager Fred Claire.

"John, what are you guys doing?" screamed Claire.

"Fred," said Hart. "We're in a different market than the Dodgers."

"John," he said. "You don't have to give these contracts now. Wait until they are in their fifth year [facing free agency]. Why rush it?"

"We can't do that here," said Hart. "We can't keep going to arbitration with guys. We have to fix our payroll."

"Well," said Claire. "Good luck with all of that!"

Hart and O'Dowd received a lot of calls from their friends with other teams.

There were questions like:

"What if the guys can't play?"

"What if they get hurt?"

"What if the contract makes them untradeable?"

As Hart said, "We asked ourselves all that—and more."

But they believed they had to stick with the plan.

Hart and O'Dowd continued to pursue players to sign extensions.

In 1993, Belle signed an extension. Kenny Lofton signed. So did Jim Thome.

"We signed Jimmy in the spring of 1994," said Hart. "He was playing third base and making a bunch of errors in Winter Haven. At one point, Dick Jacobs asked if we really needed to sign Jimmy. I kept telling Dick that Jimmy was going to be really good for us, we just had to be patient."

Thome also had some injury problems in the early 1990s.

Then Hart received a call from Reds General Manager Jim Bowden. They were especially close friends, and Bowden had more of an appreciation for what Hart and O'Dowd were doing with the contracts.

But Bowden said after Thome signed, "John, that's your first big mistake."

Hart wondered if Bowden was right, at least until Tribe coach

Buddy Bell was able to help Thome relax at third base and at least do an adequate job with the glove.

"We also were betting on people," said Hart. "We knew Jimmy, and that he was a tremendous person. Think about those guys—Lofton, Belle, Baerga, Nagy—they wanted to be great players. They were driven. We bet on the talent and the person."

Hamilton and Shapiro believe O'Dowd's influence can't be overstated—that the new approach to baseball was a true collaboration between Hart and O'Dowd.

"John appreciated how Danny had such a high capacity to work and his level of preparation and attention to detail were exceptional," said Shapiro. "There were times when Danny's preparation nearly freaked John out, it was that good. John was the big-picture guy, a great evaluator of talent and an excellent communicator of his vision."

Imagine the Indians front office as art beginning with a blank piece of paper. Hart would draw the outline of a boat on the water with some mountains in the background. O'Dowd would take the outline, turn the boat into a sailboat in the waves with storm clouds looming over the mountains. He'd add the texture, the color and the mood to the painting that began with Hart's vision of a boat on the water with mountains on the shore.

"Both men made each other better," said Hamilton.

And both men were never quite as successful after they left the Indians as they were together in Cleveland.

"Danny also was largely the architect of the farm system that produced so many good players back then," said Shapiro. "And John also was very comfortable with surrounding himself with smart, very capable people. He didn't feel threatened by them. He wanted them working with him."

And this combination of Hart and O'Dowd, and the calculated bets that they made on players with long-term contracts, would soon pay off with two trips to the World Series.

Radio

[FANS WRITE IN]

My strongest memory of the Tribe from that era was watching the playoffs in '95. I watched Game 6 of the Seattle series on TV with my father. As it became clear in the eighth that the Tribe may very well clinch the series, my father at some point shut off the sound on the TV and turned on the radio. I don't remember much of what Herb or Tom were saying as the game ticked down. What I distinctly remember is the post-game show. Herb was in the locker room attempting to interview Grover. He asked some question and Mike just screamed, "Hey Herbie, we're going to the Series!" I remember being shocked at that much emotion from Hargrove. He always seemed relatively stoic on TV. It was a powerful moment and one that will always be one of my fondest Tribe memories. I'm not ashamed to admit that I'm actually tearing up a little thinking about the experience. *—Andrew Reid, New Westminster, British Columbia*

The Indians were playing the Seattle Mariners in the AL Championship Series in 1995. It was Game 5 on Sunday, October 15, 1995. The girl I was dating and I had purchased a season pass for the Broadway Series at Playhouse Square and we were at a play during the game. During intermission, I noticed many of the guys were listening to the game on handheld radios. I was disappointed that I hadn't thought of that myself. After the play ended, we raced to the car and turned on the radio and headed for the highway so we could get home and watch the game on TV. We were stopped at Carnegie and East 9th Street when Orel Hershiser struck someone out. The roar from Jacobs Field was incredible. It sounded like an earthquake. Tom Hamilton was announcing and his voice was just booming out of the speakers with a yell of "HEEEEE struck him out!" It was just an incredible moment. *—Patrick Whelan, Rocky River*

My first true inkling of a special team was a game during the strike-shortened 1994 season where Albert Belle capped another ninth inning comeback with a liner up the middle off Boston closer Jeff Russell. I found out the results of the game while at my own baseball game by hearing my father in the stands from my left field position shouting while listening to the play-by-play on the radio. *—Matthew Pastore, Columbus*

One summer, during the heyday of the Tribe's American League dominance, I suffered an ailment that left me pretty much unable to function normally. A side effect of this ailment was severe vertigo. Even watching TV would trigger the dizziness. This, of course, made it difficult to watch the exploits of the talented Indians team. A major factor in helping me get through this ordeal was being able to listen to the Indians radio broadcasts. That entire summer, I never missed an Indians game and looked forward to listening to Tom Hamilton and Herb Score deliver the play-by-play accounts, their expert analysis, and relate wonderful baseball stories throughout the broadcasts. For some reason, with my eyes closed, and total concentration on those great voices emanating through the radio that was always at my side, I was able to get through the evening.

Years later, after my return to good health, I was fortunate enough to meet Tom Hamilton at an Indians Caravan event. I relayed my story to Hammy and told him that he is a treasure to Indians fans, that his golden voice and the way he conveyed his passion for baseball helped me get through a difficult time. Hammy was very gracious, and seemed almost embarrassed to receive the flattery. Today, even with high-definition TV, endless slow-motion replays, and a plethora of video graphics, I continue to enjoy listening to the Indians radio broadcasts. A warm summer night seems to go hand-in-hand with baseball on the radio. *—Don Sebastian, Columbus*

It's always exciting to hear Tom Hamilton call a game, but never more so than the early 1990s when the excitement was building toward their greatness. One of my favorite "calls" was a game against Seattle, really before they got good. The Indians won on a grand slam by the late Carlos

Martinez. Tom's calls were amazing, and I recorded it on tape and listened to it over and over. *—Dan Polster, Solon*

I didn't see Manny Ramirez's "Wow" home run off Dennis Eckersley live on July 16, 1995, but I remember listening to the radio. When he hit that home run to end the game, and after a few seconds of soaking in Tom Hamilton's excited voice, I opened the door of my car and looked out across the parking lot. There were at least a dozen other people all doing the same thing, smiling and shaking our heads as we got out of our cars. It felt like the entire city had been listening to that game on the radio. *—Matthew Rich, Evanston, Illinois*

I recall one evening—when passing by old Municipal Stadium with undoubtedly a sparse crowd holding out hope with Herb and Tom—that I got on the radio with Herb and Tom! On a whim, I decided to toot that Mazda horn a few times as I passed by the stadium and sure enough, a few moments later with the stadium getting smaller in my rear view mirror, I could clearly hear myself (or at least my Mazda) sounding off as Herbie called a long fly ball off the bat of Jim Thome. I am still listening to the Indians—online and without car horns—from Holland, Michigan. *—Vince Duckworth, Holland, Michigan*

The comeback vs. Seattle in 2001. I don't know how many fans remember, but on Hammy's radio call of the Omar triple he got caught up in the incredible chain of events and began shouting "Tribe wins! Tribe wins! ... Or ties it, I'm sorry." I thought that was funny and it showed that Tom was just as thrilled as all of the fans that stuck around or continued watching/listening. Obviously, it didn't happen in the '90s, but it was certainly a game from that era that I will never forget. *—Philip Sodeman, Youngstown*

I was in fifth grade during the 1995 season. My parents typically sent me to bed around the seventh inning or so on school nights, but unbeknownst to them, I had a little tiny radio that I used to sneak under my pillow to catch the last few innings. The best was of course a particular game (I don't remember exactly what year) when Jim Thome hit a long walk-off homer off Troy Percival. Hearing Hammy yell "waaaaaaaayy back ... GONE!" as the crowd went wild almost made me shout for joy, which would've blown my cover of course. I had to settle for a silent fist bump into my pillow. Hearing Tom Hamilton call a walk-off home run on the radio always brings back the excitement of those days for me. What a team! *—Paul Shaniuk, Cleveland Heights*

My grandfather started me listening to the Tribe on the radio—back then it was Jimmy Dudley (who I only vaguely recall) and then Herb Score. Although some games were televised, my grandfather told me: "On the radio, they paint a picture better than anything you can see on TV, in fact you don't need TV. Just close your eyes and listen—it's like being at the field." To this day, radio is my first choice for the Tribe, thanks to my grandfather. *—Linda Olen, Parma*

Those '90s Indians years were my high school years when kids start to break out on their own, but sitting in the car with my dad and listening to Tom and Herb call the games helped to create a stronger bond with my dad. We would laugh when Herb would call it, "Way back, Vizquel under it." And would marvel at Tom's ability to paint a picture with his voice. Then, to years later get to meet and learn from Tom helped lead me to eventually become a radio broadcaster with the Indians minor league affiliate in Mahoning Valley. *—Tim Pozsgai, Mentor*

Growing up in the '90s, my childhood was significantly impacted by the Cleveland Indians. One of my favorite memories was the night I discovered that my bedroom alarm clock had AM radio capabilities. No longer did I need a bedtime story, because I now had Tom Hamilton's broadcast to facilitate my slumber. Usually exciting, but always under control, his precise command of the ballgame truly made me feel like I was there. *—Evan Rapkin, Atlanta, Georgia*

I'll never forget the nights growing up listening to Hammy on the radio. Three to four nights a week, my dad and I would play ball in our makeshift diamond. Every night, a radio graced with an Indians sticker would accompany us. As a 7-year-old, playing baseball with your dad and listening to your favorite team is as good as it gets. Baseball is the ultimate father-and-son game. Eleven years later, as a freshman at Xavier University, I met a kid named Nick from Avon Lake, Ohio. Nick was one of the nicest kids you will ever meet, and we bonded over our love of the Indians. I soon found out he was the son of Tom Hamilton, and soon thereafter, I had the privilege of meeting Tom. It was somewhat of a surreal moment knowing that my friend's dad was the voice I admired, and grew up listening to. A few years later, after Nick was drafted by the Indians, I was watching a spring training game. I saw Nick come to the plate for the Indians, but I didn't hear Tom's voice calling the game. Instead, I saw an understandably emotional Tom in the crowd watching his son. It immediately brought me back to the days of me and my dad playing in our field listening to the Tribe. That bond and those memories are what the Tribe is all about. *—Fritz Schilling, Buckeye Lake*

October 1997. Game 6 of the ALCS was on a Wednesday evening. I remember the night because I drove my younger sister to church for youth group, but I did not go in. I sat in my car and listened to Tom Hamilton and Herb Score call the game. I thought I'd be able to walk in a few minutes late, but the game went to extra innings. Church was almost over, and Tony Fernandez stepped to the plate. I can still hear Herb. "The Indians are going to the World Series! Maybe!" The game ended in time for me to celebrate with friends after church, and take my sister home as well! *—Kyle Snyder, Hermitage, Tennessee*

Mr. Hamilton brought the Indians to life for me. Through his voice, I could feel every pitch, hit and catch. I was a Tribe fan once but high school and college got in the way. But when I returned to baseball in the mid-'90s and I heard the voice of Tom Hamilton, I was hooked. Like fine wine, Mr. Hamilton's voice is smooth but contains loads of flavor that changes with the fortunes of the Tribe. Mr. Hamilton is honest, upfront and to the point with his observations of how the Tribe is doing nightly. Mr. Hamilton has made me cheer, cry and pull the darn car over with excitement, but most of all, his voice makes me care about the Cleveland Indians. It makes me proud that he is behind the mic telling me the Indians story nightly. One of the best moments in my life was sharing Mr. Hamilton's "Yes Cleveland, you will have an October to remember!" with my then-girlfriend Sharon. It brought chills to her, and tears for me. We were winners. *—C.R. Barclay, Reynoldsburg*

I was never much of a baseball player growing up, but I loved pretending to be a member of those Indians teams. I remember spending hours in my driveway with my Fisher-Price radio blasting Herb Score and Tom Hamilton calling the Tribe, and throwing a ball against the garage door pretending to be Carlos and Omar turning double plays. There were many nights after the sun set where I'd be the only person still out on the street and the only sounds you could hear were Herb, Tom and the thump of the ball against the garage door.

While I loved those Indians players, Herb and Tom ended up becoming my real idols. I aspired to be in and around the field of broadcasting. I studied broadcasting in college and grew up to be a communications lawyer at the Federal Communications Commission (FCC) in Washington, DC. *—Adam Copeland, Alexandria, Virginia*

One of my favorite radio memories was (I want to say) Hammy's 3rd or 4th year. The BELOVED Herb Score had a senior moment. Passing the mic back to Tom he said back to you Tony. Hamilton, always the professional, laughed, and so did Herb. To me Score was already a legend as an announcer and Hamilton had just become one. *—Steve Vopicka, Fort Worth, Texas*

A NEW BEGINNING

A True New Day For the Tribe

You knew the world had changed for Cleveland Indians baseball on a snowy day in early December of 1993. That was when the Tribe called a press conference to announce the signing of free agents.

Not one free agent.

Two.

And not just two guys found at the bottom of the bargain bin at some baseball rummage sale.

In the new restaurant area of the new Jacobs Field, where a game had yet to be played, were Eddie Murray and Dennis Martinez.

The Indians never signed players such as Murray and Martinez before, even if they no longer were in their primes. If talented veterans had a choice of where to finish their careers, most would have picked the Yukon Territory before Cleveland.

But all that changed as the 1994 season approached.

"It's a whole new ballgame," General Manager John Hart kept saying . . . with feeling!!

Murray and Martinez put the two exclamation points at the end of that sentence.

Martinez arrived in town with a 15-9 record and a 3.85 ERA with the Montreal Expos in 1993.

Murray showed up with a .285 batting average, 27 homers and 100 RBI for the Mets in 1993.

"I kept thinking how the Indians NEVER signed guys like Eddie and Dennis," said Tom Hamilton. "You'd never even dare dream that they'd sign players like that. This signing was as big as it gets—maybe the biggest in franchise history. That's because it changed the mindset of people with the Indians, and how people looked at the Indians."

Martinez had come to Cleveland to finalize his contract. There were a few snags. Martinez told Dick Jacobs how he was supposed to be at a family reunion in Miami, and maybe he should go home. They could work out the details later.

Jacobs said, "Stay as long as you want. When you're done, I'll send you back in my private jet."

New ballpark. Private jet.

Martinez realized it truly was a new ballgame in Cleveland.

Martinez stayed in Cleveland, and the deal was finished.

Then Jacobs told a man standing nearby, "OK, Captain, take him home."

And Martinez was gone, on a private jet.

"My dad [Ron Shapiro] represented Eddie and Dennis," said Mark Shapiro. "One of my jobs back then was to pick up different free agents at the airport and bring them to the ballpark. I remember picking up David Wells and Sid Fernandez. We didn't get them signed. But I also brought in Dennis and Eddie."

Shapiro said that Hart would take the free agents to the new ballpark, and they'd walk around the field.

Hart would talk about sellout crowds, about the best new stadium in baseball, about young stars such as Albert Belle, Kenny Lofton and Carlos Baerga.

"And you will be right in the middle of it," Hart would say. "Eddie, you'll be batting right behind Albert—right in the heart of the order. And Dennis, you'll be starting the opener. You'll be our big-game pitcher. Look around at the ballpark. You can see it coming."

Shapiro would listen to Hart, "and it almost sounded poetic."

New ballpark.

New dream.

New team.

Hart also had some fun with the two free agents.

He told projected designated hitter Murray: "The wind usually blows out."

When touring the new stadium with Martinez, Hart pointed to the flag. It was blowing in: "That's how the wind usually blows."

He had to know that Martinez and Murray would compare mental notes, and the windy promises would come up.

But Hart also had known Martinez and Murray for years, dating back to when they were players with the Orioles and Hart was a minor-league manager in the Baltimore farm system from 1982 to 1987.

"People around baseball were beginning to understand that the talent was here; there was a real core of a good team," said Hart. "You could come to Cleveland and we could compete with New York, L.A. and everywhere else because of the talent. When we signed Eddie and Dennis, we knew they were in the twilight of their careers. But we were convinced they still had some gas in their tanks. They knew how to win and that could help us."

Martinez signed a two-year, $9 million contract.

Murray signed a one-year, $3 million deal.

Murray was 37 and Martinez was 39 when they were introduced to the Tribe media and fans on December 2, 1993. That's why their contracts were so short in length.

"Until we built the foundation of a good team and a new stadium, it didn't make sense to spend wildly," owner Dick Jacobs said at that press conference. "It would have been like throwing money into Lake Erie. I admit, a few years ago, our team was so hard to watch that there were games where I went home early."

Instead, the Indians were heading into an era when you had better buy your tickets early.

Real early.

Like how the team sold out the entire season before opening day from 1995 to 1999.

Martinez was excited at that 1993 press conference. He talked about how he hadn't been in Cleveland since 1986, and how the city had changed. He raved about the development of downtown, the new stadium, the talented team. He sounded as if he worked for the Cleveland Chamber of Commerce.

This was the same Dennis Martinez who pitched for the Orioles on one frigid night at the old Stadium on Lake Erie in 1978. When the game was over, he said, "When it gets this cold in Nicaragua [his home], people die!"

By 1994, he couldn't wait to take the mound in Cleveland.

The $12 million that the Tribe committed to Martinez and Murray was nearly equal to the $15 million spent for the team's entire payroll in 1993.

"With Eddie and Dennis, we've made a major breakthrough," Hart said at that press conference. "When our park opens in April, we will be ready to go to war. We didn't want to put a shell of a team in the new ballpark."

Most Tribe fans couldn't believe the signings. The cynics believed something must be very wrong with Murray and Martinez, or why would they want to come to Cleveland? The team had some promising talent, but its record was exactly 76-86 the previous two years.

It helped that Ron Shapiro (father of Mark Shapiro) was the agent for Martinez and Murray. Not because he'd do his son a favor. Rather, having a son in the front office meant that Ron Shapiro paid extra attention to what the Tribe was doing in terms of building a team. He knew there would be a major impact from the new ballpark.

"The composition of the team and the ballpark made the difference," Ron Shapiro said at that press conference. "The organization also really put on the full-court press."

Murray seemed happy to be away from a major media market. The previous five years, he had played in Los Angeles and New York. He was often portrayed as sullen and/or angry in the media.

"I'm just looking for some calmness," said Murray. "And that was a good, young club."

Murray was being signed to be the designated hitter and bat fifth, behind Belle.

At the time of their signings, Martinez and Murray had combined for 11 All-Star appearances.

"I knew that even if they were only 80 percent of what they used to be in their primes, that still made them better than 80 percent of the players in baseball," said Hart. "And we had to get some veterans who would have instant respect in the clubhouse from our young guys."

Hart paused, thinking back to his early days with the Tribe.

"I remember when we had our winter press tours," said Hart. "We'd be driving around in five feet of snow, and I'd be trying to sell the fans on Jose Escobar. Not many were buying that."

Hamilton said, "After that day, I realized that we were entering into an era where good players would actually want to come to Cleveland. It was an amazing change."

A New Ballpark, A New Game

Even before Jacobs Field officially opened, fans would show up and just stare.

That's right, stare at an empty ball field. Or stare at a stadium being built.

And then they'd smile.

And dream.

And take pictures.

Sometimes, it was just photos of the stadium. Other times, it was a photo of themselves with the stadium in the background.

The photos seemed to say, "Can you believe this?"

This being a new baseball stadium in Cleveland.

This being able to say, "I lived long enough to see the new stadium, and I never thought it would happen here."

This being baseball in Cleveland no longer being a joke.

"Most Cleveland fans really didn't know what a good baseball stadium looked like because they had only watched games at the old Stadium," said Tom Hamilton. "When Jacobs Field opened, we no longer had a stadium. We had a ballpark! It was made for baseball and for baseball fans."

Hamilton thought back to 1994 when Jacobs Field opened: "Now almost everyone has a new ballpark, so it's hard to imagine the impact back in 1994. But back then, only Camden Yards in Baltimore [which opened in 1992] was a real ballpark. The White Sox moved into a new stadium, but it had no real personality. But walking into Jacobs Field, I said to myself, 'I can't believe we're actually going to play here. This can't be possible!' "

Many of the fans felt the same way.

It had to be like the first time electricity flowed, turning on the lights in your house. No more candles. No more gas lanterns. Just turn a knob or flip a switch.

And yes, there was light.

Or the first time someone turned on a faucet and water flowed.

No more going out to the well.

Fans were told how the new ballpark would be magnificent. They had seen drawings in newspapers. They watched the hole being dug, then the walls going up.

"But the full force of it never hit you until you first stepped inside," said Hamilton. "You just knew that everything had changed for the Indians."

And it almost didn't happen.

For years, there was talk of creating a new ballpark for the Tribe. Or perhaps, building a dome for both the Indians and Browns. In 1984, there was a vote on a new dome. It would be used for both teams. Art Modell opposed it. He wanted to remain as landlord of the old Stadium, and he wanted the Indians as paying tenants. OK, Modell didn't say he was against a dome. He just said it wasn't needed.

As Gabe Paul often said, "There was only one man who really liked the old Stadium—Art Modell."

It didn't matter, because the project was poorly conceived and voters knew it. Not only did the measure lose, the vote against was by a 2-to-1 margin.

The next vote was in 1990. This time it was to pay for construction of a new baseball stadium for the Tribe and a new arena for the Cavaliers. It was to be in the Central Market area of downtown Cleveland.

If the vote passed, everyone in Cuyahoga County who bought a beer would pay a 1.9-cent tax. It was 1.5 cents per ounce of liquor, and 4.5 cents on every pack of cigarettes sold. This was called the "Sin Tax."

Suppose it had failed. Would the Tribe have moved?

"That seemed like the only option at the time," said Hamilton.

Six days before the May 8, 1990 vote, Commissioner Fay Vincent came to town and said that he wanted the Indians to stay in Cleveland, but without a new ballpark . . . they could move.

St. Petersburg, Fla., had a new dome and was on the prowl for a baseball team. It had nearly secured the White Sox before Chicago built them a new park. St. Petersburg now hungrily eyed the Indians.

"Dick Jacobs was an astute businessman," said John Hart. "Yes, he might have moved the team—but could he do it? I don't know if he could."

Jacobs had owned the team since 1986. One of his reasons for buying the franchise from the estate of F.J. "Steve" O'Neill . . .

Let's stop here for a moment and remember that for nearly three years, the Tribe was owned by a dead man. O'Neill purchased the franchise in 1978, and he died in 1983. And for three years, his nephew, Pat O'Neill, shopped for a buyer who would keep the team in Cleveland.

That became Jacobs, who grew up in Akron and kept his shopping mall empire primarily headquartered in Cleveland. Jacobs bought the team because the price was right, and he also was a man who knew how to cut deals and build things. He didn't buy the Indians to move them, or to sell to someone who would relocate the franchise. But he also knew that if the Tribe remained at the old Stadium, the situation was hopeless. He also didn't buy the Indians to lose—be it baseball games or money.

"We were on a plane [Jacobs' private jet] the day of the vote," said Hart. "At one point, it was 70 percent against the vote passing. The vote became closer. Later in the day, we heard it was 54-46, still against the vote. Dick said, 'It's going to pass,' and he talked about the western suburbs that had yet to report. He was right."

It was 51.7 percent in favor, enough to make the new ballpark (and an arena for the Cavs) a reality.

It also enraged Modell, who believed he had been outmaneuvered by Jacobs and ignored by the city of Cleveland. But at this point in 1990, the last thing anyone imagined was that the Cleveland franchise that would move was the Browns. There are a lot of opinions about why that happened, but there is little doubt that Jacobs was the smarter and more politically connected owner who knew how to pull off a deal of this magnitude.

As the Tribe prepared for its first game at Jacobs Field in 1994, Dick Jacobs talked about what the new ballpark meant to him.

"When I see this place, I feel something inside," he said. "It's almost euphoria. It's a field of dreams."

Jacobs' critics would say that he also saw dollar signs. Millions and millions of dollar signs.

On that day, Jacobs talked about owning 40 shopping malls, five hotels, 42 Wendy's restaurants and several office buildings.

"You can build 40 or 50 shopping malls, but there is only one ballpark," he said.

He was 68 years old on opening day of 1994. He talked about being a "buy and hold guy." He said he had sold only one significant business—a shopping mall.

"The Indians are different from anything else," he said. "I do take more satisfaction from owning them because they really belong to the city and the fans. I never had what I considered a serious offer to buy the Indians, and the team is not for sale."

Jacobs talked about leaving the ballpark early in some of those seasons where the team lost more than 100 games.

"In my business, an optimist is a guy who brings his lunch to work," he said. "But I expect us to contend. I really do."

On that day, no one knew that the Indians were entering the best seven-year span of the franchise, that two World Series appearances were coming. Or that there would be a 455-game sellout streak. But Jacobs knew the ballgame had changed, and he knew the ballpark was the main reason.

When Jacobs Field opened, there were 43,368 seats, and that included 1,564 in luxury suites.

By the time the Tribe left the old Stadium, the capacity for baseball was listed as 74,483. But in the 1940s and 1950s, some crowds were announced as more than 80,000. The Tribe media guide says the franchise record was 86,288 for Game 5 of the 1948 World Series. Game 4 drew 81,897. The last World Series game played at the old Stadium was Game 4 in 1954, with a crowd of 78,102.

No need to dwell on the numbers. The point is that when fans first walked into the old Stadium, they were overwhelmed by the sheer size of the place.

At Jacobs Field, it was the beauty and intimacy of a ballpark right in the heart of the city, about a half-mile from Lake Erie and the old Stadium.

"I remember when they were building it at the old Central Market area," said Hamilton. "There didn't seem to be enough room. It's like they were squeezing it in."

Jacobs Field consumes 12 acres of prime downtown real estate, and the cost was listed as $175 million.

"With the smaller park, people were forced to buy more tickets in advance," said Hamilton. "This was the early 1990s. The big money-makers for teams were not the local cable television deals that you see today. That came later. It was your ballpark, especially those luxury suites."

The new ballpark had 109 suites on the second deck of the stadium. The price was between $45,000 and $85,000 per season.

They had another 10 suites at field level renting for $100,000 per year.

When the park opened in 1994, all but one of those 119 suites was rented in advance. Many had five-year leases. If you do some quick math, the Indians had about $8 million in revenue from suites alone for 1994 before the first pitch was thrown.

"Our entire payroll for 1992 was about $8 million," said Shapiro. "The change in two years was startling."

By opening day of 1994, the Tribe had sold 17,000 season tickets. Compare that to 3,330 in 1992, when that team had the $8 million payroll.

The Indians had sold about 2 million tickets before the first pitch. Everyone with the Indians was sure the ballpark would be embraced by fans and ticket sales would soar.

But no one saw what would happen between 1994 and 1996.

1. There would be a baseball strike wiping out the final six weeks of the 1994 season, along with the playoffs and World Series.

2. The Browns would move to Baltimore after the 1995 season.

3. The Cavs would have a mediocre team.

4. The Cleveland economy of the 1990s would be strong.

5. The Indians would have their first contending team since 1959.

"You put all that together and you have a unique set of circumstances that had never happened before and will never happen again," said Shapiro. "When the strike hit, almost every other team was losing ticket sales in a big, big way. It's like we were walled off. We had no real pull-back. So our revenue had increased dramatically at a time when about everyone else in baseball was seeing their revenue cut back."

Tribe fans were so giddy about the new stadium and the young, gifted team that was emerging, their anger at the 1994 baseball strike was not aimed at the franchise. They just wanted baseball back. They wanted to go to the ballpark. They believed that this team would indeed deliver a World Series, and they wanted to watch it happen.

The Browns' move just made more people into baseball fans. With the football team gone, it was All Tribe, All The Time on most radio sports talk shows. The Indians also dominated newspaper coverage.

"Something else that was big in the middle 1990s was the economy so was much better," said Shapiro in a 2014 interview. "There were four more Fortune 500 companies in Cleveland than there are today. There were twice as many people working downtown as there are today. People had money to spend."

There was the new ballpark . . .

The new winning team . . .

The new sense of hope . . .

"People kept buying tickets," said Shapiro. "Suddenly, we could operate like a major-market team because our revenues were increasing while most franchises were hit so hard [by the strike]."

Consider the following:

- In 1994, the average attendance for a Major League Baseball (MLB) game was 31,256 before the strike. The Indians averaged 39,121.
- In 1995, the MLB average dropped to 25,022. The Tribe was at 39,483.
- In 1996, the MLB average was 26,510. The Tribe was at 41,477.
- In 1997, the MLB average was 28,261. The Tribe was at 42,034.

It wasn't until 2000 that the MLB average returned to 30,000. Meanwhile, the Indians were selling out every game from June 12, 1995 to April 4, 2001. That was a sellout streak of 455 games.

Furthermore, the tickets were being bought in the off-season, meaning the team could bank some of the revenue and draw interest while waiting to write payroll checks and meet other expenses during the season.

Yes, the baseball strike of 1994 was a GIANT help to the Tribe.

"And the other teams also didn't have a ballpark like us," said Hamilton. "Only Baltimore with Camden Yards could compare to what we had in Cleveland in 1994. Now, almost everyone has a new park with luxury suites. But back then, it was a big advantage for us. In a lot of ways, we could operate like a major-market team."

There was yet another factor helping the Tribe—the "no-show rate."

That's the percentage of fans who buy a ticket, but then don't show up.

"In April and May it was around 20 percent in the 1990s," said Shapiro. "It dropped to 10–15 percent in the summer. The average is about 20 percent for a season. Some years, we were very close to 10 percent. That's important, because the more people in the stands, the more revenue you can capture. They buy food. They buy souvenirs."

It seemed nearly everyone in Northeast Ohio owned a shirt, cap or jacket that featured something in Wahoo red, white and blue. The Indians became cool, embraced by young people and the casual fans.

"Revenue is one thing, but a key reason you want people in the park is the energy they create," said Shapiro. "In those first few years at Jacobs Field, the electricity and the pride about the building and the team was so transparent. You could feel it. People would go to the games, have a great time, and then want to come back."

The big crowds also helped the team retain players.

"It was so much fun to play for the Indians back then," said Orel Hershiser.

The home-team clubhouse had leather chairs and sofas. There were huge TV sets. The lockers themselves were made of high-quality wood. The carpeting was plush. The training room and weight rooms were huge and state of the art. They had indoor batting cages.

So much had changed so quickly from the old Stadium, where sometimes the showers only spit cold water and the sewers occasionally backed up in the tunnel to the dugouts. Players used to complain that the water from the fountains in the dugouts tasted like gasoline.

All the excuses were gone.

"No ballpark ever changed the perception of a city nationally like our park did," said Hamilton. "For so long, Cleveland was a punch line for jokes on national TV. A lot of that died out in the 1990s. It seemed everyone was feeling better about Cleveland."

Mike Hargrove Finally Makes it to the New Ballpark

"Hey! Get off the grass!"

Someone screamed those words at Mike Hargrove on the morning of the first regular-season game in the history of Jacobs Field. It was about 6 a.m. on April 4, 1994. It was a cold, clear spring morning in downtown Cleveland.

"One of those morning shows like 'Good Morning America' was there and they did an interview with me in the dugout," Hargrove said. "When I was done, I looked out at the field. It was clear and crisp, the grass had frost on it."

Hargrove then walked across the field behind home plate.

Actually, the exact words were: "Hey . . . get the [*bleep*] off the grass."

The voice belonged to head groundskeeper Brandon Koehnke.

"I turned around and went over to him," said Hargrove. "I got right in his face. Talk about two guys who already had the adrenaline flowing about the first game. I was yelling, 'Don't ever talk to me like that again!' and I added some others words to make the point. And remember, it was 6 in the morning.

"Now I know that walking on grass with frost like that leaves footprints," said Hargrove. "I didn't know that at the time. And I was just pumped up for the first game."

In terms of what the new ballpark meant to the fans and the city, Hargrove had the greatest appreciation of anyone in a Tribe uniform on that first day.

That's because he first came to the Indians in the middle of the 1979 season in a trade for Paul Dade. He played seven years for the Indians. Unlike many of his teammates, he never wanted to leave Cleveland. He never became so discouraged with the depressed circumstances of Tribe baseball in the late 1970s and 1980s.

"I never thought we'd see a new stadium," said Hargrove. "For so long, we all knew we needed a new ballpark. Every so often, there was a threat that the team would move somewhere. And once in a while, you'd hear that they might build a new park. But it never happened."

Hargrove paused, thinking back to the pre-Jacobs Field era.

Moving the team "seemed like the more likely scenario," he said. "And I would have absolutely hated to see that happen."

In 1990, Hargrove was in his first season as the Tribe's first-base coach. He had managed at every level in the Tribe's minor-league system. In 1989, he was named the Class AAA Pacific Coast League Manager of the Year by Baseball America. The magazine also named Hargrove its top candidate to become a major-league manager. When he was promoted to the big-league coaching staff in 1990, he was the manager in training. This was part of the plan by Hank Peters. The former Tribe president made that clear to John McNamara, who had been hired as manager that spring. Part of his job was to train Hargrove, and the 57-year-old McNamara understood his mission.

There were times after games when he would be talking to Hargrove and say, "Mike, when you're managing this team . . ."

Just as Peters was teaching young front-office executives John Hart and Dan O'Dowd, McNamara was grooming Hargrove.

And all of them were waiting and wondering if the new ballpark would be a reality.

"There was a make-or-break vote on the Sin Tax," said Hargrove. "We were playing a game in Minnesota, and many of us were wondering about the vote. After the game, we heard it passed. It had barely passed, but it passed. And finally, I knew the team would be staying in Cleveland."

President Bill Clinton was scheduled to throw out the first pitch when Jacobs Field opened. He wanted to play catch in the bowels of the stadium, near the batting cages. Tribe Vice President Bob DiBiasio asked Andy Hargrove, son of Mike, if he wanted to play catch with the president.

"Andy was about 12 and he said, 'My dad doesn't like him, so I can't play catch with him!' " Hargrove said, laughing as he recalled the story.

Can't blame Andy. He thought he was backing his father.

"Jiminy Christmas," Hargrove, with another laugh. "My son turned down the president!"

More than 20 years later, the story still amused Hargrove.

"The thing is, I did like Bill Clinton," he said. "I met him several times later when I managed in Baltimore. I never voted for him, but I really liked him."

Hargrove added that he and General Manager John Hart quickly grabbed the chance to meet the president and had pictures taken with him before that 1994 opener.

Did he ever tell the president about Andy?

"No," laughed Hargrove. "I should have—he would probably have gotten a kick out of it."

In another strange opening-day story, a fan approached Dick Jacobs and asked if the Tribe owner was "the guy who is the statue."

The fan meant Bob Feller.

Jacobs said he wasn't.

The man shrugged and walked away.

Hargrove replaced McNamara on July 6, 1991. The Indians were 25-52 under McNamara that year.

"You could see it coming," said Tom Hamilton. "In 1990, we had a decent year [77-85], at least by the standards back then. But John [Hart] and Danny [O'Dowd] thought it was a bit of a mirage. And once the vote passed, everything was aimed at putting a good team on the field in 1994. So they cut payroll, traded off veterans and brought up a lot of kids. Hank [Peters] knew it would be hard for Mac. He was at the point in his career where he wanted to win now because he knew he didn't have that many years left to manage."

So Peters turned to Hargrove.

He was 41, a 12-year major-league player with a career .290 batting average. Hargrove was picked in the 25th round of the 1972 draft by the

Texas Rangers. He came from tiny Northwestern Oklahoma State in Alva, Okla. He never played baseball in high school. He was in college to play football, and then tried baseball. So he was no one's prime prospect. Hargrove played only two seasons in the minors—never higher than Class A. Former Rangers Manager Billy Martin brought Hargrove to the majors, and he hit .323 and was the 1974 American League Rookie of the Year.

So Hargrove spent more years in the minors as coach and manager (five seasons) than he did as a player (two).

Hargrove finished the 1991 season with a 32-53 record.

There was no question that Hargrove would return as manager in 1992. But there also were doubts about his long-term future in the dugout.

After the 1991 season, Peters retired. While Hargrove knew Hart, it was not a close relationship.

"John didn't hire Mike," said Hamilton. "People forget that. Mike was picked by Hank Peters. And I always think that at some point, a general manager wants to hire his own manager. Mike would always be a Hank Peters hire."

Hart would object when his relationship with Hargrove was termed a "shotgun baseball marriage."

But that was exactly the case. The men were thrown together by Peters during a season when the team would lose a franchise-record 105 games.

Hargrove did have a few advantages. Because of his playing career with the Tribe, he was popular with fans and media. People knew he not only wanted to manage, but he wanted to manage in Cleveland. The franchise and the city were special to him. He and his wife Sharon were active in community events, and people knew the Hargroves. Both have this sense of unpretentiousness and decency about them.

Hart was the brash newcomer, a virtual unknown to the fans with no track record worthy of discussion when he took over as general manager in 1991. Most people in the media knew that Hart was behind many of the moves to slash payroll, trade veterans and lose with young players. And they knew that strategy put the manager (Hargrove or anyone else) in a hopeless position.

So just as Hart had to have patience with his young players, he had to have the same with his young manager.

And Hart was only 42, a year older than his manager when Hargrove was promoted by Peters.

As the first game at Jacobs Field approached, Hargrove stepped on to the field.

"The sun was out," said Hargrove. "It was crisp, but clear. A real gorgeous day to open the season."

He watched the Cleveland Orchestra play the national anthem. He saw the team "re-retire" the numbers of Bob Feller, Lou Boudreau, Mel Harder and Earl Averill.

"All opening days are special," said Hargrove. "To a player, every day should feel like opening day. Everything is so new. You wish you could have that feeling all season."

But there would never be another opening like April 4, 1994.

"I had been going to the park before it opened," said Hargrove. "I saw it in various stages of construction. But to see it finished for the first time—the carpet down, the lights and walls put up—everything so fresh and new . . . and I looked at the great weight room and the batting cages [under the stands] . . . I felt like I was finally in the big leagues in Cleveland. It was inspiring."

Game-time temperature was 48. Dennis Martinez started for the Tribe.

"Sandy [Alomar] got the first hit [it was in the eighth inning] for us," said Hargrove. "Randy Johnson was pitching [for Seattle]. He had great stuff. I was thinking, 'It would be a tragedy if we got no-hit on opening day,' because it looked like that could happen."

In the press box for that game was Feller, the only man to throw a no-hitter on opening day.

He was thrilled when Alomar lashed a single to right.

"I've sweated it [the opening-day record] out for 50-some years," Feller told Tony Grossi, who was working for The Plain Dealer and helping to cover the game.

"It's about the only record that I have left," Feller said. "Except for the most bases on balls [208] in one season. That's one Nolan Ryan didn't get from me."

* * *

Hargrove had survived 2½ years as the Tribe manager at the old Stadium.

"I really didn't know if I'd make it" to the new ballpark, said Hargrove. "For a manager, your first job is your most important job. Depending upon how it goes, you are going to manage a long time—or not very long at all."

And Hargrove had his doubts.

"In 1992 and '93, we got off to terrible starts," said Hargrove. "There were times both years when I wondered if I'd be around by the All-Star break."

The 1992 Indians were 8-15 in April, 36-52 at the All-Star break.

The 1993 Indians were 7-15 in April, 19-32 by June 1 and 40-48 at the All-Star break.

Hargrove had been around baseball—especially Cleveland baseball—long enough to know that managers are often fired during the season.

When Hargrove was named manager in the middle of the 1991 season, it was the fifth time in the previous 15 years (1977–91) that the Tribe fired a manager during the season.

"Most managers have a point in their careers when the season is going bad and you think, 'I'm not going to make it to the All-Star break,' " said Hargrove.

Most managers also aren't as honest as Hargrove when it comes to admitting the insecurity of the position.

The 1992 Indians rallied from that 36-52 record at the All-Star break to finish at 76-86. That was a significant improvement from 57-105 in 1991.

But Hargrove may have been fired in 1993, except for one horrible event.

On March 22, 1993, Tribe pitchers Tim Crews and Steve Olin were killed in a boating accident on Little Lake Nellie in Clermont, Fla. Pitcher Bob Ojeda also was in the boat when it rammed into a dock late at night. Ojeda was seriously injured, but survived.

Hargrove and his wife Sharon spent several weeks dealing with the players' emotional issues and grief from the tragedy. Tribe fans remember how Hargrove often was the voice of the team during those weeks following the death of the two pitchers.

"It all could have come apart after the accident," said Hamilton. "In the first half, the team was just so lost—they hadn't gotten over what happened."

The Tribe was 15-25 after 40 games.

Hart thought the 1993 Indians would be a .500 team. They were 76-86 in 1992. The key players had gained more experience. But was the problem really the manager? How can anyone evaluate the impact of the tragedy on the team? And would it seem wildly unfair to fire a manager—especially a manager so respected by the players?

He was the one who stood so strong in the middle of broken hearts and tears.

In 1995 interviews, Hart said he was on board with the decision to hire Hargrove. And Hargrove said he "never felt as if I was shoved down John's throat." But looking back, both men admitted they didn't know each other well when they began working together.

Would Hargrove have been fired if there had been no boating accident?

Yes, you can ask that question.

But you also have to ask, would the team have started so slowly if there had been no boating accident?

Suppose it was just another start to another season. Would the Tribe have played better? After all, that 1993 team finished at 76-86. That means it was 61-61 over the final 122 games after that 15-25 start.

The team played .500 ball once a sense of normalcy returned.

And Hargrove also returned for 1994 . . . and the new ballpark.

The hero of the 1994 home opener was . . . Wayne Kirby.

In the bottom of the 11th inning, Eddie Murray doubled. With two outs, he was on third base. The score was 3-3.

Kirby didn't start that game. Hargrove sent him into the game as a pinch runner in the 10th inning.

OK, here's a trivia question: Kirby replaced whom on the bases?

Manny Ramirez.

And in the 11th, when Ramirez would normally have come to the plate, it was Kirby batting—and winning the game with a base hit.

Why did Kirby run for Ramirez?

This was 1994, the first full season for Ramirez in the big leagues. In the eighth inning, Ramirez had knocked in a run with a double. And then he was picked off second base.

Hargrove didn't want something like that happening again, so he used Kirby.

And the manager didn't know that Kirby would indeed win the game—with his bat.

The 1994 season ended after 113 games because of a labor dispute. The Indians were a game out of first place.

That year delivered several messages, the first being that the Tribe was really a legitimate contender.

The next was that Hargrove was the right manager.

Albert Belle: You Didn't Want to Miss a Single At-Bat

Albert Belle.

All you have to do is say that name and Tribe fans have an instant opinion.

Make that a very strong instant opinion.

Albert Belle.

In 1996, Belle was climbing the Tribe's all-time home run list, passing the likes of Earl Averill (franchise leader at the start of 1996 with 226 career homers from 1929 to 1939), Rocky Colavito, Larry Doby, Andre Thornton and Al Rosen.

In 1995, Belle became the first hitter in big-league history to hit 50 homers and 50 doubles in the same season. Those 50 home runs passed the Tribe's single-season mark of 43 set by Rosen in 1953.

For his career, Belle was a .368 hitter with the bases loaded, including 13 grand slams.

"Albert was such a great hitter," said Hamilton. "I never wanted to miss one of his at-bats. If I was off the air and had to go to the restroom, I'd wait another minute to watch Albert bat. He was the most fearsome slugger in the game. The way he stood at the plate as if he owned it. The way he stared at the pitcher, just glaring. The way he swung the bat, everything was ferocious. I never saw a hitter quite like that."

Belle was a regular in the majors from 1991 to 2000. In those 10 years, he averaged 37 homers and 120 RBI. He did it for the Tribe, White Sox and Orioles. He did it in good lineups and bad, and he did it every day.

You can also say he did it his way—even if it sometimes happened to be the hard way.

As Mike Hargrove said, "If only Albert had done some things differently, he could have been the Michael Jordan of Cleveland."

The former Tribe manager is so right. How the fans longed to embrace Belle. The same was true of his teammates. They loved Belle being on their team, even if they didn't always like being around Belle.

"One day, Albert got four hits in his first four at-bats," said Omar Vizquel. "In his last at bat, he popped out. He threw his helmet. We won that game, and went into the clubhouse. I was really hungry, but Albert was still so mad about popping out—he had turned over the table with all the food. He could be a little kid in that way."

Vizquel also had stories about cookies and food tossed around the locker room when Belle was angry.

For years, Kenny Lofton's locker was next to Belle's.

"He was so superstitious," said Lofton. "No one was supposed to touch his bats. No one was supposed to touch any of his stuff. If he talked to Hoynsie [Plain Dealer baseball writer Paul Hoynes] and got three hits, then he wanted to talk to him again. If he talked to him and had no hits—then he wanted nothing to do with [Hoynes]."

Belle had several superstitions.

He never left the on-deck circle until his name was announced. He didn't want any music played when he came to bat. He demanded silence. He immediately erased the back line of the batter's box. After every pitch, he stepped out of the box—and took two swings. Always two swings. Then he stepped back into the batter's box.

Lofton added, "Albert would say, 'Don't touch my stuff, don't want nobody touching my stuff.' "

In 1995, Plain Dealer columnist Bud Shaw wrote a very flattering article about how Belle kept a notebook with data about opposing pitchers. Hargrove and a couple of Tribe coaches told Shaw about the notebook. Shaw never saw it. Belle read the article and was enraged. He was convinced Shaw had been looking at things in his locker. No matter how many times Shaw said he never touched his locker, Belle refused to believe it.

He loathed anyone who seemed to step into his world, even a reporter who tried to write a complimentary story.

One year, Belle said his goal was to break Al Rosen's team record of 43 homers in a season. He did that with 50 in 1995.

"Hank Greenberg had 100 RBI at the All-Star break," Belle once said. "I wanted to break that record."

He never did. But most players in the 1990s had never heard of Greenberg, a star in the 1930s. Or Rosen, a star in the 1950s.

"What I want to be is the best run-producer," Belle once said. "That's the guy who drives in more runs than anyone else. That's what I want."

Lofton said baseball people now devalue the leadoff man and the stolen base. They forget that for a player to drive in 100 runs, someone has to be on base.

"In was like when you put food on the table and [Belle] has to eat it," said Lofton. "When we got on base, he was hungry. He wanted all the RBI he could get."

In his last six years with the Tribe (1991–96), Belle averaged 39 homers and 118 RBI per season.

"He was like a genius with crossword puzzles," said Lofton. "He had charts about what pitches were thrown to him. He could tell you from this at-bat to the next at-bat, how they pitched him. He was the most intense hitter, and most prepared that I have ever seen. He was never as bad as people made him out to be."

How do you even begin to explain Albert Belle?

"He's a deep study," as former Tribe General Manager Hank Peters once said.

One Sports Illustrated story by Michael Bamberger in 1996 featured a picture of Belle on the cover with the words "Tick . . . Tick . . . Tick . . ."

He was portrayed as a time bomb.

He threw a baseball at a fan, another at a photographer. He cursed out countless members of the media, and was fined $50,000 by Major League Baseball for screaming at television reporter Hannah Storm during the 1995 World Series. He ripped the thermostat off the dressing-room wall because he didn't like the room temperature. He smashed CDs when he didn't like the music picked by some teammates to be played in the clubhouse.

"One day, I walked into the auxiliary locker room and there were bats broken and sticking into the wall," said Mark Shapiro. "We knew it was Albert. It was just the kind of thing that he did. It was amazing. The bats were stuck straight into the wall. A plaster wall, not drywall. You know how strong you have to be to do that?"

Albert Belle strong, to be exact.

There are more stories, but you get the point.

"Albert's personality was never warm and fuzzy, so you knew what you were going to get from him," said Shapiro. "We have had other players over the years who'd be warm and fuzzy one day, and the next day they were belligerent. That was harder to deal with than Albert. You knew Albert was a tough guy who was focused on himself—and he didn't want to deal with any distractions. He wasn't very tolerant of others who had a different focus than he had. Most players respected his drive and his work ethic."

Shapiro then outlined Belle's strengths, counting them off . . .

"One, he wanted to play every single day. I mean, every day. No days off.

"Two, he was driven to be great. Not just good. He would never be satisfied with being good. He had to be great.

"Three, his work ethic was unparalleled.

"Four, he was consistently focused on his own performance and maximizing it."

Hamilton said, "Albert was not going to fail. He had a hard time accepting failure. He hated, absolutely hated to fail. He wanted to be the best hitter in the game, and was driven to be the best hitter in the game."

The Indians rated Belle as a top-three talent in the 1987 draft. But they knew other teams were worried about the LSU player's attitude. The Tribe didn't have a first round pick in 1987. When the second round rolled around, Belle was still available. The Indians were delighted to pick him, believing his raw power was a bargain, and signing him for $68,000.

Give former Tribe executives Jeff Scott (who first lobbied for Belle) and Joe Klein credit for taking a gamble with Belle that delivered one of the biggest payoffs in the history of the franchise.

The Indians immediately discovered a few things about Belle.

He was so smart when it came to hitting. He studied tapes of great hitters. He read baseball history about great hitters. He was determined to be a great hitter.

Great, not good.

And he hated anything that seemed to be in the way of that goal.

That's right—hated.

He believed he had many enemies who didn't believe he'd succeed, and he wanted to prove them wrong. Oh, how he wanted to show them that Albert Jojuan Belle would become one of the greatest hitters.

Ever.

He was known as Joey when he was at LSU and in his early days in the Tribe farm system.

Belle was 6-foot-2 and 210 pounds when he signed with Tribe. He was 20 and he was mad.

He was mad about being picked in the second round. Mad about the $68,000 bonus. Mad about a suspension at LSU. Mad that he wasn't recognized as what the Tribe had secretly rated him as: The No. 3 overall player in the 1987 draft.

And he wanted to reach the big leagues . . . yesterday.

That happened two years after he signed. He opened the 1989 season at Class AA Akron-Canton, hitting 20 homers in 89 games. The Indians allowed Belle to skip over Class AAA and brought him to the majors on July 15, 1989. He was not quite ready, hitting .225 with seven homers in 218 at-bats.

He opened the 1990 season with the Tribe and was only 4-of-23 when they sent him to Class AAA.

Belle was outraged, believing the Tribe gave up on him too soon. The Indians thought he needed some time in Class AAA to develop some patience (a word he hated) when it came to handling breaking pitches and change-ups.

Belle batted .344 with five homers in 96 at bats with Class AAA Colorado Springs, but his anger was erupting. The Indians were worried that he would hurt himself. During a game in June, he was so overwhelmed after popping out, he returned to the dugout and destroyed a sink with his bat. He went to the outfield in the next inning. During warmups, a teammate threw him a ball. He caught and fired it over the outfield fence.

The Tribe suspended him for 10 games. He was summoned to Cleveland and spent 10 weeks at Cleveland Clinic. When he emerged,

Joey Belle became known as Albert Belle. He insisted he had a drinking problem, which surprised the Tribe front office, coaches and his teammates. Maybe he was a closet drinker. But he never showed signs of being hungover or smelled as if he had been drinking when at the park. Odds are the stay at Cleveland Clinic was also to address his anger issues.

"You should have seen him in the spring of 1990," said Hamilton. "I had just been hired by the Indians so I had nothing to compare it with at the time. But I've never seen a player have a spring like that since then. He hit everything. I mean, everything."

Belle clubbed 11 homers in 74 at-bats, hitting .324.

"I was in awe of him at the plate," said Hamilton. "Herb [Score] was saying it's only spring training, and you can get fooled in spring training. But after a while, Herb was saying how 'We haven't had a guy like this around here in a long while.' He was crushing the ball."

Belle hit 28 homers and drove in 95 runs in 123 games in that 1991 season. He was also suspended for a week for throwing a ball at a fan and hitting him in the chest. He was sent to the minors for a month because he failed to run out several balls. But in the end, Belle was back and hitting homers.

That year, "Albert didn't sulk when we sent him back to the minors," said Hank Peters. "We gave him credit for that. We also knew we had to be patient with Albert."

By 1992, he owned the No. 4 spot in the lineup.

"Mike Hargrove always said that you needed a leadoff guy and a No. 4 hitter to build your lineup around," said Hamilton. "We had that with Kenny [Lofton] and Albert."

Belle just scared opposing pitchers.

Each year, he seemed to get better. And better. And better.

He shortened his swing. He took more pitches, drew more walks.

"I consider myself a .300 hitter," he said, even before he began to hit .300.

By 1994, he batted .357 with 36 homers and 101 RBI in 106 games during a strike-shortened season. He missed the batting title by two points. That also was the year that he was suspended for seven games for using a corked bat. That bat was grabbed by the umpires in Chicago. The White Sox heard Belle was using a corked bat. They asked the umpires to check. When the umpires stored it in their locker room, Tribe pitcher Jason Grimsley crawled through some vents in the ceiling to grab the bat and replace it with a Paul Sorrento model. The umpires weren't fooled. They went to the Tribe dressing room, demanded bats with Belle's name on it. One was cut open and found to be corked.

Grimsley grabbed the Sorrento bat because he thought all of Belle's bats might have been corked.

Hargrove never admitted Grimsley took the bat, but he did once say that the pitcher had the type of personality "where he would storm a pillbox." In a 1999 New York Times story, Grimsley said he did indeed steal Belle's bat.

Belle always denied he used a corked bat. He implied the league officials were out to get him, wondering why they had to send the bat to the American League office in New York to be X-rayed. Why not do it at the park in Chicago, he asked.

But the bottom line on Belle was the bottom line. The numbers. The stats. The man who insisted his name be in the lineup every day.

"Albert was not that hard to manage," said Hargrove. "Yes, you had to keep an eye on him. There were times when it seemed as if he was going a little off-line [with his moods]. That's when I'd call him into my office and we'd talk."

Hargrove said he usually started the conversation with this point: "Albert, you have all these aspirations and goals. You want to put up all these numbers. And that's all well and good, but if you continue to do this [whatever was the problem], you won't be able to reach those goals."

Belle would say, "Why not?"

Hargrove would say, "Because I won't play you. If I don't play you, you can't do it. So you need to just get back and play ball like you can."

Hargrove said Belle usually calmed down and went back to hitting.

"You could just count on him, every day," said Hargrove.

The former manager denied a story about a day when Hargrove wrote out a lineup and Belle's name wasn't in it. Supposedly, Belle ripped the lineup card off the wall, took it into Hargrove's office and demanded the manager "try it again."

"Not true," he laughed. "If he did that, one of us would be dead by now."

Hargrove paused.

"A manager still has what they call a 'hammer' over the players," he said. "By that, the manager writes out the lineup card. That's the ultimate hammer, deciding who plays. And Albert wanted to play. Every day."

In 1993, Belle played all but three games—and he was suspended for those three games.

In 1994, he played all but seven games—the seven games that were his suspension for the corked bat.

In 1995, he played all but one game.

In 1996, he played 158 games and missed four (two because of a suspension).

"Some people said Albert played every day because he wanted his stats and was selfish," said Hamilton. "I don't care why he played. He played every day. He played when he was hurt. He played when he was sick. He gave you your money's worth. You could count on Albert. He never got enough credit for that. Yes, he had some defensive lapses in left field when he seemed to be still thinking about hitting. He'd look at some balls hit in the gap as if to say, 'Kenny [Lofton], go get that.' So he wasn't a great left fielder. But he was a great, great hitter."

Hargrove remembered a meeting after a season when owner Dick Jacobs asked the manager, "Mike, can you win without Albert in the lineup?"

"Mr. Jacobs, we can win without him," said Hargrove. "But having him in the lineup makes it a whole lot easier."

Nearly 20 years after Belle hit 50 homers with 126 RBI and a .317 batting average in 1995, Hargrove is mad about Belle not being voted the MVP award. That went to Mo Vaughn (.300, 39 HR, 126 RBI).

"It was just because Albert ticked off so many writers," said Hargrove. "The same with him not being in Hall of Fame. He belongs. But the writers took it personally. He should be in the Hall of Fame right now."

Hamilton still marvels at the combination of strength and intelligence that Belle brought to the batter's box.

The right-handed hitter loved to flex his huge biceps. He held the bat like a war club, ready to savage the baseball.

"But he was rarely fooled by a pitcher," said Hamilton. "That's because of all the notes he took, the video that he studied. He also had a very good memory. It's a shame that Albert didn't let others know all the work that he did to become a great hitter. Eddie Murray was the smartest hitter that I've ever been around, and Albert was right there with him."

The Indians twice nominated Belle for the Roberto Clemente Award for public service. The United Way, Multiple Sclerosis Society and Big Brothers/Big Sisters were among his favorite charities.

But Belle refused to talk about his work with them, or allow any publicity when he supported some of these causes.

Hamilton did see this side of Belle.

"We always got along," he said. "He is a complicated man. Albert was always good to me. I remember in 1995 when we were winning all the time and it seemed everyone had guests in the clubhouse. I had Nick [Hamilton's son] with me one day. Albert came up and said, 'You're part of the team, why don't you get some pictures taken with Nick and the players?' "

Hamilton said, "I don't feel right doing that."

Belle said, "Why not? Everyone else comes in here."

Then Belle led Nick into the clubhouse. Hamilton took pictures of his son with Belle and the other players.

"We have these great pictures because of Albert," said Hamilton. "I never would have done that—but Albert wanted me to do it. It was his idea."

Hamilton golfed with Belle a few times and saw how Belle was kind to different people on the course.

"You'll never believe this," said Hamilton. "He was so calm when he played golf. I was the one throwing the clubs around."

Kenny Lofton

When Kenny Lofton was on first base, he loved it.

"All the eyes were on me," said the former Indian. "The pitcher. The catcher. The opposing coach. The fans. What is he going to do? They wondered what was going on in my head."

Lofton paused, then said: "They all wanted to know what was going on in my head."

Suddenly, it was October 17, 1995. It was Game 6 of the American League Championship Series, the Tribe in Seattle.

Eighth inning, Ruben Amaro on third, Lofton on second base.

The Tribe had a 1-0 lead. Randy Johnson cut loose with a fastball that sailed and bounced off the mitt of catcher Dan Wilson.

Amaro scored easily from third.

Lofton was racing from second base to third . . .

Johnson stood at home plate, shaking his head, never expecting what would happen next . . .

"I saw the catcher had his back turned, bending over to pick up the ball," recalled Lofton.

Perhaps the fastest man ever to wear a Tribe uniform realized no one thought he could score from second base on that play.

"It was a reaction thing," he said. "I felt I could make it. The entire play was in front of me—I could see what was happening."

He actually could see it before it happened. The catcher was jogging to the ball. The pitcher was looking bored at home plate. Everyone expected Amaro to score from third base.

No one expected Lofton to come all the way home from second.

No one but Lofton.

"I hit third base, and I made a hard turn," he said. "I always made a hard turn when I was running to a base."

That's because Lofton was always thinking about the extra base. Could he catch the other team by surprise?

"The Kingdome was so loud," he said. "No one was paying attention to me."

Lofton never hesitated as he touched third, roaring into home plate.

And he slid across the plate, and then popped back up to his feet.

And he scored . . . easily. The slide was so quick, you almost needed to watch it in slow motion to realize that he bothered to slide at all. Johnson, Wilson and everyone in Seattle uniforms had no clue he was coming home.

"To me, that was not a special play," he said 19 years later. "It was my kind of play."

And that gave the Tribe a 3-0 lead.

The Tribe players in the dugout ran out to meet Lofton.

"That play was like a knife to the side" for Seattle, said Lofton. "That shut up the crowd."

The Indians won that game, 4-0, and earned a trip to their first World Series in 41 years.

"I remember that game so well not because of that play," he said. "I remember it because it got us to the World Series. I had been at the old Stadium. I remembered when we were terrible. And now we were going to the World Series. That made it special."

Two men brought Kenny Lofton to Cleveland—John Hart and Charlie Manuel.

You can give Dan O'Dowd some credit, too.

In September 1991, the Indians were on their way to 105 losses when Hart was promoted to general manager. His team was awful. His budget was about the size of a baby's piggy bank. His center fielder was Alex Cole.

One day, his phone rang.

Charlie Manuel was calling. A close friend of Hart's, Manuel was the Tribe's manager at Class AAA Colorado Springs.

"John, I've been watching this kid . . . you've just got to see him," said Manuel.

"One of ours?" asked Hart.

Both men laughed. They knew the answer. If there was a player at Colorado Springs that Hart absolutely had to see, they'd both know it.

"It's Kenny Lofton," said Manuel. "Plays for Tucson."

Hart knew that Lofton was fast. And that Lofton had been a basketball player at Arizona. He also knew that Lofton played very little baseball in college.

In fact, Lofton's baseball experience at Arizona consisted of only one at-bat. He appeared in five games, mostly as a pinch runner. He was the sixth man on Arizona's 1988 basketball team that played in the NCAA Final Four. Arizona also was big-time in college baseball, so it was common for scouts to be at every game—and several practices. A Houston scout named Clark Crist would watch some of the Wildcats' practices. He had played at Arizona. He knew Lofton from the basketball team, where he averaged 4.9 points and shot 54 percent as a junior. He was known for his pressure defense, and some outrageous dunks despite being only 5-foot-11.

Crist paid special attention to Lofton in baseball practice. The speed was almost overwhelming. A fly ball would be hit to Lofton's left, and he would break slightly to his right, then double back and easily catch the ball.

He could outrun his mistakes in the field.

At the bat, he had a long swing with a bit of a hitch.

He was raw, raw, raw.

But every step screamed one word: ATHLETE.

Crist believed you could take a gifted athlete and teach him baseball, assuming the athlete was willing to admit that he needed to learn the game. The scout urged the Astros to draft Lofton in the lower rounds.

Houston picked him in the 17th round. The NCAA had a rule that allowed an athlete to be a professional in one sport, and still play as an amateur in another. It's how John Elway played baseball in the Yankees minor-league system while also a quarterback at Stanford. So Lofton quickly signed with the Astros, and was sent to Auburn, N.Y., in the New York-Penn League. It was the bottom of the baseball ladder, a rookie league.

Lofton looked like he seldom played baseball. In that first season, he batted .214. He struck out 51 times in 187 at-bats, a terrible ratio for a guy with only eight extra-base hits. But he stole 26 bases in 48 games. If he could find a way to reach base, no one could stop him. He also was practicing basketball a few times a week, preparing to return to Arizona for his senior season.

Lofton averaged 5.5 points as a senior. One of his dunks was a finalist for Dick Vitale's "Dunk of the Year" on ESPN. Lofton thought he could play in the NBA if he had been featured in a program that pressed, such as those coached by Rick Pitino and Jerry Tarkanian. In his second pro baseball season, he batted .292 for a pair of Class A teams, and stole 40 bases in 56 games.

In 1990, it was a .331 batting average with 62 steals in the Class A Florida State League.

In 1991, he skipped over Class AA and went to the Class AAA Pacific Coast League, where he batted .308 with 40 steals and 17 triples. That's where Manuel fell in love with Lofton. Given how his team was playing, Hart was thrilled to get out of town on a scouting mission. He caught up with Lofton's team in Tucson and was mesmerized as he scouted him for five games.

"He was one of the most dynamic players I'd ever seen, even though his talent was still pretty crude," said Hart.

Then he thought of his current center fielder, a fellow named Alex Cole who wore glasses and often seemed on the verge of being hit in the head with a fly ball. Cole also was the only player Hart had ever seen who forgot how many outs there were—when it was only one out into the first inning! Two batters into the game, and Cole already was confused.

Hart and his assistant, Dan O'Dowd, had made a list of young center fielders whom they wanted to acquire in a trade. The top two names were Bernie Williams and Stan Javier. Lofton was in the middle of the pack. After seeing Lofton, Hart moved his name to the front of the list.

Lofton was promoted to Houston in September of 1991, and batted only .203 for the Astros. He struck out 19 times in 74 at-bats, and had only two steals. The Astros had another center fielder named Steve Finley. They wondered if Lofton would ever hit major-league pitching—ignoring his lack of pro experience and how fast he had bolted through their farm system.

* * *

After every season, there is a ritual known as the general managers' meetings. It is mostly a time of golf, long, fattening meals and even longer nights at the bar.

But Hart and O'Dowd set up shop in the lobby of a hotel in Miami, Fla. As other general managers went out for golf or dinner, the Tribe brass collared them to talk trade.

Their target was Houston, which had Lofton.

"We caught a break because the Astros promoted Lofton in September, and he didn't play well for them," said O'Dowd.

O'Dowd talked to Bob Watson, who was Houston's assistant general manager.

Hart huddled with Bill Wood, Houston's GM. The Astros didn't want to trade Lofton, but were willing to listen to offers. They also were in the market for a left-handed hitting catcher. But they didn't want to make any trades just yet.

A month later, the general managers were meeting again. This time, it was baseball's Winter Meetings. This time, it was in Boca Raton, Fla. And this time, the Indians didn't want to let Lofton get away. The Indians had a young catcher named Eddie Taubensee, who was also a promising left-handed hitter. The Astros wanted him, but they were still reluctant to part with Lofton. Hart also liked Taubensee and wanted to make sure the Indians should push for a Lofton-for-Taubensee deal. He gathered the staff together and asked them all to vote. Scout Tom Giordano, O'Dowd and Manuel all were for the deal. Scouting director Mickey White had doubts. Hart took White out of their hotel suite onto the balcony, where they looked at the Atlantic Ocean. White had discovered Taubensee buried in the Cincinnati Reds farm system and pushed for the Indians to acquire him, later from Oakland. It had been a great move. But now, he was about to lose his diamond in the rough just as it was starting to sparkle. Hart knew the feeling. He once was a scout himself. He comforted White and said he had done a great job—if Taubensee brought Lofton to the Indians, then White had played a huge role in the trade.

In the next four hours, Hart and O'Dowd met with several members of the Houston front office. The deal was Lofton and Taubensee, but Houston wanted other players involved. Finally, the Indians agreed to kick in a minor-league pitcher named Willie Blair.

"It was 1 a.m. and Houston wanted to wait until the morning to announce it," Hart said. "I insisted we get everyone together right now and make it public. I was afraid they'd change their minds."

At 2 a.m., it was announced that the Indians had obtained the man who would become their best center fielder since Larry Doby.

Lofton's first thoughts about being traded to the Indians?

"I was going from one last-place team to another last-place team," he said. "At least this last-place team wanted me."

In 1991, Houston was 65-97, the Tribe was 57-105.

"I also thought I had to be good enough to play on a last-place team," Lofton said.

Then he paused, still bothered that Houston would write him off so quickly.

"You tell me that I can't do something, you are in trouble," said Lofton. "I want to prove you wrong."

Lofton spoke these words 23 years after the trade to the Tribe.

"I knew I had a lot to learn as a player," he said. "I was raw. But I also knew that all I needed to do was play."

Then Lofton talked about growing up in East Chicago, Ind. He was raised by his grandmother, who was losing her sight.

"I had to learn to be a man early," said Lofton. "She was blind, but she could cook and clean. She could get the job done. They'd say she was blind and couldn't do this . . . well, not necessarily."

Rosie Person had seven children and grandchildren in her cramped apartment during some of the years when Lofton was growing up.

While many of his friends took to the streets and ended up in jail and later dead at an early age, he played baseball and basketball in high school. He graduated and went to Arizona on a basketball scholarship. Then he chased his baseball dreams. He knew he was far behind nearly every other prospect in terms of experience.

"There were obstacles," said Lofton.

More than he will ever talk about.

Watching his grandmother "made me think I could almost conquer anything," he said.

He paused.

"Don't tell me that I can't do something," he said.

In Lofton's neighborhood, you trusted very, very few people. You expected to be left on your own. Those who knew a young Kenny Lofton with the Tribe sensed he was like a teenager who was afraid someone would steal his new basketball shoes—which was an issue in his neighborhood. In the streets of Lofton's youth, it was wise to look at the world with a hard expression that threatened, "Don't mess with me."

Lofton often believed reporters wanted to trap him into saying something controversial, or perhaps they simply wanted him to look bad.

Much of his life, he believed many people didn't respect him. He found it hard to trust people, unless he had known them for a long time.

It's easy to understand why, given that Lofton's parents were not often in his young life.

The one strong male figure in the family was B.F. Collins. He was known as "Uncle B.," and he helped Rosie Person with a young Kenny Lofton.

"He never beat us, he never had to," said Lofton in a 1999 interview.

That was right after Uncle B. had died. He had been a steel worker, the kind of man who said more with a stare than a speech. When he wanted to convey a warning, he'd tell Lofton, "You can keep doing what you're doing and end up in big trouble, or you can stop. The choice is yours."

Uncle B. was the closest thing Lofton had to a father.

When he came to the Indians, Lofton was driven to stay in the majors, to prove people wrong—and to show his grandmother and Uncle B. that they were right to believe in him.

Lofton had so many great plays with the Tribe. He led the league in stolen bases every year from 1992 to 1996. The numbers are stunning. In 10 years with the Tribe, he batted exactly .300 (.800 OPS), averaging 45 stolen bases a season.

"He could be cocky," said Jim Thome. "It was almost arrogant the way he'd flip the bat away [after a walk]."

Thome spoke in awe of Lofton, perhaps the best leadoff hitter in team history.

"He was one of the reasons we just dominated back then," said Thome.

Lofton played baseball as if it were a rugged pickup playground basketball game on the asphalt of East Chicago, where he grew up.

You scowled. You gave your opponent no credit. You didn't just try to be beat him, you wanted to embarrass him. You want to take the ball right out of his hands. You wanted to dunk in his face. You wanted to rise above your opponent, unleash a long jumper and hear it jangle through the metal outdoor nets.

Then you said, "No way. You can't stop me."

So it was in baseball, when Lofton jogged to first after a walk. He danced off first base, staring hard at the pitcher.

He seemed to be saying: "You know that I'm going to steal second base. I know I'm going to steal second base. Everyone knows I'm going to steal second base. And guess what? You have no chance to stop me. NONE. ZERO. Don't even bother to try."

His body language said that, even if the words never came from his lips.

In 1992, he was facing Jack Morris, one the game's best and most intimidating pitchers.

In his first at-bat, Lofton dropped down a bunt and beat it out for a base hit. Morris didn't even try to throw out Lofton. He picked up the ball, walked to the mound—and gave the rubber a vicious boot.

Who was this kid to bunt on him, Morris seemed to be saying.

In his next at-bat, Lofton bunted again . . . for another hit.

Morris just stared at him, shaking his head. The veteran had plans for Lofton's next at-bat.

In the third at-bat, Morris uncorked a fastball right at Lofton's knees. Players who rely on speed hate it when a pitcher throws at their legs. Lofton hit the dirt, getting his legs out of the way that pitch.

On the next pitch, Lofton bunted . . . again!

This time, Morris actually threw him out.

But Lofton was saying, "You can't tell me how to play this game!"

Lofton stole 325 bases in his first five seasons in Cleveland. That's an average of 65 per year. His batting average was .316.

"He was the ultimate leadoff man," said Hart. "Any pitcher hated to face him. Kenny made himself into a good hitter. He was so much more than a speed guy."

Lofton led off, followed by Omar Vizquel.

"I loved being on first with Omar at bat," he said. "We played cat-and-mouse. Omar could bunt. He could hit to the opposite field. We could play hit-and-run. They had no idea what we'd do."

Lofton said that he and Vizquel "even had their own set of signs" that the coaches knew nothing about.

Lofton used to say that he didn't aim to lead the league in stolen bases. But in 1995, he was behind Kansas City's Tom Goodwin most of the season. He entered September trailing Goodwin by six steals.

Guess how many bases Lofton swiped in that final month?

Try 22!

And he had 14 in the final 11 games to beat Goodwin, 54-50.

"Look at what Kenny did," Hart said after that season. "He bunted. He drew walks. He did everything possible to get on base—then he took off. We had a big lead in the standings, so the stolen-base title was something else for him to shoot for. He went head-to-head with Goodwin in a couple of games at the end of the year and ran him right out of the park."

Early in his career, Lofton could have stolen 100 bases in a season. But the Indians had so much power in the middle of the lineup with Belle, Thome, Murray and Ramirez—well, it made no sense for him to pile up stolen bases. But that September of 1995 showed what Lofton could do if his main goal was stealing bases.

His speed was as intimidating as his power.

The last Tribe player to even steal 40 bases in a season was Vizquel (in 1999).

Again, in his 10 years with the Tribe, Lofton averaged 45 steals a year.

"At the start of his career, we saw Kenny's exceptional athleticism and intense competitiveness," said Mark Shapiro. "The question was how would that translate on the baseball field? It really came down to this—can he hit? He just had to put the ball in play, because his speed would help him get on base. But the remarkable thing was how Kenny developed into an excellent hitter. That was a real tribute to him, because he was not like that when he started his pro career."

He also won Gold Gloves each season from 1993 to 1996.

Lofton played center between Manny Ramirez and Albert Belle, two guys who spent a lot time in the outfield thinking about their next at-bat.

"I have to thank those guys for the Gold Gloves," said Lofton, meaning he had lots of chances to run down balls and make great plays because Belle and Ramirez were not about to cover much ground.

But Lofton believes he was underrated as a fielder.

"They talk about my speed and how I just ran down balls," said Lofton. "Look, I still had to make the plays."

Yes, a young Kenny Lofton could break the wrong way on a fly ball, then run in the right direction and make the catch.

But so often, he bolted directly to the wall, took one last huge step and then seemed to almost fly as he stole home runs with catches above the center-field wall.

Lofton believes he should have won more Gold Gloves.

And he was outraged for years about being passed over for the 1992 American League Rookie of the Year. Lofton batted .285 (.726 OPS) with 66 stolen bases, five homers and 42 RBI.

The winner, with 20 first-place votes compared to seven for Lofton, was Milwaukee's Pat Listach, who batted .290 (.701 OPS) with 54 steals, one homer and 47 RBI.

Lofton believed the media didn't appreciate his overall game, and was very angry about Listach winning the award. And that was the only good season for Listach, who played only six years in the majors and retired with a .251 batting average.

Lofton lived in Tucson during the winter after the 1992 season. He said he drove up into the Arizona mountains and screamed after he learned of losing out to Listach. In 1993, he batted .325 with 70 stolen bases, but Toronto Manager Cito Gaston failed to pick him as a reserve on the All-Star team.

That also enraged Lofton.

Even now, he believes his career is not appreciated by many baseball people and the media.

"I knew I was in trouble in 1997–98, when it was all about how 'Chicks dig the long ball,' " said Lofton. "Suddenly, those fly balls that were wall-scrapers were flying out of the stadium."

Yes, he's talking about how steroids changed the game, and how teams began to just wait for someone to hit a home run.

"It's just not fair," said Lofton. "Everyone knew what some of those guys were doing. *Some* of those guys. They cheated. They admitted they cheated. And no one says anything. I didn't cheat . . ."

Lofton quickly dropped off the Hall of Fame ballot for lack of support.

"That bothers me a lot," he said. "I know how I played the game. I'm a straightforward person. For me to go out and cheat it that way, that's not respecting the game I love. I just feel the reason these guys cheated was because of the money. They didn't care about the Hall of Fame. If you cared about the Hall of Fame, you wouldn't have even thought about cheating. I'm just sad that my numbers are not being looked at the way they should be. I really believe I had a Hall of Fame career."

When at his best with the Tribe, that certainly was the case.

"The best trade they made [in the 1990s] was for Kenny," said Hamilton. "He was the missing piece, the dynamic leadoff man. He was a game-changer. They had power hitters, they had no one with the speed of Kenny. It was such a dramatic trade because few people even knew who Kenny was before he came to Cleveland—and he ended up being one of the best players ever to wear a Cleveland uniform."

Manny Ramirez Made Hitting Look Easy

"Well, that's just Manny being Manny."

Baseball fans heard that thousands of times about Manny Ramirez.

Manny being Manny was why Ramirez stole second base in a game, then walked back to first and was tagged out. He said he thought Jim Thome had hit a foul ball. Thome had taken the pitch, which was a ball.

Manny being Manny was piling up hundreds of dollars in fines at video stores because he rented a few movies and forgot to return them—for years.

Manny being Manny was telling Manager Mike Hargrove that he couldn't play "because of a sore throat." That was in 1994.

Manny being Manny was him being hit in the chest . . . with a fly ball. He was in right field for Class AA Akron-Canton. He fell down as if shot by a bazooka. It went for a four-base error.

Manny being Manny was a paycheck left in his locker for months, in one of his cowboy boots. And it was bundles of $100 bills stuffed in his glove compartment.

Manny being Manny was a young player who took bats out of teammates' lockers and used them in games. And he took their belts and uniform pants, and wore them in games.

Manny being Manny was jumping on the back of former Akron Beacon Journal baseball writer Sheldon Ocker and expecting Ocker to give him a ride. Ocker is about 5-foot-7, and Ramirez is 6-foot-1, 205 pounds. And it's Manny agreeing to be interviewed by another writer, but stopping after two minutes: "I have to brush my teeth." He left and never came back.

Manny being Manny was having two different agents representing him at the same time in 1999. And three different ones in 1995. Whenever Manny became friends with a player, he sometimes gravitated toward that player's agent—creating problems for himself and his team.

Or as Tom Hamilton said, "To me, Manny being Manny was a very young guy who became perhaps the best right-handed hitter that I've ever seen. He was even better than Albert [Belle]. The only one who comes close is [Detroit's] Miguel Cabrera."

The Manny being Manny that Hamilton saw with the Tribe was the story of a young man from the Dominican Republic via Washington Heights in New York City. He reached the majors and found life overwhelming. While it's not that simple, there is quite a bit of truth to it—at least when he was with the Tribe.

"We never saw the worst of Manny," said Hamilton. "That happened after he got big money and went to Boston."

The most Ramirez made with the Indians was $4.2 million in 2000, his final season. He then signed an eight-year, $160 million contract with Boston.

Early in his life, Manny discovered that he could do one thing better than about anyone else—hit a baseball. And in his Dominican culture, so many boys and young men longed to do what Manny could do when he held a bat in his hands.

Because he could hit, exceptions were made and some excuses for selfish behavior were accepted.

Ramirez and his family moved to the Washington Heights section of New York when Manny was 13. His father drove a cab, his mother was a seamstress. Washington Heights is at the northern end of Manhattan. The vibe is definitely Dominican, the soundtrack a combination of salsa music and rap. English is a second language . . . a distant second. It was like that when Ramirez grew up there in the 1980s, and not a lot has changed. Drugs have been an epidemic. The walls of buildings have long featured colorful gang graffiti. It is two different worlds, one during the day and one at night. When the sun is out, so is the best of Washington Heights. The bodegas and restaurants are filled with working people, with senior citizens, with smiles and laughter coated with the smell of rice and beans.

During the time when Ramirez lived there, the nights were when too many drug dealers and thugs controlled the streets. The rest of Washington Heights retreated to their apartments. Doors were locked. Lots and lots of locks on the doors.

Manny went to George Washington High School. It opened in 1925, a lavish building with pillars in the front. It looked like an old lavish theater with marble floors and high ceilings. Among the famous alumni are Henry Kissinger, Jacob Javits, Harry Belafonte, Alan Greenspan and broadcasters Edwin Newman and Marvin Kalb.

And the school also had two Hall of Fame caliber hitters: Rod Carew and Manny, although Manny's use of steroids definitely puts his Cooperstown credentials in question.

This was once an elite academic school, but it was more of a baseball powerhouse when Manny was there. At one point during Manny's time at the school, there were about 4,000 students—at least 1,000 too many, according to a New York Times story. During Manny's time, there were bars on some of the school windows, metal detectors at the doors. Security men patrolled the halls. It was a preview of how many other urban schools would have to deal with the problem of keeping students and teachers safe.

The school has since been split into four branches, returning to its strong academic roots.

Manny's coach was a man named Steve Mandl, who was inducted in the National High School Baseball Coaches Hall of Fame. That was in 2014, also Mandl's 30th year teaching physical education and coaching at the same school.

Mandl was conflicted when talking about Manny in a 1997 interview.

Because of Manny, Mandl won a lot games and received a lot of media attention. In Manny's senior year, the New York Times did an eight-part series on his high school team.

Let's repeat that: In Manny's senior year, the New York Times did an eight-part series on his high school team.

At the heart of most of the stories were Manny and Mandl.

"I never had a player work harder," Mandl often said of Manny.

Mandl tells stories of Manny running through the streets of Washington Heights, a rope around his waist attached to a huge tire. He dragged it along a place called Snake Hill. He tells of how Manny would show up hours early for games or batting practice, but would skip team pictures and some meetings.

"He was a great talent, absolutely obsessed with baseball, especially hitting," said Mandl.

The coach talked about Manny's fear of being embarrassed and his tendency "to be a follower." Mandl battled to keep Ramirez attending class. Ramirez never did graduate from George Washington, although he reportedly did later pick up a G.E.D.

Over the years, Ramirez would visit his high school. Once in a while, he'd take some of the players to a store and buy them equipment. But Mandl had asked him to purchase uniforms and help with the team in others areas. For a while, it seemed Manny agreed to do so, but he never followed up.

Later, their relationship became strained. Some believe it was because Mandl suggested to a few reporters that Manny may have had a learning disability. Or else, Manny just drifted away from his old coach for whatever reason. But it seemed Manny missed an opportunity to re-invest in the school and the team that helped launch his career.

When the 1991 baseball draft dawned, Manny Ramirez was no secret.

The Tribe had a scout named Joe DeLuca based in the New York area. He first saw Ramirez play as a sophomore. Ramirez also played in the summer for Mel Zitter, who had elite amateur teams. Zitter has said more than 20 of his players have been selected in the draft.

As late as 2012, Mandl had two players picked: Nelson Rodriguez (15th round, Indians) and Fernelys Sanchez (21st round, Braves).

So the question was not about drafting Ramirez, but how high should he be selected?

DeLuca had sent in rave reports about Ramirez. Tribe scouting director Mickey White also was aware of Ramirez for a few years. By Manny's senior year, White and DeLuca were wondering if they had "another Roberto Clemente."

And if Manny was indeed a once-in-a-decade amateur hitter, should the Tribe use the No. 13 pick in the first round on him?

He batted .650 as a senior. In 22 games, he hit 14 homers, drove in 41 runs and stole 30 bases. But the competition was very uneven. Manny didn't play in any of the national showcases for high school players that are available today. In general, players from the South and West had a distinct advantage because the weather was better and they played more games.

Furthermore, Mandl's program was composed primarily of kids who came from poor economic backgrounds. The coach often was buying them equipment. When scouts watched George Washington play on its old AstroTurf surface with the right-field fence only about 280 feet from home, they wondered exactly what to make of it.

It's one thing to sign raw, talented kids from the Dominican Republic, who aren't subject to the draft. It's another to pick a player such as Ramirez in the first round and have him flop.

The risk was high, and the chance of looking foolish was very real.

"But Manny had the prettiest swing that I'd ever seen," said Mickey White.

This was in 1991, when the Indians drafted him. It was long before anyone knew Manny would be Manny, the Manny whose stats scream Hall of Fame except for the steroid suspensions that came later in his career.

White "pounded on the table" when it came to Ramirez. That's a scouting term, meaning when you advocate for a player with your bosses, you pound on the table to make a point.

You also recruit people to your point of view.

John Hart had the final decision on the first pick in the 1991 draft. White took Hart to Washington Heights to scout Ramirez.

They approached the field, and Hart heard a distinct *whap*, the sound of a bat meeting the ball in the ultimate sweet spot.

"Manny?" asked Hart.

"Manny," said White.

Hart loves to tell this story, because it's an example of how you could hear a hitter and know he was something special before even seeing him swing a bat.

As the 1991 draft approached, the Indians were conflicted.

Scouting director White loved Manny. Hart was intrigued, perhaps even infatuated with Ramirez.

But the Tribe was in the process of losing 105 games. This was the first draft for Hart as the general manager. Some in the Tribe front office liked Aaron Sele, a terrific pitcher at Washington State. He was a member of the 1990 Team USA. He was the opposite of Ramirez, the raw high school kid. Sele was a polished college pitcher who had competed against elite college competition. He could reach the majors quickly.

Sele had a very solid career with 148 major-league victories.

There was another factor in favor of drafting Ramirez. He definitely would sign. In 1989, the Tribe selected Calvin Murray with the No. 11 pick in the draft. He was a high school player from Fort Worth. The word before the draft was that he planned to attend the University of Texas. That's exactly what happened. He turned down the Tribe and went to college.

That was not an option for Manny.

The Indians had the No. 13 pick in the 1991 draft.

Here were the top 13 selections:

1. Brien Taylor, Yankees.
2. Mike Kelly, Braves.
3. Dave McCarty, Twins.
4. Dmitri Young, Cardinals.
5. Ken Henderson, Brewers.
6. John Burke, Astros.
7. Joe Vitiello, Royals.
8. Joey Hamilton, Padres.
9. Mark Smith, Orioles.
10. Tyler Green, Phillies.
11. Shawn Estes, Mariners.
12. Doug Glanville, Cubs.
13. Manny Ramirez, Indians.

By far, Ramirez became the best player on that list. The next-best player in the first round would have been Shawn Green, who went No. 16 to the Blue Jays. He finished with 328 big-league homers, batting .283.

As for Sele, he went No. 23 to Boston.

The pick was a huge risk by the Tribe. In some ways, it was like the 1987 draft when they didn't have a first-round pick. That year, they went with Albert Belle in the second round, despite Belle's attitude problems and discipline issues at LSU.

If you check the history of players drafted from George Washington High, you find 24 names. Only five made the majors. Even more significant, the only other player with a big-league career of note was Alex Arias, drafted in the third round of 1987. He played 11 years and was a career .265 hitter.

After the draft, Manny quickly signed for $250,000. He bought a BMW and headed to Burlington, N.C., to start his pro career.

"After we signed Manny, it was a race," said Mark Shapiro.

What does that mean?

"He was such a great hitter that we knew his bat was going to move him up fast," said Shapiro. "We tried to develop him as more than just a hitter. He needed to work on his base-running, his defense in the outfield, professionalism, maturity . . . just about everything except hitting."

Manny was homesick in his first month at Burlington, N.C., in the Appalachian League. He racked up a $400 phone bill. After a few weeks, he told some teammates that he was "going home" to New York. He didn't leave, but the Indians had to be very careful with him.

His stats from that first season in rookie ball are incredible: He batted .326 with 63 RBI in 59 games, ripping 19 homers. His slugging percentage was .679.

The next year, he batted only .278 at Class A Kinston, but he was leading the Carolina League in homers (13) and RBI (63) when he broke a hamate bone in his hand on July 4 and missed the rest of the season.

"Manny did view baseball as more than just hitting," said Shapiro. "But he was such a gifted hitter that he advanced too quickly through the farm system. He didn't get enough repetitions in the outfield or on the bases to really become a finished product there. Just look at his stats."

In 1993, he hit a combined .333 with 31 homers and 115 RBI in 129 games between Class AA and Class AAA. His OPS was 1.031, a stunning number.

At the age of 21, Ramirez arrived in Cleveland when the 1993 rosters expanded in September. He had played only 269 games in the minors.

"For guys going from the minors to the majors, one of the big adjustments is playing the outfield," said Shapiro. "The ball travels faster and carries much farther than it does even in Class AAA. The hitters are stronger. It's not uncommon for some prospects to struggle in the outfield when they first come to the majors."

That was true of Ramirez. But it didn't matter much.

That's because Manny could hit.

When Charlie Manuel managed Ramirez in 1993 at Class AAA Charlotte, he said, "Manny hits off his front foot, just like Hank Aaron."

Manuel added that "Ted Williams would love this guy because of his plate discipline."

Manny struggled when coming to the Tribe in 1993. He was 9-of-53 (.170) with two homers and five RBI.

In the spring of 1994, Manager Mike Hargrove thought it would be wise for Manny to open the season at Class AAA. It made sense. He struggled with the Tribe in September. He had played only 40 games in Class AAA. He was still 21 years old.

"In the middle of spring training, we had a meeting about the roster," said Hart. "I asked Grover how he saw his team. He said his outfield was Albert [Belle] in left, Kenny [Lofton] in center and Wayne Kirby in right. No Manny. I didn't say a word."

There were more meetings, but the final one was a few days before the team would leave Winter Haven. Once again, Hargrove listed his starting outfield without Manny.

"I've never done this before," said Hart. "But I'm going to say this . . . Manny is breaking camp with us and he's going to be our opening day right fielder. Wayne Kirby will be our fourth outfielder. I'm going to sign Wayne to a three-year contract, and that will make him happy. It's not like we're throwing him under the bus or anything—but it's time for this kid.'"

Ramirez played 91 games for the Tribe in that strike-shortened 1994 season, hitting 17 homers with 60 RBI, a batting average of .269.

But he nearly was sent to the minors. In May, he was trying to pull nearly every pitch. Suddenly, he was thinking about home runs. That month, he batted .132 with two homers.

That came after hitting .313 with six homers in April.

The Indians told Manny to just be the Manny that they signed—the guy who hits .300, hits the ball to all fields.

He batted over .300 in each of the last three months of a season that ended on August 11 with a labor dispute.

Orel Hershiser tells a story that is very revealing about a young Manny.

"He called me 'Papi,' " said Hershiser. "He sometimes followed me around like a puppy dog."

Hamilton noticed that the older players treated Ramirez "like a little brother." It was a playful relationship, but one where "the veterans always took care of Manny, even protected him a bit."

In the early days of Jacobs Field, there were two rows of benches in the dugout.

"I'd sit on the upper row on the days when I wasn't pitching," said Hershiser. "When the [opposing] starting pitcher was warming up, Manny would come by and sit right below me in the lower row. He'd leaned back and I'd rub his shoulders. We'd watch the pitcher together."

After a few throws, Manny would ask, "What's you see, Papi?"

Hershiser might talk about the pitcher's breaking ball, or the sink on his fastball.

"Sometimes, a reliever would come into the game," said Hershiser. "Manny would come by and sit under me. The pitcher would throw two warmups, and Manny would ask, 'What's you see, Papi?' I'd laugh and ask him to at least let me watch him finish warmups so I could see all his pitches."

Then they'd talk baseball.

Hershiser would say something like, "This guy has a good two-seamer and it's sinking good on the inner half of the plate, but he can't throw it for a strike. So early in the count, don't swing at it. If it's inside, it will be a ball. Watch his fastball . . . it's staying up high and away. But you can hit it a long way. Look for that pitch."

This would go on a few times each game.

Very few hitters ever asked Hershiser to scout opposing pitchers for them. But Manny knew Hershiser was one of the smartest pitchers in the game. Even as a player, Hershiser viewed the game as a coach. So Ramirez asked Hershiser for advice.

Manny would watch Eddie Murray take batting practice and notice how the veteran seldom hit the ball over the wall. Murray worked on keeping his swing short, mostly hitting the ball up the middle or to the opposite field. Power hitters tend to get into slumps when they try to swing too hard and pull everything. Murray's approach to batting practice was to stay away from the home-run swing.

Soon, Ramirez began to take batting practice that way.

Once he began swinging with a high front leg kick and messed up his timing.

The Indians wondered why Ramirez was doing that. He had been watching veteran Harold Baines use this unorthodox approach, and thought it would work for him.

That caused batting coach Charlie Manuel to almost have a migraine, as it took him several days to convince Manny to return to his natural swing.

Ramirez also was tempted by the power of suggestion when it came to switching agents. He'd become friends with a veteran, and soon, that veteran's agent was representing Manny. At least twice in contract talks over the years, the Indians dealt with two different agents claiming to represent Manny in his quest for a new deal. Eventually, it would be cleared up—until he changed agents again.

But in the end, it came down to this: Manny hit and hit and hit.

One of the keys to the success of Manny being Manny was that when it came to hitting, he continually looked for ways to get better.

As his high school coach Mandl said, "Manny was obsessed with hitting."

That remained true during his career with the Tribe.

Once he came to the majors to stay in 1994, Manny averaged 33 homers and 114 RBI a season, batting .315 in the next seven years with the Tribe.

"I always found Manny to be very pleasant," said Hamilton. "He was not one to hold a long conversation, but we got along well. And at 7:05 when the game began and he came to the plate, he was a guy who made you want to stay in your seat and watch him hit. That's how I'll always remember Manny."

Going to Jacobs Field

[FANS WRITE IN]

During the sellout streak, I would get online early to try and buy tickets when they went on sale. I would have a list of games we wanted to attend in order of importance. I would spend all day and all of my dad's allotted money on tickets for the season. I just remember how crazy it was to try and get tickets during this time—the Indians website would be bombarded with requests. *—Jennifer Kline, Lakemore*

My dad had seen over 40 games in the 1948 championship season. He saw his first Indians game in the 1920s at League Park. His father, my grandfather, had seen games before that. My son and I also had taken in games at the old stadium when he was a pre-teen. We also had the privilege of seeing many of the 1990s players in the minors in Charlotte, North Carolina, which is now our home. But we saw the 1997 team in Jacobs Field—our first visit there—so that we could say our family, dating back four generations and over nearly a hundred years, had seen Tribe baseball in all of the different venues. *—Phil Williams, Charlotte*

My first visit to Jacobs Field was actually the very first game that was played there, the exhibition game against the Pirates. I will never forget the moment when I actually saw the field itself. I stopped short on the way to our seats, looking all around me in awe and disbelief. I had never expected to see such a beautiful ballpark, with so many wonderful features. I have been to several other ballparks and I have to say that the one "at the corner of Carnegie and Ontario," to quote Tom Hamilton, is my favorite. *—Cindy Chadd, Madrid, Spain*

July 16, 1995. My father, brother and I were on our way to church that Sunday morning when we got stopped by an older couple that my father knew. Turns out they had four tickets to the Indians game but could not go and asked if we were interested in going in their place. We went to church every Sunday, but my father decided we should take this rare opportunity to take in the ballgame. Unlike today, Indians tickets were very hard to come by. When we got there, we saw the tickets were six rows behind the Indians dugout. We couldn't believe it! It was a great experience for my first ever game at Jacobs Field and a moment I will never forget sharing with my father. *—Joshua Czech, Hartville*

I remember going to the first game at Jacobs Field, the exhibition game against the Pittsburgh Pirates on April 2, 1994. Walking around the park before the game, I kept thinking, "Are we really in Cleveland? Do we really get to keep this place?" After seeing dozens of games at the Stadium, this was such a surreal experience. *—Ramin Meshginpoosh, Madison*

I got a job in Grand Rapids, Michigan, soon after college and that's where we raised our family. I lost count of the many five-hour trips we made from Grand Rapids to Cleveland to watch the Tribe. We were able to secure tickets for Opening Day 1994. We arrived the day before and stayed at a hotel near the Jake. After dinner, we walked over to the stadium just to see if we could catch a glimpse of the field. I was standing near the main gate marveling at the new stadium, thinking to myself, "This can't be true, this can't be Cleveland." Of all the Indians stars of the '90s, I never would have guessed it would be little-known Wayne Kirby who would be the hero for that game. The ride back to Grand Rapids after that game was one of our all-time best. *—Gregg Hagley, Byron Center, Michigan*

I had seen Gateway being built in school trips to Tower City. I still wasn't prepared for how massive the Jake was when I arrived for my first game. The energy that pulsed through the stadium, even before the game started, was electric. We had nosebleed seats along third base and every seat was packed. My sports heroes seemed larger than life, even from those seats. The post-game fireworks rivaled any fireworks display that I had seen at Lake Anna growing up in Barberton. *—Scott Snowden, Laurel, Montana*

John Adams and his wife, Cathy, would drive us to games in his big van after they moved to our street in Brecksville. We would have a great time as all of the neighborhood kids and my brothers and sisters would throw peanut shells on his drum before the Indians would do something good. We would wait sometimes what seemed forever for that moment to happen. Then, when the Tribe would finally do something good, shells would go flying everywhere as John would strike up the drum to the delight of me and my friends and brothers and sisters. Some of my best memories as a kid were sitting in the bleachers with John. *—John Houser, Abilene, Texas*

While The Jake was being built I walked down at lunchtime to the site, just to stare at the hole in the ground and dream of what was to come. I wasn't alone. Dozens, maybe more, of similarly suited men were doing the same thing. We didn't talk to each other much, lost in thoughts of our own "Field of Dreams"—or maybe "Major League"! But we smiled, nodded, some of us young again as we urged our fathers to throw the ball higher and higher in the back yard. Others looked forward to holding our son's or daughter's hand as we passed through those yet-to-be-built gates. The anticipation was palpable. We craved to be rid of The Curse. That construction period was like one long, sweet spring training. Just thinking about that time again makes me smile. *—Kurt Landefeld, Huron*

I knew Jacobs Field was special the first time I went. It was the first night game, the third game of the season. I was sitting with my brother and friends in the bleachers. I screamed to Seattle's center fielder Ken Griffey Jr. that we were going to the World Series before his Seattle Mariners. Then, the strangest thing happened. He turned around and smiled. He had heard me, and was laughing. When you sat in the bleachers at Municipal Stadium, we had screamed "respectful" taunts at players and teams for years, and I don't think anyone had ever heard us. But his reaction, and subsequent interactions, was joyous. I had never felt like I was a part of the game like I do now when I go to The Jake. *—Paul Wilson, Camas, Washington*

HEART OF THE ORDER

Omar Vizquel

Tribe fans will remember his smile, which could electrify a Cleveland night brighter than any Jacobs Field light tower. They'll remember how he sometimes caught ground balls with his bare hand, rather than his glove. Then he'd grin when it was over, like a magician knowing he had just pulled off his favorite sleight-of-hand trick.

They'll remember how he ran down pop-ups, his back to home plate, the ball softly dropping into his mitt like a bird landing in a nest.

They'll remember how during warmups he'd juggle a baseball with his feet the way he did a soccer ball when he was growing up in Venezuela. How he was just a little kid in a 30-something body having fun playing ball.

They'll remember Omar Vizquel as the best Indians shortstop of this generation, if not any generation—with all due respect to Lou Boudreau. Veteran Cleveland baseball writer Hal Lebovitz saw both shortstops and said it was no question, Vizquel was the superior fielder.

But no one knew that in December 1993.

That's when Tribe General Manager John Hart and his assistant Dan O'Dowd were debating this question: Mark Lewis or Felix Fermin, which would be the best bet at shortstop when the Indians became a contender?

Manager Mike Hargrove also was brought into the debate: Fermin or Lewis?

Lewis was the Tribe's first-round pick in 1988, the No. 2 overall selection in that draft. He was destined to be a mediocre major-league infielder, and that was obvious after the 1993 season.

Mark Lewis? In 1992, he was given the starting shortstop job and made 25 errors in 121 games, batting .264 with five homers and 30 RBI.

Felix Fermin? In 1993, he started at short, batting .263 with two homers and 45 RBI in 140 games. He also made 23 errors.

As Hart, Hargrove and O'Dowd considered the shortstop situation, they came to this conclusion: None of the above.

Not Lewis. Not Fermin. Not if the Indians wanted to be a contender as they moved into the new ballpark.

The Indians had to upgrade their shortstop position. As usual, the Indians were on the prowl for pitchers. The Mets expressed an interest in Fermin, in a deal that would involve pitcher Bobby Jones.

Then O'Dowd heard something. The Mets had no plans to keep Fermin. They planned to send him to Seattle for Omar Vizquel.

That led to another meeting.

Omar Vizquel. Everyone in the room smiled. Omar Vizquel had just won a Gold Glove. He made great plays, and all the easy ones, too. Now there was a shortstop for a team with World Series dreams.

The Indians stopped talking to the Mets and called Seattle.

"In the past, this deal never would have happened," said Tom Hamilton. "Usually, we were the team trading a guy like Omar because he was making too much money. When I heard we were talking about getting Omar, and this came after we signed Eddie [Murray] and Dennis [Martinez] . . . well, I thought, 'We're now playing the game like the big boys do.' We were trading for a guy who was becoming too expensive for someone else."

So why would Seattle trade Omar?

Mariners General Manager Woody Woodward had a problem. His owner had just spent close to a million dollars to sign a young shortstop named Alex Rodriguez, the first pick in the draft. Rodriguez was supposed to be a superstar, ready for the big leagues as soon as 1995. Vizquel was going to be a free agent at the end of the 1994 season. He was earning $2.3 million and would command more. No way Seattle could afford Rodriguez and Vizquel.

Why keep Vizquel for a year, then lose him to free agency?

Meanwhile, Hart was in Puerto Rico to attend a banquet honoring Carlos Baerga as that island's top professional baseball player in 1993. As is usually the case with Hart, if he's in town and there is a game to scout, he does a little scouting. He attended a Puerto Rican Winter League game, at which he talked to Edgar Martinez, whose summer job was to DH for the Mariners.

"What kind of a guy is Omar?" asked Hart.

"The best," said Martinez. "He is so special, not just as a player, but as a person."

"How good is he at short?" asked Hart.

"The best," repeated Martinez. "We love Omar."

Hart called O'Dowd. The message was clear. They had to cut a deal for Vizquel.

As was the case with so many things in the 1990s, the Indians found that they were in the perfect position to make the perfect move. Woodward had to trade Vizquel. He had to find a stop-gap shortstop until the young Rodriguez was ready. He already liked Fermin, as the Indians knew from their trade talks with the Mets. The deal started with Fermin and Vizquel, but Seattle wanted a little more.

"What about Reggie Jefferson?" asked Woodward.

Jefferson was a promising designated hitter, but had suffered one injury after another with the Indians. Furthermore, the Tribe had Murray as the DH.

Jefferson and Fermin for Vizquel?

Done deal.

About midnight on December 19, 1993, the phone rang at the home of Omar and Nicole Vizquel.

"It was my agent," Vizquel said. "He told me that I was going to be traded to Cleveland."

The sound of the telephone woke Vizquel's wife. He told her the news of the trade.

She cried.

How could the Mariners trade her husband? Didn't they know the Vizquels planned to live in Seattle? Or that Nicole was from Seattle? And Cleveland? Who wanted to live in Cleveland? Vizquel was shaken by the deal, too. He felt even worse as he watched the tears roll down his wife's face. He tried to tell her that the Indians were going to play in a new ballpark. The city supposedly was getting better. Things would be all right.

But neither of them was sure about that.

When the Vizquel deal was announced, it was greeted with yawns by most Tribe fans. Their team seemed to have traded one shortstop for another. So what? Because Omar played in Seattle, he was seldom on national TV, or even on ESPN's SportsCenter. But after a month, Tribe fans realized they had never seen a shortstop with the acrobatic grace of Vizquel. They were in love with the little guy from Venezuela who seemed happy just to be playing baseball.

Within a year, Hart was calling Omar "the heart and soul of our team."

Omar signed a five-year deal to stay in Cleveland in December 1995. He was in love with the baseball palace that was Jacobs Field. The fans were wonderful. The city was in the midst of a revival, and some of the suburbs were very nice.

The team really was a contender. This was what Vizquel had always wanted. To be the shortstop on a good team. At home, smiles replaced the tears.

"Within a few months, I knew we'd be good and that I was in the right place," said Vizquel. "I looked at the roster we were putting together—Eddie and Dennis, along with Kenny, Carlos, Albert and those guys . . . I knew we had a chance to win and I sensed my career would take off."

The date was April 16, 1994.

It was the day that Omar Vizquel made three errors.

"That's still hard to believe," said Omar, almost 20 years later. "One year [2000], I played 156 games and made only three errors."

That's right, three errors all year.

But that windy, chilly and sunny afternoon in Cleveland, he made three in one game.

"I'll never, ever forget that game," he said.

It's true that you can learn a lot about an athlete when he has a stinker of a day.

Does he hide?

Does he alibi?

Or does he act like Vizquel?

"No excuses," said Vizquel on that day. "I messed up the whole game."

Vizquel sat quietly in front of his locker after the Indians lost 12-9 to Kansas City.

"This never happened to me before," he said.

Never?

"Never," he said quietly. "I still can't believe it."

In the third inning, Greg Gagne hit Vizquel a grounder—and he dropped it.

"I wanted the next ball hit to me," he said. "Whenever I make a bad mistake, I want the ball hit to me, right away."

And it was—by the next batter—and Vizquel kicked it. His two errors in the third inning opened the door to four Royal runs. We could have heard talk of tricky hops, of uneven infield dirt or of Lord knows what else. Many ballplayers have an infinite supply of rationalizations when they need something to cover their butts.

But consider what Vizquel said about the wind-blown pop-up that popped out of his glove in the eighth inning.

"I had it all the way and I just dropped it," he said. "First time in my life that I've ever dropped a fly ball like that."

And that caused three more runs to score.

Add it up, and Vizquel's glove coughed up seven runs—this from a guy who made only seven errors in 136 games in 1992.

He was so smooth, so composed, so professional.

"It was God's gift," he said. "Like I was meant to play shortstop. Just like some guys always could hit. They don't know why, they just can."

That's why he was as shocked by that Saturday as the 36,439 fans at Jacobs Field, most of whom booed him.

"It bothered me to hear that," he said. "But I understood it. The fans pay good money for a good show, and I just screwed up the whole day."

Vizquel ended that post-game press conference promising, "This will never happen again."

And it never did.

"When I give speeches to kids and young players in the minors, I talk about that day," he said. "That was my first month with a new team, and the fans and media probably wondered, 'Why did they ever trade for this guy?' I heard some media people say that after the game. I just laughed. I knew they didn't know me, but I also knew it took time to earn respect from people. I needed to make some good plays, get some big hits—and then people would know that everything was cool."

Vizquel made only three more errors the rest of the 1994 season. He had a streak of 51 errorless games. He won another Gold Glove.

"You have to face the media when you have a bad game," said Vizquel. "I remember guys saying that they were going to take a quick shower and eat real fast and leave before the press got there. But the press is there for every game. They write the good and the bad. When you make three errors, it's bad. And that's what they write. I decided to be good to them no matter how I played. That's being a professional."

Vizquel's mother was a kindergarten teacher, and she preached honesty to her children, at home and in school.

"I was raised not to make excuses," he said. "Most excuses are really just lies, so why say them?"

But something must have happened on April 16.

"OK, I'll tell you about it," he said, years later. "I was sick that day. You can ask [infield coach] Buddy Bell. It was the only day that I didn't take infield practice all year. But I wanted to play, and I just made a mess of things."

A young Jim Thome watched Vizquel that day.

"What Omar did taught me a lot," said Thome. "It taught me that I have to face the writers and fans even when I have a bad day."

Like Vizquel, Thome never ran from the media.

"The remarkable part is Omar is not from this country, he's from Venezuela," said Hamilton. "But he became enormously popular not only because he was a great shortstop, but because he could talk to the fans. He loved to be with the people. His English is excellent. He wanted to communicate."

Now consider that Vizquel came to America knowing one word in English—eggs.

"My first year in baseball, all I ate was eggs," he said. "They'd ask me what kind. I'd just say, 'Eggs.' I didn't know what kind of eggs."

Instead of sunny-side up, the 16-year-old Vizquel thought they meant what kind of eggs as in what color or what size. He laughs as he talks about it now, but it had to be confusing and down-right scary in 1984.

"That was in Butte, Montana," he said. "It was my first year in the Seattle farm system. They signed 10 Latin players and put all of us in this big house."

He was playing in front of miners and cowboys, guys in big hats and boots who chewed more tobacco than the players. In Butte, they consider people from Utah to be foreigners. You can just imagine how a Latin kid felt.

"That never bothered me much," said Vizquel. "A lot of the guys wanted to go home. I was homesick, but I never thought of leaving. I was going to be a big-league shortstop, and if I was going to make it, I had to learn how to live in America."

Then Vizquel smiled as he remembered something about Butte.

"The infield," he said. "All the American players said how hard it was and how bad. To me, it was a dream. I never saw a field that nice. I couldn't understand what they were complaining about. I wanted to play on fields like that for the rest of my life."

Vizquel's father worked at an electrical plant in Caracas, but played with his son in the summer on infields that were nothing but gravel pits.

"Ground ball after ground ball, and it was on rocks and hard dirt," said Vizquel. "My father would tell me to expect every ball to take a bad hop . . . then you're not surprised by anything. My father is the man I most admire and he made me a good fielder."

Vizquel said there was a field near his home.

"As a kid, I played without a glove on dirt with rocks," he said. "The ball was taped. So that's where I learned to bare-hand those ground balls. We played without gloves. Everything was bare-handed. When I got to the big leagues, it was natural to do that on some plays."

Vizquel's first heroes were the pros who played in the Venezuelan winter league.

"When I was 10 years old, [former White Sox shortstop and Caracas native] Chico Carrasquel was at one of our games," said Vizquel. "I met him and I told him that I was going to be a big-league shortstop just like him."

Vizquel paused, a bit embarrassed.

"I can't believe that I said that," he said in 1994. "But now when I see Chico, he says, 'You told me that you'd make it.' He remembers."

The scouts began to notice Vizquel when he was 15.

"The Red Sox wanted to sign me," said Vizquel. "But the scout talked to me and said he was afraid I was too young, that I didn't know any English and I would have a bad time in America. He said he'd see me in a year."

But two weeks later, a Seattle scout approached him.

"He asked me if any other teams were watching me," said Vizquel. "I told him about the Red Sox, and he asked me if I wanted to play now. I said, 'Where do I sign?' He gave me a $2,500 bonus and a plane ticket to the U.S."

It took Vizquel five years to make the big leagues to stay, and about five minutes to be recognized as one of the game's most graceful and steady shortstops. Not only did he make the great plays, he didn't botch the routine plays because he knew there was nothing routine about a ground ball.

Omar Vizquel Sr. taught his son well.

"Of the 10 of us in that house my first year in Butte, I'm the only one who made the big leagues," he said.

If you want to judge a batter, there are so many statistics—everything from the batting average to home runs to slugging percentage to on-base percentage.

As for pitchers, statistics exist for everything short of how many times he spits on the mound.

But what about fielders?

"It's in the eye," said Vizquel.

He meant that you can't put a number on it, you have to see it. Yes, there are fielding percentages. But making the fewest errors doesn't mean you are a good fielder.

"It may mean that you don't get to a lot of balls," Vizquel said. "You may catch most balls hit at you, but if you don't reach many, then you are not a great fielder."

There are new stats that measure a player's range, his arm strength and other fielding attributes. But even those who bow at the altar of stats admit these are far more subjective than the numbers attached to hitters and pitchers.

So what makes a great shortstop?

"He is a man who makes all the routine plays—that's the most important thing," Vizquel said. "But he also makes a lot of great plays. He can do both."

Managers and coaches in each league are asked to select the top defensive players at each position. So the coaches and managers vote—but they are not allowed to pick players on their own team—and that is how the Gold Glove winners are chosen. Vizquel won eight Gold Gloves with the Tribe, 11 in his career.

He is the only Tribe shortstop ever to win the award.

But Gold Gloves weren't awarded until 1957, so that is why a Tribe great such as Lou Boudreau never was so honored. Along with its relatively short historical span, the award is subjective. It is done "by the eye."

"And too often, they vote for a guy who is a good hitter," said Hamilton. "For example, Derek Jeter was a Gold Glove. I'm telling you right now, Jeter was a great all-around player, but Omar was a much better shortstop. It's not even close."

Some managers and coaches supposedly have voted for lesser players on other teams to dilute the vote so that their own players would win the award. So politics also has played a part. But in the end, most managers and most coaches take it seriously, and their collective judgment is sound because it is their job to know the strengths and weaknesses of every player in their league.

"I wish I had a chance to see Ozzie Smith play [in his prime]," Vizquel said. "I've seen him on TV, but never live. I know he is more flashy than me. But I would have liked to see him even take ground balls during infield practice. That would have been nice."

Smith won 13 consecutive Gold Gloves with the Cardinals from 1980 to 1992, but his era is past.

Yes, Smith made sizzling plays in the field, but Vizquel wasn't exactly a glass of lukewarm water.

Fans absolutely loved his bare-handed grab and quick throws off those slow rollers.

"My managers and coaches hated it," he said, "I mean, they really hated it. [Seattle Manager] Lou Piniella once said if I ever dropped a ball like that, he was going to punch me out. He also hated it when I caught a pop-up, and I snatched it out of the air with my glove [sort of flipping his glove downward with the ball]. I did that with the bases loaded and two outs in a 3-2 game, and Piniella ran down the dugout at me. He screamed, 'If you ever drop a fly ball like that, you'll never play for me again!' "

The amazing thing is Vizquel never dropped a ball with his bare hand or on one of those pop-ups.

By the time he reached the Tribe, he was already considered a great shortstop.

"I never cared how Omar caught the ball," said Mike Hargrove. "I just wanted him to catch it."

Vizquel said that he knew of other infielders who tried to bare-hand ground balls and "ended up breaking their fingernails, or they jammed their fingers."

Never happened to him.

Why not?

"Because I treat the ball like an egg," he said. "You open your hand real wide. You let the ball hit the hand, you don't grab for it—like if you grab for an egg, you break it."

Vizquel said he played a game called "wall" as a kid, where he threw a rubber ball against a wall and practiced catching it with one hand.

"When I came to Cleveland, it was like people have discovered me," he said. "When I played all those years in Seattle, you are so far west that you are lost. On the Mariners, they know Randy Johnson and Ken Griffey Jr. and that's all."

The biggest surprise about Vizquel is that he came to Cleveland and began to hit.

He batted .255 with two homers in 158 games for Seattle in 1993. In parts of five years with Seattle, Vizquel was a career .252 hitter with little power. Part of the reason was that he first arrived in the majors at the age of 21.

"I had started switch-hitting for only a year before I got to majors," he said. "So I was trying to learn how to switch-hit in the majors. I knew if I could do it, I'd be a better player because batting left-handed would help with my speed."

In 11 years with the Tribe, he was a .283 hitter. He often led the team in sacrifice bunts. He knew how to steal bases.

"When I came to Cleveland, they batted me second between Kenny [Lofton] and Carlos [Baerga]," he said. "I started seeing a lot of fastballs because they didn't want to walk me to get to Carlos. And with Kenny on base, they threw me a lot of fastballs," because it's easier for a catcher to throw out a stealing baserunner on a fastball than a breaking pitch. "It was perfect for me."

Vizquel also joined a team where everyone expected to hit, yet he was not supposed to be a key part of the offense. There was no pressure on him at the plate.

"I had doubts when I was young," he said. "But with Cleveland, I started to think of myself as a hitter."

Vizquel also tried to help some of the younger Latino players. For example, he worked with rookie infielder Enrique Wilson in 1997:

"Now write the word—socks," Vizquel said.

Slowly, Wilson wrote S-O-C-K-S in a notebook.

"Good," Vizquel said.

Wilson smiled.

"Now, try—pants," he said.

Carefully, Wilson wrote the word, making a mistake.

Vizquel corrected him. Wilson tried it again.

"P-A-N-T-S," Vizquel said. "That's good."

Vizquel always believed it was imperative that Latino players learn English. It made the adjustment to a new team and new country easier, and it also helps a player gain respect of teammates and fans when he is able to communicate with them.

But nothing spoke as loud as Vizquel's glove.

In the 2000 season, he made only three errors in 156 games. He won Gold Gloves each season from 1993 to 2001.

"I was awestruck by how Omar played," said Mike Hargrove. "I don't think anyone in the history of the game has ever played shortstop like him."

In 2004, Vizquel was 37 years old. It was his final season with Tribe, and he batted .291 (.741 OPS) with 20 sacrifice hits, 19 steals and made only 11 errors in 147 games.

The Indians had Jhonny Peralta in Class AAA, where he was the Most Valuable Player in the International League. Vizquel had played a better shortstop than anyone ever had at the age of 37.

Could he do it again at 38?

Did it make sense to even find out, when the Tribe had a cheaper and much younger alternative in Peralta?

The Indians decided to let Vizquel become a free agent. He signed with the San Francisco Giants, and won Gold Gloves in 2005 and 2006 in the National League. At the age of 39, he made only four errors in 152 games, batting .295.

"I never wanted to leave Cleveland," he said. "I wanted to retire as an Indian. I remember looking around one day and all the old guys were gone—Kenny, Albert, Charlie, Thome, Manny. I was the last one standing. It was at that moment that I realized they'd let me go, too. It's business. But it was still sad, and it still hurt."

Vizquel played until the age of 45, a starter at 40. He defied time for years and years.

"I didn't think I'd play that long," he said. "When I went to San Francisco, I thought I had a year or two left. I won two more Gold Gloves. I could still play."

Vizquel loves coming to Cleveland.

"I was here longer than anyone [from those great teams of the 1990s]," he said. "Eleven years with one team is a long time. I have always appreciated all the love the fans give me. Maybe it's because I signed a lot of autographs. I wasn't one of those guys hitting a lot of homers or anything, but I connected with the fans."

Vizquel said he has a Twitter account, "and most of the followers are from Cleveland—even though I haven't played here since 2004."

Vizquel should be a first-ballot Hall of Famer, but his best years were in Seattle and Cleveland. His ticket to Cooperstown is his glove, which often doesn't lead to an easy entrance in an era where voters put a premium on offense.

"I try not to think about it," he said. "I think I have the numbers, but who knows?"

Any voter who really watched him play should know . . . and find it very easy to vote for him.

Eddie Murray: A Great Teammate

The first move made by the Tribe that showed it was indeed a different ballgame was the signing of free agents Eddie Murray and Dennis Martinez.

Both were introduced to the media together before the 1994 season, just as the team was preparing to go into the new stadium.

"There are certain guys in baseball, that when they walk into a room, there is instant respect," said Tom Hamilton. "Not many have that. But Eddie Murray had that."

Hamilton believes that Tribe fans will never fully appreciate what Murray coming to Tribe at just the right time meant to the team.

In 1994, the core of the team was outrageously talented. Consider the names: Albert Belle, Jim Thome, Omar Vizquel, Manny Ramirez, Sandy Alomar, Carlos Baerga, Charles Nagy and Kenny Lofton.

Not only were they physically gifted, but some of them were explosive personalities. Not all of them majored in maturity. They were preparing to unleash their power and athleticism on the American League. But that doesn't always translate into a team that wins big.

While General Manager John Hart pushed for the signing of Murray and Martinez, it was Dick Jacobs who approved it.

"He didn't blink," said Hart. "He didn't want us to go into the new park with the shell of a team."

The new ballpark was driving the Indians forward, forcing them into the free-agent market. In the new stadium, ticket prices went up. Some luxury suites sold for $100,000. As a result, the Indians could not put a team on the field that belonged under a blue-light special.

Caught up in the excitement of that day, Jacobs said, "I think we have a great team now."

It seemed outrageous at the time, but it turned out Jacobs would be right by 1995.

That's why Murray was so important.

Yes, Martinez mattered. A veteran starting pitcher is important, and Martinez had won 208 games. He was 39 and in incredible condition. But starting pitchers rarely become team leaders.

But someone who was in the lineup every day . . .

Someone who had played for a long time . . .

Someone who played nearly every game . . .

Someone who had been an All-Star and played in the World Series . . .

Someone destined for the Hall of Fame . . .

Someone such as Eddie Murray was exactly what the Tribe needed in 1994. Murray was 38 years old. He was coming off a season when he batted .285 with 27 homers and 100 RBI for the Mets. He hated playing in New York, but he was in the lineup for 154 games in 1993.

"There are certain guys who simply show you how to play the game the right way," said Hamilton. "And how to conduct yourself off the field the right way, Eddie did that for us."

From 1977 to 1993, Murray missed an average of six games per year. In six of the seasons, he played at least 160 of 162 games.

That means Murray played through bruises, cuts and muscle pulls and strains. It means he played through upset stomachs, viruses and days when he simply didn't have any energy.

For nearly all of his career, Murray was like the national anthem—there for every game.

In some ways, that was a surprise in 1994.

Once upon a time, there was a Sports Illustrated article entitled, "Is It Twilight Time?"

It was about two players who were supposed to be at the end of their careers. The first was Jim Rice, and the other was Murray. The article appeared in March 1988, and author Peter Gammons was half right. Rice had come to the end of the line.

But Murray?

Why would Sports Illustrated try to write off a guy at the age of 32, a guy who had 30 homers and 91 RBI in 1987?

In a 1995 interview Hank Peters said, "You had to be there to understand what happened to Eddie."

Peters was the Baltimore general manager when Murray came up with the Orioles in 1977 when he was only 21, and was the American League Rookie of the Year. From 1977 to 1985, the Orioles won at least 90 games six times and won two pennants. Murray was good for 29 homers and 103 RBI.

Everybody loved the guy until July of 1986.

"Then Eddie pulled a hamstring," recalled former Orioles Manager Earl Weaver in 1995. "It was the first time he went on the disabled list."

It also was the last time, but no one would know that.

"Edward Bennett Williams had bought the team, and it was changing," Peters said. "It was not the same Orioles that Eddie grew up with, because Williams was signing all these free agents who really weren't the kind of people we usually had in Baltimore."

In 1986, the Orioles also were in the midst of a miserable season.

"Williams loved to hold clubhouse meetings," Peters said. "The first time he did it, the players were enthralled. Williams was an attorney and a great orator. The second time, the guys were still interested in what he had to say. After that, it became ho-hum."

But Williams wanted to have one more meeting.

"He went into the clubhouse and gave this big speech about how we all were a family and should stick together," Peters said. "I looked at the players and they were completely bored. That night, the game was rained out. The reporters went to Williams for his opinion about what was wrong with the team, and he attacked Eddie."

Murray was set to make $2 million a year starting in 1987. Williams implied that Murray wasn't worth the money, and that he was taking a very long time coming back from his hamstring injury.

"Eddie saw that in the paper, and he was outraged," Peters said. "He had good reason to be. Williams was being completely hypocritical. Eddie came into my office and asked to be traded."

What the Orioles' owner didn't know, or intentionally failed to tell reporters, was that Murray wanted to play.

"Eddie told me that he wasn't 100 percent, but to put him in the lineup," Weaver said. "The doctors wouldn't clear him to play. They said he couldn't slide. I told them, 'Hey, Eddie won't slide. If he hits the ball over the fence, he won't have to slide.' They wouldn't listen. Then I sent Eddie up to talk to the owner, hoping they would smooth things out. Instead, they got into an argument and it just made things worse."

Murray finished the 1986 season with a .305 batting average, 17 homers and 84 RBI in 137 games. The Oriole fans took Williams' lead, designating Murray as the team's scapegoat. In the words of Sports Illustrated, Murray became "an exile in his home park, scourged, booed and singled out for his team's position in the second division."

"Eddie was never the same player in Baltimore after that," Peters said. "He felt betrayed and it was as if his spirit was broken."

In Weaver's words, "Eddie never was a guy for phony hustle, but some people look at him and think that he doesn't care."

All of that is true, but Murray believed that the Baltimore fans should have known better. Didn't they remember the good times? Couldn't they see that it wasn't he who changed, it was the team around him? Murray couldn't understand why the fans and media turned on him, and it didn't help the situation that he really started looking at the world through what Jim Palmer called "Eddie's Darth Vader face."

In 1987, a disillusioned Murray still put up Eddie Murray numbers: 30 homers, 91 RBI and a .277 batting average. But the Orioles were 67-95, and that set up Sports Illustrated's doubt-raising article in the spring of 1988.

"Eddie wasn't happy and made no bones about it," Peters said. "He was very hurt by what happened, and he had good reasons for feeling that way. It just turned out to be a bad situation for everyone, but Eddie showed how strong he was by what he has done since."

Murray moved to the Dodgers from 1989 to 1991. He spent two stormy years in New York with the Mets. Next, he came to the Indians in 1994.

"It's a piece of cake compared to other places I played," Murray said after he arrived.

Everywhere Murray played, he hit. But under that gruff exterior, there is a very sensitive man who felt every arrow fired in his direction. He withdrew from the media and sometimes the fans. He did his job, but his years in Los Angeles and New York were not that much different from his final days in Baltimore.

Cleveland changed all that.

Instead of being called a "clubhouse cancer" by some sportswriters who either didn't know or want to know Murray, he was considered one of the Indians' team leaders, a true elder statesman in 1994–1995.

Tom Hamilton loved to watch Murray take batting practice.

"He started by hitting the ball to the opposite field," he said. "Then, he'd hit the ball up the middle. Then, he'd pull the ball. He wasn't interested in putting on a show of home run derby. He wanted to perfect his swing and timing. Soon, Manny [Ramirez] and Albert [Belle] were taking batting practice the same way."

In 1995, Murray was chasing his 3,000th career hit. It happened on June 30 in Minnesota's Metrodome.

"I liked going for it more than I thought I would," he said. "They put up that banner at Jacobs Field, and every time I got a hit, they'd take a number down—and the fans would cheer. You know what made it really special? How the fans wanted me to get the record. I was amazed at how hard they pulled for me."

In 1995, Murray batted fifth, protecting Belle in the lineup. Murray batted .323. Remember, there were few cheap hits as his 40-year-old legs were not about to help him beat out those slow rollers. He also drove in 82 runs, impressive since he batted behind Belle, who hit 50 homers. Murray often came to home plate with the bases empty. But when there were runners in scoring position, Murray's batting average rose to .351.

"Albert was a great hitter, but some of those big numbers were due to Eddie batting right behind him in the order," said Hamilton. "You couldn't just walk Albert because Eddie could hurt you, too."

Murray finished his career in 1997 with 504 homers.

Most long conversations with Murray ventured into his trials and tribulations in Baltimore, L.A. and New York. Mostly, they dealt with his difficulty with the media. In 1995, he was named one of the 10 biggest jerks in baseball by Sports Illustrated.

In the spring of 1996, he said that didn't matter, having learned a long time ago that he can't control how people view him, or what they write.

"You don't hear about me cussing out fans," he said before the 1996 season. "I don't even cuss out writers. Does it make me a jerk when I say, 'No thank you, I don't want to do an interview?' True or not, negative stuff sells. I just want to be a man about it, but the media is out of control."

Hamilton said he never saw Murray being impolite with a member of the media, or anyone else during his time with the Tribe.

"I'd imagine every player with the Tribe during that time would rate Eddie as one of the best—if the not THE best—teammate that they had."

Murray was underrated for his entire career. Maybe it was because he never had that monster, 45-home run season. Maybe it was because of his uneasy relationship with the media. Maybe it was because early in his career, he was unfairly stereotyped as a natural athlete who happened to be playing baseball.

"Some people acted like the game came easy to me," he said. "They thought I really didn't push myself, that I didn't think about the game."

Those people forget that he won three Gold Gloves at first base. They forget he made himself into a switch hitter, and that he was best after he had seen a pitcher before—because he studied that pitcher's tendencies.

"Eddie was such a smart hitter," said Hamilton. "No hitter knew the strike zone better than Eddie."

Hamilton gave this example of Murray's leadership. Hamilton had criticized Ramirez for not hustling after a ball in the outfield.

The next day before the game, Murray spotted Hamilton and asked, "Gotta minute?"

They were near the batting cage, no one else was around. Murray made a point of the conversation being private.

"I heard you last night [on the radio when Murray was in the clubhouse]. You may have been a little hard on Manny because you said you didn't know if he went after that ball very hard. Here's what happened . . ."

Murray explained there were some unique circumstances.

"It's your call," said Murray. "But you may want to think about this in the future."

Hamilton told Murray, "I will think about it . . ."

Then Hamilton told another story about Murray. In the week where he was approaching his 3,000th hit, Murray agreed to do a long interview that could be cut up into five parts and shown on the stadium video board.

"In those days, we gave a player $50 for each pregame interview," said Hamilton. "I put $250 in an envelope and gave it to Eddie."

Handed the envelope, Murray asked, "What's in here?"

"It's the money we give you," Hamilton said,

"I don't want any money," said Murray.

Murray then called one of the clubhouse workers and handed him the envelope: "I don't know what's in here, but it's yours."

Hamilton said, "Eddie, there's $250 in there."

Murray said, "I don't care if there's $10,000 in there. I'm not doing this for money. Those guys work hard, they need it more than I do."

Hamilton said, "I always judge people by how they treat those who aren't in their same league economically, or people who really can't help you get ahead," said Hamilton. "And when he was with the Indians, Eddie was always great to those people. He never did stuff for show or to impress others. I'll always remember him for that."

Dennis Martinez and the Greatest Game

Tom Hamilton still isn't quite sure how it happened.

Exactly how did Dennis Martinez beat Seattle's Randy Johnson?

Beat the best pitcher in the American League in the biggest game of the season for the 1995 Indians.

"I doubt anyone thought Dennis would win that game," said Hamilton. "Not if you were being realistic."

That game was Game 6 of the American League Championship Series. It was played in the old Seattle Kingdome. In 1995, virtually every visiting team hated the Kingdome. Its artificial surface seemed like a putt-putt green over cement. It was a great place to dribble a basketball. It was where ground balls sometimes reacted like old-fashioned Super Balls—they appeared to gain speed with every hop.

It also was where Rick Manning beat out a bunt for a base hit. This was in 1977. Manning was a young center fielder for the Tribe and appeared to be headed to several seasons on the All-Star team.

"I tried to steal second base," said Manning. "I did my normal slide into second base, but they had the little dirt area around the base too wet. I slid wrong and broke my back. I was never the same player after that."

Manning was a career .281 hitter before the injury, .250 after.

"I hate this place," Manning said right before the 1995 playoffs in Seattle. He was the Tribe's broadcaster and like everyone else who cared about the team in Wahoo red, white and blue, Manning was worried on the night of October 17, 1995.

Yes, the Indians had a 3-2 lead in the best-of-7 series.

Yes, the Indians had the superior team, seemingly a team of destiny.

But this was Seattle, where the Mariners were 46-27 in the regular season. It also was where they knocked off the heavily favored Yankees in the first round of the playoffs.

And on the mound was Randy Johnson. It's difficult to truly characterize how intimidating it was to face Johnson in 1995. Start with the fact that he was 6-foot-10. And his arms were so long, it appeared as if he could touch the sun—or at least the roof of the Kingdome—if he raised them both above his head and stood on his toes. His hair was long, scraggly, wild. His eyes often were wide, piercing, as if on the edge of rage.

And the man could throw close to 100 miles per hour.

With those long legs, long arms and a whip of windup from the left side, it appeared as if he was releasing the ball about 10 feet away from home plate.

No one wanted to bat against Randy Johnson in 1995.

In the regular season, he was 18-2 with a 2.48 ERA. He averaged 12 strikeouts per nine innings.

He faced the Tribe once in the regular season, and threw nine innings in a 5-3 victory. Only two of the runs were earned.

In the first round of the playoffs, Johnson beat the Yankees twice.

That meant he was 20-2 heading into the series against the Tribe.

Johnson started Game 3 in Cleveland, and had a no decision in the 5-2, 11-inning win. He allowed only one earned run in eight innings.

Orel Hershiser said the Tribe had a "lineup for the ages" in 1995. Johnson had one of the greatest seasons in baseball history. At the age of 31, he was at the peak of his powers. He was surly, cocky and more than a little mean when he took the mound in the Kingdome, where fans nearly blew off the roof with every rocket of a fastball that he unleashed.

"It was so loud in the dome for that series, it was impossible to hear yourself think," said Hamilton. "The roof kept all the noise inside and it felt like the walls were shaking at times."

In 1992 and 1993, Johnson led the league in hit batters—a combined 34 times. No one wanted to be drilled with a Randy Johnson fastball. Not unless black and blue were your favorite colors.

In 1995, he had plunked only six batters. But his reputation as a guy who loved to throw inside and watch batters flop down and grovel in the dirt was well earned. When Johnson came close to a batter with a pitch, there was a sense that he wanted to hurt someone.

"I feel like I'm going into the mouth of a lion," Dennis Martinez told two baseball writers a few hours before that Game 6.

The Kingdome was also dark, mostly gray. In some ways, it felt like a baseball tomb until 1995 because most of the Mariners teams were terrible and the crowds miniscule.

But in 1995, Seattle was rocking, much like Cleveland. This was the best team in Mariners history.

And Johnson was seemingly unbeatable.

The day before the game, Martinez talked to a few friends in the media.

"I'm wasted physically," he said. "Earlier in the year, I hurt my knee. That caused my elbow to hurt. Now, my elbow is a little better, but my shoulder aches."

He paused then added, "A mess, that's what I am."

On October 17, 1995, Martinez was 41 years old. He had just become a grandfather. He talked as if he were ready for a rocking chair and bottle of Ensure.

"Guys like Randy Johnson, I'm not in his class," said Martinez.

The Indians allowed Martinez an extra day of rest because his shoulder was cranky. He was supposed to pitch Game 5 in Cleveland, but Manager Mike Hargrove gave Martinez a little more rest. Instead, Orel Hershiser started with only three days of rest (rather than the usual four), and beat the Mariners, 3-2. At this stage of his career, Martinez wanted opponents to dismiss him. He played the role of the creaky, aging pitcher with no life left in his arm, and barely one strong beat remaining in his heart. Listening to Martinez, you wondered how he had enough energy to even walk all the way from the dugout to the pitcher's mound without a cane.

When Martinez lost the opener of the Seattle series, 3-2, the veteran sat in the dugout long after his teammates had retreated to the clubhouse. He had a towel wrapped around his head, down over his jaw. It was as if he had about six teeth in need of root canals. Martinez had allowed three runs in 6⅓ innings. While he was charged with loss, it was not as if he earned it. The Indians just didn't hit enough.

On the morning of Game 6, Martinez was sitting by himself in the lobby of the Crown Center Hotel in Seattle. He spotted two Cleveland writers and yelled, "Hey, what are you guys doing?"

The writers were headed to lunch, but they knew this would be entertaining. Martinez wanted to pitch his night game at noon. He was ready to talk, prepared to list all of his ailments. He then discussed how the series should have already been over, how the Indians could have won it in five games. But there were times when the hitters didn't hit, when the manager made some questionable moves, when the pitchers . . . actually, he really didn't blame the pitchers at all, now that he thought about it.

Suddenly, he was talking about how he liked to cut his own lawn.

"I could pay someone to do it, but I like to do it myself," he said.

The two writers looked at each other, realizing this was a strange turn of conversation even for Martinez.

"It's not like I'm cheap," he said. "I just like to cut my own lawn."

"Nothing wrong with that," said one of the writers.

Martinez and the writers noticed a lot of people going into a conference room.

"Looks like a meeting," said one of the writers.

"I should go," said Martinez. "I always talk at meetings."

He meant Alcoholics Anonymous meetings. He had a drinking problem in his 20s. He had quit at 31.

The writers explained it was some kind of business meeting.

"But I bet they'd rather listen to you anyway," said one of the writers.

Martinez agreed.

Martinez had been the opening-day pitcher since joining the Indians in 1994. He often complained about how he had to be the one facing the other team's best pitcher. And here he was, 41 years old and feeling 444 years old.

On October 17, 1995, Martinez had been in the majors longer than the Seattle franchise. He came up to the Baltimore Orioles in 1976, and Seattle joined the American League in 1977.

"I just hope the guys don't think, 'If we don't get them tonight, there's always Game 7,' " said Martinez. "The pitcher can only do so much. You can feel real alone out there. Look, I can't win this game by myself. They have to have their heads in the game."

Martinez was making an excellent point. Did the Indians really want to go to a Game 7 . . . on the road?

The pressure would be on them. The weight of history could be crushing. It would be another one of those, "Why does this have to happen to us?" stories for Cleveland sports fans.

As Martinez also mentioned, "I really want to win the game that puts us in the World Series. That is something people would always remember."

Long before the game began, Martinez had one request for Hargrove. Most of the season, Martinez threw to veteran catcher Tony Pena. For example, Pena caught the opening game of the Boston playoff series, his home run winning it in the 13th inning. Martinez pitched six innings in that game, allowing two runs. That was not a knock on Sandy Alomar. It was just that Martinez had teamed up with Pena most of the season. Hargrove did that as a way to make sure Alomar received a day off at least once a week, as the star catcher often battled injuries. Hargrove was weighing what catcher to use when Martinez made his request for Pena.

The manager went with Pena.

Now, a few words about Pena's mitt. It seemed to be caked with dried mud, gunk, tobacco juice and who knew what else.

"Nasty," said Orel Hershiser. "Real nasty."

Consider that Martinez had something called "an emergency pitch." He never explained what the emergency pitch was, or when there was such an emergency that demanded its use. It probably was not a spitball.

But it was . . . something.

And maybe the something had . . . well . . . something to do with all the gunk on Pena's glove.

Or maybe not.

But if Martinez ever needed to have an emergency pitch available, it was this night in the Kingdome when 58,489 fans jammed the place and seemed to shake it on every pitch.

"When Dennis asked for me, that made my heart feel good," said Pena. "We could be like the hand and the glove."

And they were.

Martinez threw about five different pitches from a few different angles and with a variety of speeds. Sidearm sliders away. Overhand fastballs that seemed to ride in a bit into the fists of right-handed batters. Change-ups that dipped away from lefty hitters. Most pitches were right at the knees, on what the hitters called "the black."

The black is the edge of the plate, the inside and outside corners. Dennis Martinez was born in 1954, the year of the Tribe's last trip to the World Series. Despite a 19-year big league career, he took the mound on that Seattle night never having won a game in the postseason. He had started four postseason games in his career with Baltimore and the Tribe, and three times allowed three or fewer runs.

But no victories.

"Mr. No Decision," said Martinez.

But not on this night.

"Dennis brought a sense of urgency," said Hershiser. "You could feel it."

Urgency . . . emergency . . . whatever.

It was seven scoreless innings.

"He was masterful," said Hamilton. "That atmosphere was one of the loudest, most intimidating that I've ever been in for a baseball game. Dennis never blinked. He was in complete command. That building was waiting for Seattle to do something, so the fans could explode. Dennis wouldn't let that happen."

Johnson was blazing away . . . his eyes . . . his whip of a left arm . . . his fastball lighting up the radar gun at 95 . . . 96 . . . 97 . . . 98 . . .

Even a few were 99 miles per hour.

At times, Martinez seemed on the verge of exhaustion. He'd stand behind the mound, leaning over a bit. Pena could sense it. He walked a few miles to the mound by the end of the night—giving Martinez time to regroup mentally and physically. Yet, Martinez also ran off the field after every inning ended, and ran back to the mound to start the next inning. He had been doing that since he was a kid playing on a dust-bowl of a diamond in Nicaragua, and that was not about to change.

Few fans outside of Seattle recall that the 1995 Mariners had a lineup that nearly could match the Tribe.

They had three hitters with at least 111 RBI—and none were future Hall of Famer Ken Griffey. He battled injuries that season and played only 72 games, still hitting 17 homers.

There was Tino Martinez (.293, 31 homers, 111 RBI), Edgar Martinez (.356, 29 homers, 113 RBI) and Jay Buhner (.262, 40 homers, 121 RBI). A guy named Mike Blowers hit 23 homers.

Martinez sliced them up and shut them down.

"A surgeon out there," Seattle Manager Lou Piniella said after the game.

The Indians scored their first run in the fifth inning, an RBI single by Kenny Lofton.

Then came the top of the eighth.

The Tribe had Ruben Amaro on third, Lofton on second base. Johnson cut loose with a sailing fastball and it bounced off the mitt of catcher Dan Wilson.

Amaro scored easily from third.

Lofton was racing from second base to third.

"I saw the catcher had his back turned, bending over to pick up the ball," recalled Lofton.

He kept running, scoring all the way from second base on a passed ball. One pitch that bounced off Wilson's glove led to two runs and a 3-0 lead.

Then Carlos Baerga hit a home run, turning that 1-0 lead at the start of the eighth to 4-0.

Julian Tavarez and Jose Mesa relieved, preserving the victory for Martinez.

Digging deeper into that eighth inning, it began with a double by Pena, the personal catcher of Martinez. Amaro ran for him. Then Lofton beat out a bunt, sending Amaro to third base. Lofton stole second base. In several ways, Lofton's legs dominated the inning.

That set up the passed ball, the two runs scoring.

Martinez threw 90 pitches, 56 strikes. He allowed four hits, walked one.

"I think this was the biggest game that the Tribe won in all my years covering them," said Tom Hamilton. "Yes, there would have been a Game 7 if we lost—but who knows what would have happened? Seattle seemed like a team of destiny at that point. Did you really want to play them in a Game 7 in the Kingdome? I wouldn't."

The Mariners won a single-game playoff over the Angels just to reach the Division Series. Then they beat the Yankees in the first round. They were 4-0 in elimination games, and Johnson had won three of those. "It's hard to believe that after all these years, the Cleveland Indians finally are going to the World Series," Hargrove said after that game. "It's a feeling of disbelief, like this can't really be happening. It is happening, but there was a fear that it never would."

By throwing seven scoreless innings, Martinez made sure the dream did become reality.

A strong argument can be made that this was the biggest game in Tribe history since October 4, 1948.

The Tribe and Boston Braves had finished the 1948 season with 96-58 records, tied for first place in the American League. There was a one-game playoff, and Gene Bearden beat the Braves, 8-3. He delivered a complete game, and did it pitching on only one day of rest. In the final 10 days of the season, Bearden started four times—and threw four complete games. He allowed only four earned runs.

So what Martinez accomplished that night in Seattle doesn't exactly compare to what happened with Bearden. But 20 years later, the performance by Martinez might not be fully appreciated.

One man who really understood was Bob Feller.

The Hall of Famer never won a postseason game. Of course, when he played for the Tribe the only postseason was the World Series. He started twice and was 0-2 in 1948, including a 1-0 loss to the Boston Braves.

Feller traveled with the Indians to Seattle for that 1995 game. He talked with Martinez in the afternoon.

"He wished me luck," said Martinez. "I told him that I'd take all I can get."

Then he went out and pitched a game for the ages in front of one of the game's greatest pitchers.

Orel Hershiser: Climbing Twin Peaks

In the spring of 1995, Orel Hershiser was 36 years old.

It's worth remembering that—Hershiser being 36 when he came to the Indians.

Just as it's important to know that no one saw what was coming from Hershiser. Not the Dodgers, his old team. Not the Indians, his new team.

Not even Hershiser.

"Could anyone believe he'd win 20 games that season?" asked Tom Hamilton.

That's right, Hershiser was a 20-game winner.

Yes, only 16 were in the regular season, but he won four more in the playoffs and World Series.

Add it all up, and Hershiser was 20-7 in all the games that he pitched in 1995.

The previous three years, he was 28-35 for the Dodgers.

In the spring of 1995, baseball was still shut down because of a labor battle. Hershiser was one of the players on the union's negotiating committee.

"When we finally settled, I didn't have a contract," said Hershiser.

That's because, in the words of Hamilton, "No one was sure if Orel had anything left."

Consider that Hershiser was Mr. Dodger. He made three All-Star teams (1987–89). He was a Cy Young Award winner in 1988, a World Series MVP in 1988. But this was 1995. And all that had happened before Hershiser had career-threatening shoulder surgery in 1990.

"The Dodgers' theory back then was to get rid of a guy a year too early rather than a year too late," said Hershiser. "I remember talking to [owner] Peter O'Malley, [general manager] Fred Claire and [manager] Tommy Lasorda and some others. They were saying they appreciated all that I had done with the Dodgers. They were very nice. But their offer was at least 50 percent under what I could get elsewhere."

In 1994, Hershiser had earned $3.3 million with the Dodgers.

The contract he signed with the Tribe for 1995 was for $1.5 million.

That means if Hershiser's memory looking back is correct, the Dodgers wanted to cut his pay from $3.3 million to $750,000.

"Later, I figured out that they already had spent the money to sign Hideo Nomo," said Hershiser.

Nomo was a star in Japan, and he signed a $2.1 million deal with the Dodgers.

Los Angeles believed Hershiser's tank was empty, his arm hanging by a string—one more pitch away from another serious injury.

So they were content to say goodbye to a guy who had a 134-102 record with a 3.00 ERA for them, a guy who completed 65 of his 303 starts. Even in 1994, he was a respectable 6-6 with a 3.79 ERA in 21 starts.

Hershiser tried not to take any of this personally, but it had to hurt.

"I knew I could still pitch," he said. "I was throwing in the off-season and I could feel my body healing, my arm coming back. I was five years away from shoulder reconstruction surgery."

And he wanted to prove people wrong—especially the Dodgers.

He was talking to the Dodgers' biggest rival, San Francisco.

Then John Hart arrived with an offer from the Indians. He was selling a chance to pitch for a team with a legitimate shot at the playoffs, and possibly the World Series. He was talking new ballpark, sellout crowds, a city in a baseball frenzy and a team of young sluggers belting baseballs over the walls.

"John also talked to me about leadership," said Hershiser. "He wanted me to join with Eddie [Murray] and Dennis [Martinez]."

"We are looking for winners," Hart told Hershiser. "And we want guys who have won, know how to win and still can produce."

After being rejected by the Dodgers, the passion and respect shown by Hart had a dramatic appeal to Hershiser.

Hart was treating Hershiser as if he were still The Bulldog. Hart's research revealed that during that 6-6 1994 season, Hershiser had nine no-decisions in games he left with the Dodgers leading or tied. "I told Orel he should come to the American League where we wouldn't have to pinch hit for him" because of the designated hitter, said Hart in a 1995 interview. "We brought Orel and his wife to town and showed them the new ballpark. We took them to Johnny's [an upscale restaurant in downtown Cleveland]. I told him to start to think about winning 15 games again."

Hershiser said the contracts offered by Tribe and Giants "were almost the same."

He picked Cleveland over San Francisco. Think about that for a moment. It just shows how Cleveland had become a desirable baseball destination.

"I knew I was coming to the end of my career," said Hershiser. "I had been a Dodger and a National Leaguer all my life. So the American League had some appeal. But mostly, it was the Indians. They were a young team. They could average five, six, seven runs a game. I'd never experienced anything like that with the Dodgers. I looked at the bullpen and saw some good arms. I realized that I wasn't going to throw a lot of complete games any more. I needed a team that could score with a good bullpen."

Hamilton correctly recalls that there was interest about Hershiser signing with the Tribe, but not the excitement that came when Eddie Murray and Dennis Martinez signed in 1994.

"It's easy to be skeptical when you get a starter from the National League," said Hamilton. "Usually, you can add a half-run to his ERA [because of the designated hitter batting, rather than the pitcher]. And Orel pitched in Dodger Stadium, a great park for pitchers. It's really hard to hit there."

Hart later confessed that he was hoping for 10-12 victories from Hershiser, that he could be a solid fifth starter.

He signed a two-year deal with the Tribe, paying him $1.5 million in 1995 and $1.75 million (a team option) for 1996. In other words, the Tribe only had to guarantee Hershiser one season. This turned out to be perhaps the best veteran free-agent signing made by Hart.

"I agreed to sign with the Indians at about 3 a.m. [April 8, 1995] and I was throwing for Mike Hargrove and [pitching coach] Mark Wiley later that day in Winter Haven," said Hershiser. "It happened that fast."

Something else appealed to Hershiser, who has a tremendous

appreciation of baseball history. "I knew the Indians hadn't been to the World Series for over 40 years," Hershiser said. "And I knew that the Cleveland team that got there would always be remembered. I wanted to be a part of that."

At 6-foot-3 and 195 pounds with geeky glasses and a chest that he admitted is "kind of concaved," how could anyone call this man a bulldog? He looked more like a sandhill crane when he stood on the mound, seemingly squinting at the catcher when trying to see the signs.

And what kind of name is Orel Leonard Hershiser IV?

"I once had a roommate in the minors named Wickensheimer," said Hershiser. "We pitched a doubleheader and won. Wickensheimer and Hershiser, sounded like a doubleheader won by a law firm."

Part of Hershiser's persona was to look like an underdog, the "non-athlete" as he has sometimes called himself. He's often said, "I wasn't even the best player on my team."

Hershiser has sometimes indicated he was cut twice from his high school team in Cherry Hill, N.J. Well, he was cut twice from the varsity. As a freshman, he pitched for the freshman team. As a sophomore, he pitched for the junior varsity. He spent the final two years on the varsity. As a senior, he was 9-1 and made the all-conference team.

Bowling Green was the only Division I school to offer Hershiser any sort of aid for baseball, and it was minimal. His father, Orel III, ran a very successful printing business, so money was not an issue.

At Bowling Green, Hershiser was a 6-foot-3, 155-pound freshman. He threw in the low 80s, and only dressed for home games as a freshman and sophomore.

Here's the background, according to the Bowling Green website, featuring a story of when Hershiser was inducted into the school's Hall of Fame:

> Hershiser didn't even make the team as a freshman. The disappointment in being cut along with failing grades caused him to leave school abruptly, hitchhiking his way east until the car he was riding in was involved in an accident in Pennsylvania. With hitchhiking further out of the question (it was illegal to hitchhike

on an interstate in Pennsylvania), Hershiser found a motel and called his parents in suburban Detroit. The next day, he arrived home, with a promise to return to Bowling Green.

Orel enrolled in summer school at BG, and his grades improved. However, when tryouts came around again for the Falcon baseball team, he was left off the team once again. Working at his father's paper company the following summer, Orel's lanky frame began to fill out.

Returning to Bowling Green that fall with fifteen pounds added to his body and a fastball five miles an hour faster, head coach Don Pervis gave Hershiser a spot on the roster, and he didn't disappoint. Hershiser made the all-MAC first team his junior year, which included a no-hitter vs. Kent State on May 4, 1979. At the end of the year, he accepted an offer to attend the minor league camp of the Los Angeles Dodgers, who had drafted him in the 17th round of the MLB June Draft.

By the time he was drafted, Hershiser had added 30 pounds to that 6-foot-3 frame, and weighed 185.

A 17th-round pick is more of a "suspect" than a prospect. He was put in the bullpen in the minors, as he started only 28 games in five years. He did have 51 saves, but from 1980 to 1983, his minor-league ERA was 3.99. In 1980, he was ready to quit after being shelled for eight runs in a Class AA Texas League game. The San Antonio coaching staff convinced him to stick around. He was 5-9 with a 3.55 ERA that season. He was sent back to San Antonio in 1981, and was 7-6 with a 4.68 ERA.

He had doubts that he'd ever make the majors.

"People have always underestimated Orel's toughness and intelligence," said Hamilton. "He once told me that he made a point of always being around the pitchers who were the higher draft picks. He ran sprints with them. He threw with them. He stayed in their group so that the coaches would notice him, because he knew the coaches paid more attention to the higher draft picks."

That's because the bigger the bonus a player receives, the more the team wanted the player to succeed. It was a way of making the investment pay off.

"He was as smart as he looked, and Orel looked like a college professor," said Hamilton. "And he out-worked everyone. For him to make it, you know he had to be relentless."

Tommy Lasorda kept Hershiser on the Dodger roster in 1984.

"I was the 10th pitcher on a 10-man staff," said Hershiser.

In 1983, Hershiser was 10-8 with a 4.09 ERA for Class AAA Albuquerque. He started 10 games, and completed six of them. He also had 16 saves. Lasorda figured Hershiser could help as a long reliever, and perhaps a spot starter if someone was injured.

On May 26, 1984, Hershiser had a 5.96 ERA pitching sporadically in relief. He was summoned into Lasorda's office. He feared that he was being sent back to the minors. Lasorda was signing a baseball. He looked up, handed a ball to Hershiser and said, "It's your ball, you're starting today."

The Dodgers were playing the Mets in Shea Stadium. Scheduled starter Jerry Reuss was injured. Hershiser was given his first big-league start and delivered 6⅓ innings, allowing one run.

If he had been hit hard, would he have been sent back to the minors? Who knows?

His next start was June 7, allowing six runs in five innings. Then, he pitched a complete game with one run on June 29. And back-to-back shutouts on July 4 and July 14.

Then Hershiser put together a streak of 33⅔ scoreless innings. He threw four shutouts in five starts at one point that season. He finished that 1984 season with an 11-8 record and a 2.66 ERA.

The next year, he was 19-3 with a 2.03 ERA.

He had developed a nasty sinker. His fastball was in the low 90s. He was turning into an ace.

"Then he had one of the greatest seasons ever," said Hamilton.

That was in 1988, when Hershiser was 23-8 with a 2.26 ERA. He completed 15 of 34 starts, including eight shutouts. He threw a major-league-record 59 consecutive scoreless innings.

In September and the postseason of 1988, Hershiser threw seven shutouts. He was 7-0. He even came out of the bullpen to pick up a save. He was the MVP of the 1988 World Series, winning two games.

This was before baseball embraced pitch counts or how lots of innings impacted the arms of pitchers.

From 1985 to 1989, he averaged 252 innings per season. He completed 50 of 171 starts.

He led the National League in innings pitched in 1987, 1988 and 1989.

And in 1990, his shoulder was scrambled eggs.

Hershiser had a torn rotator cuff, several stretched ligaments and other damage in the shoulder area. Dr. Frank Jobe did major surgery, and there was no guarantee Hershiser would ever come back. Or if he did, could he even come close to his domination in the late 1980s?

Hershiser did come back after 18 months of rehabilitation. He was still a solid pitcher, but the Dodgers were sure his arm was fragile.

And that's why they wrote him off after the 1994 season.

Hart knew Hershiser's history of comebacks.

And he knew that even a repeat of that 3.79 ERA that he had for the Dodgers in 1994 would translate into far more than the six victories that he had for Los Angeles. The Tribe's emerging offense would guarantee that.

Hershiser lived in Orlando when he signed with the Tribe. After the team left spring training in Winter Haven, they arrived in Cleveland to find . . . winter.

"The first day of baseball for us in Cleveland was running down to the store to buy the kids snowsuits," said Hershiser. "We played baseball with the kids in the front yard—in the snow. We were living in Westlake. The lady across the street from us called a friend and said she didn't know where her new neighbors were from, but 'They're not from here.' She talked about us playing in the snow. She had no idea that I was with the Indians. We later became friends, and that's how I heard that story."

Hershiser credits former Tribe strength coach Fernando Montes with helping him regain some of his old form. Montes pushed Hershiser to strengthen his arm, his legs, his "core" as it's now known.

On June 22, Hershiser was 5-3 and went on the disabled list. He had strained his back during a workout, and pulled it again when pitching on June 21. Would he be out for a long time? Would he return and battle the balky back for the rest of the season? That could happen with a 36-year-old pitcher.

But Hershiser returned to the mound on July 7, and was 11-2 in his last 14 starts.

"Guys started telling me that the bite was back in my curveball and that my sinker was back like it used to be," he said.

The Bulldog was baring his teeth. He went from a fastball in the 84-87 mph range to throwing slightly above 90 mph.

Hershiser said playing for the 1995 Tribe fueled his confidence.

"We were never out of a game," he said. "We pounded people. I didn't worry about giving up a few runs. Just keep getting some outs. We'll score. There was a six-game stretch for me during the season where we scored about 60 runs when I started. I had never pitched for a team that hit like this. I'd be on the mound, look up at the scoreboard and we'd be ahead something like 7-1. That didn't happen to me much with the Dodgers."

Hershiser joined Dennis Martinez, Eddie Murray, Sandy Alomar and Tony Pena to be the team leaders. Murray and Martinez had won big in Baltimore. Pena was respected by virtually everyone in baseball because he was a veteran catcher. Alomar was the leader of the young players who came up in the early 1990s.

"Not enough was said of all the guys on those teams with leadership qualities," said Hargrove. "Charlie Nagy later grew into a leader, too. They policed themselves in many ways."

Hershiser told a story of how Albert Belle was "upset about something," and didn't want to play in the All-Star Game.

"Eddie Murray and I had a long talk with him," said Hershiser. "I loved Eddie Murray. He could get Albert's attention. Of all the guys I played with for all those years, Eddie Murray was in the top five in terms of being a great teammate. We were so close. He had a knack of knowing how to cajole and convince the young guys to do the right things. When it came to influencing the young guys, Eddie was off the charts."

And yes, Belle did play in the All-Star Game.

Hamilton believes Hershiser was critical to the development of Nagy.

"For years, the burden of being the ace of the staff was on Charlie," he said. "But he was just a young guy, like all the rest who came up in the 1990s. First, we added Dennis [Martinez] in 1994. And then we signed Orel. Now, Charlie didn't have to start the opener and all the big games. He also saw how those guys prepared to pitch in those games."

Mark Shapiro remembered a story told by Ross Atkins, now the Indians' minor-league director. Atkins was a minor-league pitcher at the time. For some reason, Hershiser was working out at the minor-league complex in Winter Haven that day.

"He said Orel then ran with the pitchers," said Shapiro. "And Orel was running about all of them into the ground. He was 15 years older than most of those guys."

When the drills were over, Hershiser was asked to speak to the young pitchers. He only said a few things, ending with: "If you want to be great, you have to ask that much of yourself."

Then he walked away.

Hershiser said the racial mix was a key factor in the Tribe having strong leaders.

"You had a black guy [Murray], a white guy [Hershiser] and some Latin guys [Martinez, Pena and Alomar]," he said. "And we all worked together to teach the younger guys how to win. It gave the team a real sense of purpose. That's a story in itself, how baseball cuts across racial and ethnic lines, and how we all became good friends and spoke the same language . . . baseball."

Hershiser finished the regular season with a 16-6 record and 3.87 ERA.

Then came the playoffs.

"I had heard about how great Orel was in the postseason with the Dodgers," said Hamilton. "I thought about 1988 when Orel broke Don Drysdale's record [58 consecutive scoreless innings] Everyone said that was unbreakable. You couldn't make one mistake . . . not even an unearned run . . . and break that record. How do you do that for 59 straight innings, like Orel did?"

Hershiser allowed only 41 base runners (31 hits, 10 walks) in those 59 scoreless innings.

In that 1988 season, he threw 267 innings while winning 23 games. In the postseason, it was another 42⅔ innings, allowing a total of five earned runs. He beat Oakland in Game 5 of the 1988 World Series to give the Dodgers the title.

At that point, Reggie Jackson was quoted by Sports Illustrated as saying, "Orel Hershiser is the real thing. He's 24 carat. He's 99 and

44/100 pure. He's Ivory Snow. He's Post Toasties. He's a rainy day for the other team. Hell, he's a smog alert."

By the time the Tribe was in its first postseason in 41 years, Hershiser had turned 37.

So maybe he was a little more like oatmeal than Post Toasties. Perhaps he wasn't quite 24 carat, but nor was he fool's gold.

"I always thought we could win when I saw Orel on the hill in a big game," said Hamilton. "He'd get into a jam, and he'd throw that sinker and get that double-play grounder. He'd slow the game down when other guys felt their heartbeat rising."

Hershiser offered a different explanation.

"People have told me that I rise to the occasion when the pressure is on," he said. "No, it's the other way around. People would sometimes melt under the pressure. I just wanted to stay the same, pitch my normal game. Dennis, Eddie . . . all the older guys talked to the younger guys about remaining steady. Don't give in to all the exuberance and adrenaline. You can't stop the noise, the energy and the adrenaline rush that you feel. But focus it. Stay with your plan."

After beating Seattle twice in the American League Championship Series (ALCS) to earn the MVP award, Hershiser said, "If you play at the same level in the playoffs that you do in the regular season, maybe the pressure will get to the other guy. And while you're playing your normal game, it will look like you rose to the occasion."

In two games against Seattle in the ALCS, Hershiser threw 14 innings, allowing three runs (two earned). Two more victories.

After he beat Seattle, 5-2, in Game 2 of the ALCS, Hargrove approached Hershiser with an idea.

Yes, he threw eight innings in that Game 2, but could the veteran come back and pitch Game 5?

"How do you feel?" asked Hargrove.

"I feel great," said Hershiser.

"How are you on short rest?" asked Hargrove.

"I feel fine," insisted Hershiser.

"I'm thinking of starting you Sunday," said Hargrove, meaning Hershiser would get three, rather than the usual four days of rest between starts. "I feel good about it," said Hershiser. "Whatever you decide."

Hargrove handed Hershiser the ball, and the result was a 3-2 victory.

In the World Series, he was 1-1 with a 2.57 ERA.

"Put a black cape and a hood on him, stick a scythe in his hand and he'd look just like the Grim Reaper," Hargrove said during the 1995 World Series. "The more pressure, the more concentration he brings. Look at him staring at the plate—like a laser beam. You could just feel him bearing down."

In his three years with the Tribe (1995–97), Hershiser was 45-21 with a 4.21 ERA.

"Going to Cleveland gave me a chance to climb to the pinnacle again," he said. "Everyone remembers me as a Dodger, but coming to the Indians was a chance to rise up to another mountain top. No one season for me can compare to what happened in 1988. That was the highest peak. But being with the Indians for three years and going to two World Series—that was like climbing twin peaks. To me, Cleveland fans were amazing. All that volume. Some of the most exciting moments of my life were pitching for the Indians. I still get goosebumps thinking about it."

Charlie Manuel

Most people think they know Charlie Manuel, but they don't.

"They think Charlie showed up with the Indians and had all these great hitters," said Hamilton. "And all he had to do was throw batting practice and pat them on the back. And Charlie was never interested in taking credit for all those great hitters—but he had a lot to do with their success."

It's easy to reduce Manuel to a cartoon character. He seldom exits the same sentence that he enters, assuming he gets around to finishing that sentence. His drawl oozes Virginia's Blue Ridge Mountains, where he grew up in the town of Buena Vista—not far from Roanoke. It's coal and cow country, where people work the land with calloused hands and aching backs. It's where Manuel was the son of a "Holiness preacher," as Charlie described his father. They lived in several mountain towns where his father gave loud, emotional sermons in a tent, leading to people being saved, some with tears pouring down as Brother Manuel laid hands on them and prayed.

"I sat through all of his sermons," said Manuel, shaking his head. "He made me do it."

When Manuel tells stories, he touches your arm to make a point. He loathes self-pity and excuses, preferring humor.

"Charlie was one of 11 kids," said Hamilton. "He'd joke that he never slept alone until he was married."

But what Manuel doesn't talk about was what happened to his father. When Manuel was a senior in high school, his father committed suicide. He was suffering from diabetes and other physical problems. He left Charlie a note telling his son to look after his mother, brothers and sisters. Manuel was already a high school basketball and baseball star. He also worked in a lumber mill. And he was about to be married. So when the Minnesota Twins offered him $20,000 to play pro baseball, he couldn't wait to sign.

"People have no idea what Charlie has been through," said Hamilton. "It's why I admire him so much."

The majority of Tribe fans noticed Manuel in 1994, when he was named the team's batting coach just as the franchise was moving into what was then called Jacobs Field.

But Manuel already had been the Tribe's hitting coach, hired by former president Hank Peters in 1988.

Two years later, he was demoted . . . sent back to coaching in the minors.

"I replaced Bobby Bonds [as hitting coach]" said Manuel. "I didn't know why he was fired. The players really liked Bobby. They had never met me before. Even [Manager] Doc Edwards didn't know me because it was Hank Peters' idea to hire me."

Manuel had been a manager in the Minnesota Twins minor-league system for six years. He was a nobody to the players, and his Blue Ridge accent didn't help.

Standing around the batting cage, Manuel introduced himself to Joe Carter. Carter nodded and said, "Nice to meet you, but we had a good batting coach."

Next was Cory Snyder, who said, "I don't need a batting coach. Brett Butler and my father work with me."

Then Mel Hall said, "Hey, you stay out of my way and I'll stay out of yours."

After that Manuel went into the clubhouse and saw a newspaper story, questioning Bonds' firing and his being replaced "with a minor-leaguer, a guy who hit .198 in the big leagues."

"That was my first day," Manuel recalled. "It was the only time in my life that I didn't feel like getting up the next morning and coming to the park."

Manuel had played 10 years in the minors, six more in Japan. In five Class AAA seasons, he was a .320 hitter (1.008 OPS). But he was in the systems of Minnesota and the Dodgers, two teams loaded with outfield talent.

"It would have helped if they had a DH back then," he said. But for most of Manuel's time in the minors, they didn't, and he was a hitter first and last. He had 384 big-league at bats over six seasons. Then he became a star in Japan, followed by six years of coaching and managing in the minors. When the call to the Tribe came, Manuel thought he had earned a shot as a big-league coach. He was never accepted by those Tribe players in the late 1980s.

After the 1989 season, Peters told Manuel, "You're an excellent hitting coach."

Manuel paused.

"Then he said I was fired," he said. "They sent me back to the minors. It hurt bad, real bad."

Because part of Manuel wondered if he'd ever get another chance.

Manuel began the 1990 season as the Tribe's minor-league hitting coach. In July, Manager Bob Molinaro was fired at Class AAA Colorado Springs and replaced by Manuel. Manuel never had a losing record and won two titles as the Tribe's Class AAA manager.

Hamilton loves to tell this Manuel story. In 1993, Manuel had an 86-55 record at Charlotte and won the International League. His knack of understanding frustrated players was critical to his success. He also had a quirky sense of humor.

In one game, pitcher Dave Otto was trying to convince Manuel not to go to the bullpen. This was at Class AAA Colorado Springs.

As they met at the mound, Otto said, "I feel strong."

Manuel said, "That may be, the outfielders are dying out there chasing after all those balls . . . it's Rocky Mountain shower time."

And he took Otto out of the game.

Manuel managed and/or coached players such as Jim Thome, Albert Belle, Manny Ramirez, Chad Ogea and Carlos Baerga in the minors. When it came time to hire a batting coach in 1994, General Manager John Hart (a Hank Peters disciple), who also managed against Manuel in the minors, had only one person in mind. Charlie Manuel was getting a second shot in the majors.

"This time, it was with players who knew him from the minors and spring training," said Hart.

It was the idea of General Manager John Hart to promote Manuel to the 1994 coaching staff. Mike Hargrove was the manager, and he didn't have any major objections to Manuel. The former batting coach was Jose Morales. The young hitters coming up from the minors were raving about Manuel, who had managed in Class AAA from 1990 to 1993. He also spent a lot of time with the hitters in the minors.

While no one said it, Hart believed Manuel could be an effective big-league manager. The two men became close friends. Hart relied on Manuel's judgment in some trade discussions. Manuel had managed against Kenny Lofton in the Class AAA Pacific Coast League, and he begged Hart to trade for the outfielder. Hart also wanted Lofton, but Manuel's strong endorsement inspired Hart to accelerate his efforts, and that led to the Indians trading Willie Blair and Eddie Taubensee for Lofton.

It's one of the biggest steals in Tribe history.

You can say that Manuel arrived just in time with all the great young Tribe hitters. But virtually all of them—except Lofton—played for Manuel in the minors.

Albert Belle was stubborn and suspicious, but he trusted Manuel. A favorite story is that when Manuel was throwing batting practice to Belle at Fenway Park, in a cramped batting cage, Belle sizzled a liner right back at Manuel. The ball broke through the protective screen and hit Manuel on top of his head.

Manuel quickly wiped off the blood, and then went back to business.

"He didn't quit hitting and I didn't quit pitching," said Manuel. "He looked at me and asked if I was all right. I just kept throwing."

Manuel didn't have to say a word to prove he was just as tough and determined as Belle, who was almost maniacal about hitting.

"As a coach, Charlie had time for everyone," said Hamilton. "No one was too insignificant. He worked with the 25th guy on the roster as if he were Belle and Thome. He worked with the clubhouse kids on their hitting after he was done with big-leaguers. Everyone was important to Charlie, and that's why the hitters loved him so much."

Manuel never tried to mold the hitters.

"Think about all the different styles of hitters on the Tribe in the 1990s," said Hamilton.

Thome had a big swing from the left side of the plate. Belle was powerful, but his swing from the right side was remarkably compact. At his best, Lofton slapped at the ball. Eddie Murray was a switch-hitter who could be like a tennis player, almost serving the ball to different parts of the field. And think about the different personalities and backgrounds—Latino players, black players, white players . . . players from college . . . from high school . . . from the city . . . from farms.

"Charlie wasn't trying to become the next batting coach like Charlie Lau and invent a new way to hit," said Hamilton. "He didn't clone hitters. There was no 'Charlie Manuel Way' to hit. He knew there were a couple of basic fundamentals of hitting, then he took what the player had and worked to that player's strength."

Hamilton said the players "hit and hit and hit." It was on the field, in the batting cages. Repetition. Muscle memory.

"Charlie has the ability to communicate with anyone," said Hamilton. "Albert Belle loved him. He knew there were no hidden agendas with Charlie. You might not like his answer, but you also knew he was telling you the truth because he cared about you. He never tried to appease players, but he spent so much time with them—they knew he had their best interests at heart. He never got the credit that he deserved for how those teams hit. Yes, they had tremendous talent, but he got the most out of it."

In 2013 when Manuel was managing the Phillies, he looked back at those 1990s Tribe teams and said, "I've been lucky since I started managing in the minors, I've always had great talent. That's what makes a good manager or coach."

Manuel had another battle, one that he doesn't like to talk about often. It's his health.

In 1991, he had two quick heart attacks during spring training. His chest felt as if a horse was kicking it. He went to the hospital, where they did an angioplasty, put him on a strict diet and told him to be careful. This was much better than heart surgery.

"I had a warning," he said.

And he was careful—for a while.

But then he began to feel better. He began to eat whatever was around, especially the free food in the clubhouse. He began to gain weight.

At the start of the 1998 season, he stood on a scale

"I figured I weighed about 235," he said. "It was at 258."

Not long after that came chest pains. He knew right away.

His heart.

He thought about all the relatives he knew, and how so many of them had died from heart disease—a lot of them before they were 60. He thought about how doctors were going to saw his chest in half, rip it open—stop his heart—and how this was supposed to make him better. By 1998, he was established not only as the Tribe's batting coach, but as one of the best teachers of hitting in the majors. So he knew that when he had heart surgery on July 6, 1998, his job would be waiting for him.

Assuming he lived through the operation.

Later, he'd laugh as he talked about how they "put you in one of those stupid hospital gowns that leaves you flapping in the wind." They tell you to sleep, but every 90 minutes someone is coming into your room, poking at you. They tell you everything is going to be fine—right after they tell you all the things that could go wrong in the surgery.

As he faced that surgery, Manuel told himself that he had to live. His fiancée, Melissa Martin, was battling breast cancer. She was right in the middle of chemotherapy as he was heading for heart surgery. As the surgery approached, he received a call from Eddie Murray. That meant a lot. Murray already was a future Hall of Famer when he joined the Tribe in 1994, Manual's first season back as batting coach. And Murray treated him with respect, the two men working in the batting cage.

The first time with the Tribe, hitters avoided him. Now, they lined up to have Manuel help them.

Five weeks after a quadruple bypass, Manuel was back as batting coach.

"I'm not even sure of everything they did," he said. "Sometimes, my chest felt so sore. And my back, it killed me. But it wasn't the heart."

It was the pounding in his chest and back from the surgery—all that cutting and moving him around. It was the fluid that filled part of a lung about 10 days after surgery, and how he had to go in and get it drained.

"They stick a big needle into your lung," he said. "Now that is scary."

Manuel added, "I used to think that I was a tough guy. But having something like heart surgery, you find out that you're not that tough. Not when they have all those tubes sticking in you. Not when they want you to get out of the hospital bed, and all you want to do is lay there and moan . . . You find you're not that tough at all."

But those who knew Manuel believe pure Blue Ridge Mountain grit was why he persevered.

"All I know is that I need baseball a lot more than baseball needs me," he said. "It was nice when the players said they missed me. But I'll tell you the truth, I missed them even more."

By the late 1990s, there was some tension between Mike Hargrove and Manuel. The reason was John Hart—or simply, the fact Hart believed that Manuel would be an excellent manager. Hart's friendship with Manuel predated his relationship with Hargrove. And it was no secret that Hart was prepared to fire Hargrove in the middle of the 1997 season until owner Dick Jacobs asked his general manager to reconsider.

"I never once heard Charlie say, 'I need to be a manager,' " said Hamilton. "He was happy being the batting coach and working with all those great hitters. He believed he could manage, because he had done it in the minors and won championships. I'm sure he thought he could do the same in the big leagues. Charlie and I were close, and he never mentioned managing the Indians to me or said anything critical about Mike and the job he was doing."

By 1999, Hargrove was in his ninth season as manager, an eternity in the world of Major League Baseball. He had taken the Tribe to the World Series in 1995 and 1997, and the pressure was building to win it. No longer was making the playoffs . . . being in the World Series . . . enough. The desperation to deliver the first championship for a major Cleveland sports team since the 1964 Browns was weighing down the franchise. At the start of the 1999 season, Hargrove and Manuel didn't know it, but Hart sensed that Dick Jacobs was thinking about selling the team. Hart wanted to get the Tribe back to the World Series once more.

In 1999, the Indians had a tremendous regular season team, winning 97 games (the most since 1996). They won the Central Division by 21½ games, and it was a lineup loaded with stars: Manny Ramirez, Jim Thome, Sandy Alomar, Omar Vizquel, Travis Fryman, Robbie Alomar, Kenny Lofton and Charlie Nagy. They faced Boston in the first round of the playoffs, and won the first two games. This looked like a team built to return to the World Series. They won Game 2 by a score of 11-1.

But trouble was ready to kick down the door. Game 3 starter Dave Burba left after four scoreless innings. He had been pitching with a sore arm for several weeks.

In one of the worst collapses in playoff baseball history, the Tribe lost the next three games to Boston. It wasn't just the three losses in a row leading to elimination; it was also how the games were lost. They were outscored 44-18 in the final three games.

Hargrove was criticized for altering his rotation, using Bartolo Colon and Charles Nagy on three days' rest between starts rather than the usual four. There was a sense that the team lost its will, and the manager was helpless to change what happened in the playoffs. The usual reports that the players were "tired of Hargrove" and the manager no longer could motivate the team surfaced. Nothing original, just what you hear when a good team trashes a playoff series. But it was enough to convince Hart to fire Hargrove and replace him with Manuel. At this point, Jacobs was in the process of selling the team to the Dolan family, so he was not about to stop the decision.

Hargrove did not lose his job because Manuel somehow undercut him. He lost his job because of the ever-rising expectations around the team, the "World Series or Bust" mentality that was part of Tribe baseball in the late 1990s. Hargrove also was worn down by the criticism from the media and fans, and what he sensed was a lack of full support from Hart. The amazing thing wasn't that the baseball marriage between Hargrove and Hart ended, but that it survived for nine years in a profession where most managers last about as long as a one-term president.

From the moment Manuel accepted the job, his body seemed to rebel. When he arrived in spring training for the 2000 season, he didn't feel well. In early March, he was rushed to the hospital and had emergency surgery. It was first reported as a ruptured colon. He also had diverticulitis. A large chunk of the colon was removed. He missed two weeks of spring training. When he returned, he had to wear a colostomy bag. On May 5 of that 2000 season, he had more surgery to have his colon reattached. He missed 12 days.

By this point in his life, the 56-year-old Manuel had a long scar down the front of his chest from the heart surgery. He had scars on his side from the two colon surgeries. It was not reported at the time, but during one of his surgeries, it was discovered that Manuel had a cancerous tumor, which also was removed.

"Charlie was deathly ill," said Hamilton. "More problems than ever became public. Here, he finally gets that chance to manage in the majors, and he could have died. I still don't know how he got through all that he did."

The Tribe was 90-72 in Manuel's first year, missing the playoffs on the final game of the season.

In 2001, the Indians were 91-71 and made the playoffs. But Manuel went into the Cleveland Clinic on September 25 of that year with an abdominal infection. He was back in time to manage the Tribe in the playoffs, which they lost in five games to Seattle.

"It's like about everything that could go wrong, did go wrong for Charlie," said Hamilton. "The team still won . . . he showed he could manage."

By 2002, the Dolan family was feeling the financial squeeze. The once strong farm system was nearly barren. The front office had to cut nearly $30 million in payroll and go into a major rebuild. Veterans were traded, young players added. Manuel was viewed as the wrong manager for the new Indians, and lost his job during the 2002 All-Star break.

"Charlie was in the last year of his contract, and he wanted a commitment for the next season," said Hamilton. "He was going to talk to [General Manager] Mark Shapiro during the All-Star break."

Manuel told Hamilton, "I don't know if you'll see me when I get back. I need an answer from Mark."

Hamilton said, "Don't do that. You can't put your boss into a corner like that because you may not like what he's forced to do."

Manuel said, "I don't care, I need to know."

Shapiro made no promises for 2003. The general manager sensed it also made no sense to keep Manuel for the demanding rebuild, so he was fired.

"After all the health problems and everything else he had been through, Charlie isn't like many managers," said Hamilton. "He didn't want to get fired. But he also knew that he had to be true to himself. If the front office didn't want him, then he didn't want to be there and just finish off the season."

In many ways, being fired is exactly what Manuel needed. It gave him time for his body to heal, for his mind to relax. At the start of the

2003 season, he was hired as special assistant to the general manager by the Philadelphia Phillies. Two years later, a healthier Manuel was the new Phillies manager.

By 2013, Manuel was in his ninth year managing the Phillies. He had managed them to the playoffs five times, taking the team twice to the World Series and winning it in 2008. In Philadelphia, there was discussion of 2013 being his last season, as he was in the final year of his contract. And the Phillies were in no rush to extend his contract, despite all the success.

"I don't think Charlie is respected enough as a manager," said Hamilton. "People say he had all this talent, which was true—and all he did was not mess it up. That's not fair. It takes a special person to handle all those egos."

Hamilton said part of the reason was that Manuel didn't "care who got the credit. He hates self-promotion. He's a smart guy who has no interest in letting the world know how smart he is."

There's another factor—the Blue Ridge accent.

Manuel knew that some broadcasters and fans imitated his accent, and the implication was that he was some hick from the mountains.

"When Charlie managed the Indians, we did the manager's pregame show together," said Hamilton. "I'd hear someone on the radio mocking him, and I'd come into Charlie's office all upset because these people were gutless. You never saw them around the park. They didn't have the guts to face Charlie. He'd just shrug."

But one day, he told Hamilton, "People don't even know me, and they are making fun of me. How can they do that when they don't even know me?"

And a few moments later, it was as if Manuel didn't remember saying that—and he never mentioned it again.

"It's a form of discrimination," said Hamilton. "If you made fun of him because of his color or nationality, it would be discrimination. But make fun of him because he's from the mountains of Virginia? That's OK? You tell me. That's not right."

After they taped the manager's show, Manuel sometimes would ask Hamilton, "How did the show sound?"

Hamilton once said, "I think we've made up two or three words in combinations that I never heard before."

Manuel laughed and said, "Now you know why I made two of my kids English majors."

Another time, Hamilton was amused when Manuel asked, "How come my five-tool players only show up with three tools?"

Manuel meant Milton Bradley, who was labeled by scouts as "five-tool player" because he supposedly could run, throw, hit for average, hit for power and play great defense. Other times when Bradley sulked, Manuel would tell Hamilton, "Where's Milton's tool belt today?"

Hamilton believes Manuel is one of the Tribe's most unheralded heroes from the 1990s.

"Charlie is one of my favorite people and he made a huge impact on our team," he said. "Then he proved how sharp he is by what he did in Philadelphia, one of the toughest towns in which to manage."

In Buena Vista, Va., there is a sign that says, "HOME OF CHARLIE MANUEL."

"Got one on each side of town," he said. "One coming, one going... and it's a town with only one stoplight."

Manuel then joked that "they'll take down the signs when I get fired."

Hamilton said, "That's crazy, after all you've won, you don't have a new contract?"

Manuel said, "If I get fired, I get fired. I'll get a job someplace . . . I can always go somewhere and teach someone how to hit."

Manuel was fired by the Phillies on August 17, 2013. It came two days after he won his 1,000th game as a big-league manager. He also left as the most successful manager in the 130-year history of the Philadelphia franchise. At the age of 69, he made it clear that he wasn't done with baseball. He was ready to manage or coach elsewhere.

"That's Charlie," said Hamilton. "Baseball is his life."

Jim Thome and the Statue

It still seems strange that of all the players from the 1990s, Jim Thome is the one who received a statue at Progressive Field.

Thome is the Tribe's all-time home-run hitter with 337. His 612 total home runs should be a ticket to a first-ballot entrance to the Baseball Hall of Fame. But as Thome said, "There were so many great players on those teams."

Thome stayed longer than most—parts of 13 seasons. He didn't have the flair of Omar Vizquel, or the powerful rage of Albert Belle. Kenny Lofton was far more athletic and electric. Manny Ramirez was a prodigy with the bat.

That's why Thome said this about the statue: "I'm not sure how to feel about it. You never start playing baseball thinking about a statue . . . I feel overwhelmed and incredibly thankful."

Thome knows he's only the second Tribe player honored with a statue. The first is Hall of Famer Bob Feller. The third will soon be Larry Doby, who broke the American League color line in 1947.

"It's just surreal," said Thome. "I'm kind of uncomfortable because there were so many great players when I was with the Indians. It's a great gesture."

Thome was the strongest player on the Tribe of the 1990s. His home runs were space shots.

He also was one of the most humble.

"You look back, you feel proud," he said. "But where I come from, you don't brag on yourself."

Feller grew up in Van Meter, Iowa. It really was a farm, and his father built a small baseball diamond for Feller and his friends.

Thome's story is a bit different He grew up in Peoria, Ill. "My friend and I would find a wall, paint a strike zone on it," he said. "Then we'd play baseball with a tennis ball—pitching to a batter who stood in front of the wall. You just play because you love it."

He has no Feller-like stories of playing catch with his father in a barn when snow was piling up during a Midwestern blizzard.

"My father was a foreman at the Caterpillar plant," he said. "My older brother worked construction. About a mile from our house was the inner city. It was where the best basketball games were played. I'd go over there all the time. I usually was the only white kid in the games, and they respected me because I kept coming back."

And it was his father who started him with hitting tennis balls while his father pitched to a wall.

"I began playing at the old tennis court in the city," Thome said. "He'd pitch to me, and I remember thinking that I'd never be strong enough to hit the ball over that big fence, the fence that was around the tennis court. Then he'd hit me ground balls."

On the concrete?

"Sure enough," Thome said. "He'd hit me those regular baseballs on the cement. We sure wore out a lot of balls that way."

Thome's father was a star softball player. His aunt, Carolyn Thome Hart, is in the Women's Softball Hall of Fame.

"When I grew up, my brother was my hero," Thome said. "My dad would compare me to him all the time. My father was tough on me, pushing me. I remember when I scored 36 points in a state tournament basketball game. It was one point off a school record. I thought my dad would be happy, but that night he talked about the mistakes I made on defense and in rebounding.

"I didn't like it back then. I appreciate it now."

"Playing for the Indians was living a dream," he said. "I remember playing in high school, playing American Legion ball, then playing in junior college—and wondering if I'd get a chance to play pro ball."

Scout Tom Couston signed Thome for $15,000. He was picked in the 13th round in the 1989 draft. Thome said Couston approached him between games of a doubleheader when Thome was with Illinois Central (Junior) College.

"I first saw Jimmy play in high school," Couston said in a 1996 interview. "He was tall [6-foot-4], but pretty thin. He was a shortstop, and that wasn't his position. But he had a quick bat. I wrote that down. I remembered it. But I heard that he was headed to a junior college, and I thought that was a good idea."

Couston was the Tribe's Midwestern scout, based in Chicago.

"The next time I saw Jimmy play was when he was with Illinois Central College," Couston said. "I wasn't even there to see him. There was a shortstop on the other team that was considered a prospect, and a lot of scouts were there to see him."

Then he noticed Thome.

"In that game, Jimmy came to the plate four times and hit four rockets," Couston said. "He still was pretty thin, but he was only 18 years old. He hadn't grown into his body."

Couston recalled five other scouts at the game, but they weren't there to see Thome. This is where memories collide.

"I had a bad first game and I was down because I knew some scouts were there," said Thome. "We were playing Lincolnland Community College in a doubleheader."

Remember, Couston said Thome hit "four rockets."

Anyway, the stories now start to mesh.

"Tom came up behind me," said Thome. "I started to turn around, and he said to keep staring straight ahead. He didn't want anyone to know I was talking to him."

"I told him to keep his back to me and I'll keep my back to him," Couston said.

This confused Thome.

"I thought I had done something wrong," Thome said.

Couston told him, "I want to talk to you, but I don't want you to look at me. I'm Tom Couston, a scout for the Indians," he said. "If we draft you, will you sign?"

"I sure will," said Thome.

He began to turn around, but stopped when Couston said, "Don't move! I don't want the other scouts to know I'm talking to you."

Thome stopped.

"OK, you'll be hearing from me," Couston said.

By the time Thome did turn around, the scout was gone.

"Donny Mitchell was my scouting supervisor," Couston said. "I told him that once we get to the 10th round, they should take this kid Thome. Donny had never heard of him. No one had. None of the scouts from other teams who did see Jimmy thought he could play. But Donny went to bat for the kid."

Thome was not on any of the other Tribe scouting lists. Nor was he considered even a fringe prospect by other teams. In the 13th round of the 1989 June draft, the Indians called the name of Jim Thome. He was the 333rd player selected. The only other player in the 13th round to make the majors was pitcher Mike Oquist, who had a 25-31 record with a 5.46 ERA. The 1989 draft was a strange one for the Tribe. Top pick Calvin Murray didn't sign. Their next three picks were Jerry Dipoto, Jesse Levis and Alan Embree. All had marginal big league careers. But in the 17th round, with the 437th pick, they found Brian Giles, who later became a star with Pittsburgh and San Diego.

"Jimmy's parents are great people," Couston said. "But Peoria is really middle America, very small town. They were worried about Jimmy signing a contract, going away from home. They wanted to make sure someone would watch over their son."

Thome could skip the draft and return for his sophomore year in junior college. Couston was certain that if Thome went back to school, another team would find him in the spring of 1990. The scout was authorized by the Tribe to offer Thome a $10,000 bonus. His family wanted more. Couston had to lobby with his bosses to offer a $15,000 bonus.

"I knew I was going to sign, whatever they offered," said Thome. "It was my dream to play pro baseball. I thought about it when I played summer Legion ball, when I played in high school and the one year at junior college. I went to St. Louis for a tryout [with the Cardinals], but it never panned out. There was a scout from the Twins—Ellsworth Brown—who was at a lot of our games. But nothing came of it."

Just as Couston was fearful the Indians would miss out on Thome, the then 18-year-old was afraid the Indians would change their minds and he'd never get a chance to sign with any team. So when Couston offered the $15,000, plus money to finish college if Thome wanted to return to school, Thome and his parents agreed to the deal.

* * *

Not long after he signed, Thome was sent to the Tribe's Sarasota team in the Gulf Coast League. It was rookie ball, the bottom rung of the minor-league ladder. He was scared. He was homesick. He felt overwhelmed. Couston warned the Tribe's front office that patience would be required with Thome. He was a two-sport athlete in junior college, not the product of attending elite summer baseball camps. Nor was he a gifted athlete. But he was a young man with a smooth swing from the left side of the plate—and a very quick bat.

Thome batted .237 with no homers in 186 at bats at Sarasota. He was on none of the lists of the Tribe's top 10 minor-league prospects. He was just another low-round pick, a skinny kid who seemed to be a very long shot to make the majors.

It's fascinating to look at the 1989 Sarasota Indians. Thome opened as the regular shortstop, and he made 14 errors in 40 games. He was moved to third base, and that led to seven errors in 17 games. That Sarasota team had 34 different players. Thome is the only one to have a significant big-league career. The others who at least made the majors were Ken Ramos, Bill Wertz, Turner Ward and Willie Canate.

That makes 5 of 34. Most teams believe that about 1 of 8 players who sign a professional contract eventually make the majors. No one who saw Thome in 1989 would have ever guessed that he'd become an All-Star. That's because those players at that rookie level are so raw, and some (like Thome) feel overwhelmed in their first exposure to pro ball.

"Trust me, it took a long time for me become comfortable thinking that I could make it as a major-league player," said Thome. "I thought I could, but deep down—I didn't know."

Thome began to hit in 1990, a combined .340 with 16 homers in 67 games in Class A and a different rookie-league team. The next year, he was at Class AA Canton-Akron, hitting .337 to open the season.

"That was the first time that I thought I could maybe make the big leagues," said Thome. "I knew I'd be moving up to [Class AAA], but part of me wondered if I'd still hit there. That was always in the back of my mind—how I'd do at the next level."

Suddenly, Thome was on the fast track. He was promoted to Cleveland in September of 1991, only two years after being a nondescript 13th-rounder.

"I came to a team that was going to lose 100 games," said Thome.

Actually, the 1991 Indians would finish 57-105.

They were desperate, rushing all their top prospects to Cleveland. Thome played 84 games in Class AA, then 41 in Class AAA. If he had been the product of a major baseball college such as Stanford or Texas, the rise to the majors in less than two seasons perhaps would not have been so dramatic. But Thome played only one year at Illinois Central, a junior college in East Peoria.

"I wasn't ready for the big leagues," said Thome. "That was especially true defensively."

He was 21, and listed at 6-foot-4, 215 pounds. He decided it was best to try to hit for a high batting average. He seldom pulled the ball with any power. Many of the hits produced by his sweet left-handed swing went to center or left field. In parts of two seasons (1991–92) at Class AA, he batted a combined .337, but had only six homers in 114 games.

The Indians wondered if he could ever become even an adequate infielder. They decided to make him a third baseman. But in 1990, he had 19 errors in 66 games. In 1991, it was 23 errors in 122 minor-league games.

When he came to the Tribe in September of 1991, he had eight errors in 27 games at third.

"I was real worried about my fielding," said Thome. "It was real humbling."

He was 25-of-98 (.255) with one homer and nine RBI in that first September with the Tribe. He was only 1-of-20 (.050) against lefties. But his one home run was memorable.

"Steve Farr was pitching for the Yankees," said Thome. "I wasn't hitting that well, and wasn't even sure what bat to use. Joel Skinner [a backup catcher] handed me his bat. The pitch was a fastball, and I hit it . . ."

Yes, he did—into the upper deck in right field of old Yankee Stadium.

"Even when he was so young, there were times when you could see that Jimmy had power," said former Tribe General Manager John Hart. "But it took Charlie Manuel to show him how to use it."

Playing a combined 234 pro games in 1991–92 at Class AA, Class AAA and Cleveland, Thome hit a grand total of 13 homers.

With the Indians in 1992, he batted .205 with two homers in 117 official at-bats. He also made 11 errors in 40 games.

"That was a bad year because I kept getting hurt, too," said Thome. "I hurt my wrist, then my shoulder. It seemed like nothing went right."

Then he played again for Charlie Manuel in 1993. Manuel was managing the Tribe's Class AAA Charlotte team. Manuel watched Thome take batting practice and said, "Son, you need to start pulling the ball."

Manuel had played 242 games in the majors between 1969 and 1975. This was before free agency raised salaries. If you wanted to make money, hit for power. Manuel batted only .198 with four homers in 384 big league at-bats. But in 1976, he went to play in Japan. A 6-foot-4, lefty hitter (like Thome), Manuel began to swing for the fences in Asia. From 1977 to 1980 he averaged 42 homers a season. He made enough yen in Japan to drive a very big American car when he went home to the Blue Ridge Mountains of Virginia.

"Charlie made Jim Thome into a big-leaguer," said Tom Hamilton. "Because Jimmy was willing to work and listen and had a great teacher in Charlie, Jimmy became a great player."

By 1993, Manuel and Thome were both carrying something around—doubt—because both had been to Cleveland, and then sent back to the minors. Manuel looked at Thome and saw a little of himself. Rather than being from the mountains of Virginia, Thome was from the plains of Peoria, Ill. Both came from small towns. Both are not going to overwhelm you with their perfect English. Both can easily be dismissed as not being especially bright by those who fail to get to know them. Both are 6-foot-4. At one time, both were so skinny, they couldn't cast a shadow wider than a fungo bat.

In many ways, Manuel saw a younger version of himself in Thome.

And Thome saw an older man who seemed to instantly understand him, without the need for Thome to explain himself.

"Charlie Manuel is the reason Jim's in the major leagues," said Chuck Thome, Jim's father, in an interview with USA Today's Hal Bodley. "They sent Charlie out to check on a kid who had received a big bonus and was supposed to be a hot-shot prospect. [This was with the Tribe's rookie team in Sarasota.] Well, after a few days Charlie told the Indians he didn't know about that player but said, 'This kid Thome is doing everything asked of him, and he's going to hit. You better find him a job.' " So think about this for a moment. In 1993, you have Manuel, recently fired as batting coach, a guy who never achieved his dream as a big-league player. You have Thome, scared that his baseball career would be over at 22. Twice, he had been promoted to Cleveland, and then sent back to the minors. While it was not their first meeting, it was the first time they were together for a full season, and it changed the lives of both men.

"Pull the ball," said Manuel.

Over and over, that was Manuel's message.

Look for a pitch you can pull, a pitch that you can hit a long way. Don't be afraid to strike out. Home-run hitters do that. And you can become a home-run hitter.

In 1993, with Manuel's gospel changing Thome's thought process and lifting his heart at the same time, the left-handed batter ripped 25 homers and batted .332 in Class AAA.

"I used to hit out of a closed stance," said Thome, meaning his front foot was closer to the plate than his back foot. It was a way of making sure that he could hit an outside pitch. But it also created a swing that was powered mostly by his arms and wrists. The best hitters also bring their hips and upper legs into the swing.

Manuel helped Thome do that by opening up his stance.

"I had never done that before," said Thome. "We were playing a game in Scranton, and it was a doubleheader. I got something like four hits and two homers. I hit the ball hard, really pulling it. And Charlie just stood there, looking at me with the biggest smile on his face."

Thome hit 25 homers with 102 RBI for Manuel in Class AAA during the 1993 season. And in 1994, the Tribe also made Manuel their hitting coach.

"I still may have been a big-league player if I had never met Charlie," said Thome. "But I never would have bloomed like I did. He had a way of making you feel good about yourself as a hitter. Most guys from that era [with the Indians] will tell you that."

Manuel made up nicknames for Thome: "Thome Dome and Thomenator" were Thome's favorites.

He loved the attention from the coach.

"Another thing I learned from Charlie was self-control," said Thome.

He told a story of being in Class AAA with Manuel. He made an out, came back to the dugout and slammed the bat into the rack. It was as if Thome thought he should throw the bat because other players did when they made outs in clutch situations.

"After the game, Charlie called me into his office," said Thome. "He asked me why I slammed the bat. I said I really didn't know."

Manuel paused for a moment then said, "The way you are hitting, you don't need to throw bats."

After that, Thome never threw a bat again.

Manuel did something else for Thome. When he came to the plate, he'd take a practice swing where he'd point the bat at the pitcher.

"Charlie saw the movie 'The Natural' where Roy Hobbs did that," said Thome. "Charlie told me to do it. I tried it and liked it. It was like setting the trigger before I'd swing at a pitch."

Thome in that stance, pointing the bat at the pitcher, became the model for the statue.

Thome also credits former Tribe coach Buddy Bell with rescuing his career.

In the spring of 1994, Thome was making a lot of errors at third base. General Manager John Hart was nervous, asking Mike Hargrove to find a way to help Thome at least make the routine plays.

"Buddy began to work with me," said Thome. "He was a great third baseman. I listened to everything he said."

Bell took a different approach. He believed many of Thome's troubles on basic plays were not the result of physical errors, but a lack of confidence. Many of Thome's errors were on throws. Thome would be nervous as he caught a grounder, dreading the throw to first base because of all the bad throws that he'd made before.

But Bell took a different approach.

"Jimmy, there really isn't much wrong with you at third," said Bell. "It's the throwing, right?"

Thome agreed.

"It's not a big deal," said Bell. "It's your arm slot. It's a little inconsistent."

So Bell and Thome worked on a way for Thome to throw the ball from the same arm angle each time. He improved.

Bell believed it was easier for a player to correct a physical error than to tell him, "You need more confidence."

A player thinking he "needs more confidence" ends up believing that he has no confidence.

But tell a player to do something slightly different in his arm motion, and the player thinks, "That's not hard. I can do that."

Thome was never a good third baseman, but he became adequate. In his three big-league seasons at that position, he made 15-16-17 errors.

"I can't thank Charlie and Buddy enough," said Thome. "I would get down on myself, but Buddy and Charlie—they had faith in me."

Twenty years after coming to the Indians for good, Thome still sounds in awe talking about the Tribe of the middle 1990s.

"Sandy [Alomar] was always great with me," said Thome. "He helped me with my confidence. He's a natural leader. Eddie Murray was a quiet leader. I learned from him not to let anything that happened on the field change my attitude. Albert Belle was so intense, so focused. But Albert never argued balls and strikes. I learned that from him—don't argue balls and strikes with umpires."

Thome talked about how Dave Winfield invited him to lunch.

"That was in 1995," said Thome. "I barely knew him. I admired him. He was such a great player. Dave talked to me about what it meant to be a professional, how to conduct yourself—and how to be careful with the money you make. We hugged after we talked that day. Every time I've seen Dave after that, we've hugged."

His favorite year was 1997.

"That was when all the guys pulled up their socks to wear them high [like Thome] for my birthday [August 27]," said Thome. "We got hot and went to the World Series that year. But it meant a lot to me for the guys to do that—and a lot of them kept their socks up high for the rest of the year."

High socks. Teams who care. Coaches who helped.

When Thome talks about his time with the Tribe, he tends to end up discussing others.

"With Jimmy, it's about humility, work ethic and appreciation of the game," said Mark Shapiro.

The Tribe's president talked about how the Indians were in the middle of trading for Matt Williams before the 1997 season. Williams was a Gold Glove third baseman. After all the work that Thome had put in to play third, would he now move to first base?

"That would be a new position for him," said Shapiro. "He was still a young guy [only 26]. First base was often considered a place where an older player moved after he came to the majors at another position. But Jimmy saw right away that getting Matt Williams made us better, so he quickly agreed to move to first base."

Thome recalled the conversation and how he said, "If you can get Matt Williams . . . do it."

Looking back, Thome realized, "That was one of the best things that ever happened to me, because that was a better position for me."

Some fans and media members were conflicted about the Thome statue.

Part of the reason was how Thome left as a free agent. In the spring of 2002, he gave several interviews saying that he could never imagine playing anywhere but Cleveland—how he loved the Indians and the city.

But after that season, he went to Philadelphia for $85 million over six years. The Indians offered $62 million for five years. The Tribe was rebuilding and tearing down the payroll. The front office was almost relieved when Thome went to Philadelphia, because his contract would have been a huge bite out of an ever-shrinking budget.

But fan reaction was harsh.

"I understand that, I really do," said Thome. "It hurts when someone leaves."

Thome came back to the Tribe near the end of the 2011 season.

"I felt anxious," he said. "I didn't know how people would receive me. In that first game, I got a standing ovation. I still think about that. I get goosebumps talking about it right now. It made me feel so good."

Thome admitted that the statue brings back some of the same fears.

"I never wanted to hurt anyone," he said. "The fans have always treated me great. I really want this to be a way of giving something back to them. They were as much a part of those great teams in the 1990s as anyone—we fed off their energy. I've always wanted the fans to know how much we appreciated them. They filled the park, they'd cheer and cheer for us. When Kenny [Lofton] and I came back, they kept giving us standing ovations. We've talked about how we'll never forget that."

Thome paused, then added: "There were so many guys back then just as deserving of a statue as me. I hope [the statue] can represent those great teams and great times. We went to the World Series twice. We won a lot of games. It was not one or two guys, we had great teams."

Thome made baseball history the same way he played: Don't brag. Respect the game. Have a grateful heart. This doesn't make a "good story," unless your idea of a good story is about good people doing good things.

Perhaps the statue can represent some of those virtues.

Don’t Forget About Charlie Nagy

When Charlie Nagy was a young pitcher with the Tribe, his manager sometimes called him Steve—as in Steve Nagy.

Maybe John McNamara was thinking about Steve Nagy, who was a big-time pro bowler.

“It was like that my entire rookie year,” said Nagy. “I’d come off the mound and he’d say, ‘Way to go, Steve!’ ”

What did Charlie Nagy do?

“I just gave him the thumbs-up sign,” said Nagy.

That’s classic Charlie Nagy.

As Tom Hamilton said: “Charlie would never talk about himself. I mean—never. He’d be happy to talk about the other guys. He was the consummate pro and teammate.”

Hamilton mentioned how Nagy made a point of waiting in front of the dugout between innings when he pitched, congratulating a teammate who’d made a good play in the field behind him. Or how Nagy would quickly move in the dugout to a teammate who scored a run when that player came off the field.

“I told my son [Nick Hamilton] that the one player I want you emulating as a person and teammate is Charlie Nagy,” said Hamilton. “There is nothing phony about him. He’s just a humble guy.”

When Mike Hargrove began to relate this about Nagy, he searched for the right words to express his admiration for the former Tribe pitcher.

“You know how some people wear those bracelets that say WWJD—What Would Jesus Do?” asked the former Tribe manager. “If you are a baseball player, it should be WWCD—What Would Charlie Do? There are certain people you should follow because of the example they set.

Charlie kept his mouth shut, unless you asked him something. You knew he was always in shape, always prepared, always doing what a player should do to be prepared."

In many ways, Omar Vizquel became the face of the Tribe in the 1990s and beyond because he was with the team for 11 years: 1994–2004. But Nagy spent 13 years with the Tribe, from 1990 through 2002. Like Vizquel, he was there for the glory years of the 1990s.

"One of the things that I feel good about is that I spent nearly all of my career here," said Nagy. "I never wanted to play anywhere else. I never looked to go anywhere else when my contract was up."

Nagy pitched 12⅓ innings with San Diego in 2003. The Tribe had not resigned him after the 2002 season. He was battling elbow problems. Over the years, very little has been written about Nagy other than the basics. He pitched and he won. He pitched and he lost. He had some arm troubles. He healed and came back (as he did in 1994). Or he healed and tried and never could come back (as happened starting in 2000). It seems Nagy would rather gargle with unleaded gasoline and razor blades than talk about himself.

"I was just raised that way," he said.

Mark Shapiro remembers how Nagy often asked about family members.

"In the 1995 playoffs, there were about what seemed to be a thousand reporters around his locker," Shapiro said. "Charlie had met my brother David only a few times. He spotted David and stopped his interviews to ask David how he was doing. I was just the minor-league director at the time. My brother was playing football at Amherst College and Charlie really wanted to know how it was going. He treated everyone with respect. He is just so authentic and gracious."

Nagy was a first-round pick by the Tribe in the 1988 June draft, No. 17 overall. He pitched only 51 games in the minors and was in Cleveland by the end of the 1990 season.

"I always liked the old Municipal Stadium," said Nagy. "It was where I came to the majors. It was fun when we had those big crowds for the opener and the Fourth of July. I was always happy to be in the big leagues."

Nagy started the final game at the old Stadium, on October 3, 1993.

It was his first game since May 15. He had shoulder surgery for his torn labrum on June 29. "That last game was important because the old Stadium meant so much to the fans," he said. "It also was good for me because it showed I could still pitch after the surgery."

But Nagy knew the new ballpark would change everything.

"You could see our team was getting better," he said. "We had some great young players—Kenny [Lofton], Carlos [Baerga], Albert [Belle], Jimmy [Thome], Sandy [Alomar]—all those guys. Then John [Hart] traded for Omar. He signed Eddie [Murray], Tony Pena, Dennis Martinez and Orel [Hershiser]. Guys on other teams were telling me that we were going to be a good team."

Then the fans packed the new ballpark.

"At first, they came to see the new park," said Nagy. "Then they came to see us."

Years later, it's hard for both men to talk about it.

Nagy was supposed to start Game 7 of the 1997 World Series in Florida.

"Charlie has been one of my favorites . . . forever," said Hargrove. "I absolutely respect and admire him. But at that time, my job was to make decisions with my head—not my heart. It was Charlie's turn to start. But Jaret Wright was pitching great in the postseason. I had to pick the guy who gave us the best chance to win in Game 7."

Nagy had started Game 3 of the World Series, allowing five runs in six innings. He walked four. The Indians lost 14-11 to the Marlins.

He had walked six and allowed four runs in 3⅔ innings in Game 3 of the Division Series against New York.

So Nagy was struggling, especially with his control. His arm seemed tired. He was trying to keep his pitches on the corners of home plate, falling behind in the count.

But in between the loss to the Yankees and the loss to Florida, Nagy had thrown 7⅓ scoreless innings in what became a 1-0 victory over Baltimore. That game lasted 11 innings and it sent the Tribe to the World Series.

As Hargrove met with his coaches, the discussion was about which Nagy would show up for Game 7. The Nagy that had a terrible time in two postseason starts, or the one who shut out Baltimore for those 7⅓ innings?

"There was a divided camp," said Hargrove. "Some guys felt Jaret gave us the best chance to win, others thought Charlie deserved a shot. I couldn't argue against either line of thought. In the end, it was totally and completely on me to make the decision. If it works—great. If not, they'll want to run me out of town. I went with Jaret, knowing if Jaret didn't pitch well, I'd look like a real dumbass. If he did, then it was 'He went with his gut and it paid off.'"

So Hargrove picked Wright in what he called "the hardest decision" that he had to make in his eight-and-a-half seasons as Tribe manager.

"I couldn't sleep at all," said Hargrove. "I just felt Jaret was the right call, but I hated doing that to Charlie."

"I found out after Game 6," said Nagy. "I won't kid you, it was disappointing. It was my turn to start. I wanted to start."

But Nagy accepted the decision with no argument.

"I said I'd be ready," he said. "I picked up my glove and went to the bullpen. It was Game 7, all hands on deck. "

Hargrove's decision to start Wright was wise. The rookie allowed one run in 6⅓ innings. Jose Mesa failed to hold a 2-1 lead in the bottom of the ninth, and the game went into extra innings.

Nagy entered the game in the 11th. He was charged with the loss.

What does he remember?

"The [Edgar] Renteria line drive," he said. "It tipped off my glove. I really wish I could have caught it."

That drove in the winning run. What Nagy doesn't mention is that earlier in the 11th inning, Tony Fernandez booted a ground ball at second base that could have been an inning-ending double play.

When that is mentioned to Nagy, he just shrugs.

No excuses from him.

Most people forget that Nagy was 15-11 with a 4.28 ERA for the Tribe in that 1997 season. He seems to also ignore that fact.

"I wish I had caught that liner," he repeated. "I was the in bullpen, the phone rang—I got up and warmed up when they told me. And just like that, I was in the game."

That was only the second relief appearance of his career.

"I see the play on TV every year during the World Series . . ."

His voice trailed off.

Nothing else to say.

* * *

"Charlie Nagy was a big reason that we made the 1997 World Series," said Hamilton.

Nagy faced Mike Mussina in Game 6 of the American League Championship Series in Baltimore. The Tribe had a 3-2 lead in that best-of-7 series. Just as was the case against Seattle in 1995 in the ALCS, had the Tribe lost Game 6—there would have been Game 7.

"That's Game 7 on the road," said Hamilton. "No one wants to play Game 7 on the road."

In that Game 6, Mussina appeared nearly as unbeatable as Randy Johnson was in Game 6 of the 1995 playoffs in Seattle. Mussina had a 1.71 ERA in three previous postseason starts, striking out 31 in 21 innings. He gave up only 10 hits. He fanned 15 against the Tribe in seven innings in Game 3.

Mussina is one of baseball's most underrated pitchers. He finished with a career record of 270-153, with a 3.68 ERA. He primarily pitched in the Steroid Era, when starters rarely had ERAs under 4.00.

Meanwhile, Nagy had problems with Baltimore in the 1996 postseason, and again in his first start in 1997. In those three games, his ERA was 6.88, allowing 13 runs in 17 innings.

Mussina appeared to have a huge advantage over Nagy.

"I thought Charlie just pitched a great game," said Hamilton. "People don't remember it, because the game lasted 11 innings. And Charlie was in trouble all game, but he didn't give up a run."

Nagy threw 7⅓ scoreless innings. He allowed nine hits, and walked three.

"That was a great game, but I sure didn't pitch great," he said. "I had guys on base, inning after inning. It was one jam after another and Mussina was making it look so easy."

Mussina's fastball was in the 94-97 mph range. His slider was sharp, his change-up deftly dropping under the bats of hitters. The Indians had one hit, two walks and struck out 10 times against Mussina in eight innings.

"Mussina appeared unhittable," said Hamilton. "Our only break is eventually he left the game."

After those eight excellent innings, Mussina's pitch count was 107. Orioles Manager Davey Johnson went to the bullpen. The Indians eventually won this game, 1-0, in the 11th inning on a home run by Tony Fernandez.

"People have different memories about that game than I do," said Nagy. "I just remember being always surrounded by base runners."

He shrugged again, just as he did when talking about Game 7 of the 1997 World Series.

From 1991 to 1999, Nagy threw at least 210 innings in six of nine seasons. He averaged 13 victories.

"I pitched a lot of innings," he said. "They weren't always pretty innings—but there were a lot of them."

"Charlie was an elite athlete," said Mark Shapiro. "Early in his career, he threw between 91 and 94 mph, and had great movement. He lost some of that as he got older. But he made up for it by staying in such great shape. He worked so hard in the weight room. He ran a lot. He knew how to prepare."

But in those glory years of the mid-1990s, Nagy was not just in the shadows of the big hitters such as Belle, Ramirez, Thome and the rest. The Indians also had two veteran, media-savvy pitchers in Orel Hershiser and Dennis Martinez.

That was fine with Nagy.

"What I'm proud of is being a part of some great teams here," he said. "When we moved into the new stadium [in 1994], it was amazing. There were sellouts every night. The fans believed in us. We could be down eight runs, and they still thought we'd come back."

He paused, then said, "Teams hated playing us. I'd talk to pitchers, and they were happy when it wasn't their turn to start against us."

Pitching was never easy for Nagy. His fastball was in the low 90s. He relied on a sinker and the natural movement of his pitches. He never smiled on the mound. This was a man at work. It's serious business.

Former General Manager John Hart once called him, "the classic stoic New Englander."

From 1994 to 1999, Nagy won 90 games, the sixth-best in baseball during the span. His record was 90-51.

Yet, he doesn't want to talk about his career.

"I think it's because it didn't end well," he said. "I kept trying to pitch . . ."

His voice trailed off.

Nagy signed a four-year, $24 million deal with the Tribe. He delivered a 17-11 record with a 4.95 ERA in 1999. But after that, he had elbow problems. He went on the disabled list on May 16, 2000. That ended a streak of 192 consecutive starts. While he didn't use these exact words, you can tell that Nagy felt bad about signing that last contract—the biggest of his career—then getting hurt. He had an 8-17 record and 7.67 ERA in his last three Tribe seasons.

He should realize that fans appreciate how he was there from the old Stadium to the new, from a Tribe team that lost 105 games in 1991 to a 1995 team that was 100-44.

"The fans here have always been great to me," he said. "Cleveland has always felt like home to me. I got to play on the big [postseason] stages and with some great players. Really, I got to go along on a great ride with them."

The 1995 Season

[FANS WRITE IN]

I experienced so many wonderful moments with the Tribe during the 1990s, but I have to say that the game on September 8, 1995, when the Indians clinched the Central Division title, has to be my favorite. I was born in 1955, so that was my first time in my lifetime that the Tribe had won anything. My memories of that game remain so vivid, I can still feel the lump in my throat as the championship banner went up the flag-pole while "The Dance" played. I can still see the "CLINCH!" on the big scoreboard and the tears in my sister's eyes that mirrored my own. I can still hear the pounding rhythm of Led Zeppelin's "Rock and Roll" and feel the elation that swept through the entire ballpark as complete strangers hugged and high-fived each other. While there were magical moments galore during that fabulous era, this one perfect night eclipses them all for me. *—Cindy Chadd, Madrid, Spain*

I was born in February 1948. When the Tribe won the World Series that year, Mom said I hit the bottle hard, drank too much, and threw up. I always wanted to do that again. For the next 40-some years, my dream was to someday sit on the front porch on a late summer evening, water the lawn, and listen to the Tribe in a pennant race. And it finally happened, and I am grateful for that. *—Marty Stevenson, Strongsville*

I remember going to Jacobs Field on September 8, 1995 like it was yesterday. It was shortly after Cal Ripken Jr. had broken the streak. Baltimore was in town, and Ripken received a huge standing ovation. The Indians won the game, and had clinched their first Central title. I remember the joy on the fans' faces, and the players as they raised the championship banner. The stadium was still packed, and all through downtown after the game, car horns were blaring. I was only 14 at the time, and I thought it was great that they had finally played well enough to make the playoffs. I couldn't imagine what it had been like for people who had never seen them win anything. *—Chris Jones, Elyria*

Like many, I grew up in the old stadium with lots of memories and losses. My wife and I were living in Florida when the Indians clinched the '95 pennant. This was before the Internet and satellite, and since we lived out of state, most of our game updates during the playoff run were from phone calls home or the scrolling update on the bottom of the TV screen. The morning after they clinched, I was on my way to work, stopped at a busy intersection waiting for the light to change. I was listening to NPR "Morning Edition" and they always start the hour with a news tidbit accompanied by their theme music. So there I sat, still on a high, couldn't believe we were really going to the Fall Classic, and I hear Bob Edwards say "For the first time since 1954, the Cleveland Indians are going to the World Series." I sat there and cried. I finally felt validated in being a Cleveland fan. I have to admit, the emotion still runs strong and I get a little teary eyed. *—Brian Cook, Twinsburg*

In '95 while stationed in San Antonio, Texas, I remember staying up watching CNN because they were the only channel that constantly scrolled the scores. It really seemed like when the Indians were down by two or three in the 9th, it was right where they wanted them. It was so much fun waiting for that ticker to scroll and seeing that the Indians had won! *—Bob Gorman, Aurora, Colorado*

I was due in October of 1995. My father, a lifelong Tribe fan (he attended Ten Cent Beer Night), was worried I would be born during the playoffs or World Series. He told my mom, "I'm going because I don't know the next time the Indians will be in the World Series. We can do this [have a kid] again in 9 months." Luckily, I was born early, in September of '95, and my father and I had our first sports bonding moments watching the '95 Indians. *—Alex Kaufman, Cleveland*

I have been following the Indians devotedly since 1955, when I was 6 years old. So the playoff runs in the '90s were an incredible time. Since I started following the Tribe, they had never had a postseason game. So 1995 was indeed memorable. The first playoff game took place on Yom Kippur night. And I live in New York, and the game was not televised here. My friend Chip, also from Cleveland, worked at NBC and planned to watch the game in his office. I went to temple, then rushed into a taxi that took me to NBC to catch the end of Game 1 vs. the Red Sox. The game, of course, went a lot longer than expected, ending with Tony Pena's extra-innings home run, which must have been at about 2 a.m. Chip and I were still watching and cheered loudly, with me still wearing my suit from temple. The home run was an exhilarating and memorable moment: The first Indians postseason game, one that I had waited 40 years to watch, ended in a great victory. *—Jim Miller, Yonkers, New York*

When the Indians made their World Series run in 1995, I was 12 and my sister 9. In the playoffs, we begged and begged to stay up late to watch the ends of the games. Because the games ran so late and we had school the next morning, we weren't allowed to stay up to watch them to completion. So my dad came up with the perfect system. He would use our children's chalk board to write the complete box score along with any necessary highlights or commentary. Waking up excited to read the chalk board, neither of us will ever forget the morning we woke up and the chalk board told us that Tony Pena had hit a walk-off home run in the 13th inning to win the game for the Tribe. *—Emily Scheetz-Mazzone, Cleveland*

I went into labor during the 1995 World Series, during Game 4. I waited for the Indians to make their comeback, but during the eighth inning I decided I better get to the hospital. During the car ride, in the ninth inning, Manny Ramirez hit a home run and I considered returning to the game. We were down three runs, however, and my husband wisely kept driving to the hospital. The game was such a distraction from labor and resulted in the quickest and easiest delivery of my third child, Molly. *—Mary Goodwin, Westlake*

My story is Game 5 of the 1995 World Series. I was a 21-year-old college student and had little money, but with the help of my parents and my brother, my best friend Alex and I scraped up $350 each to buy our bleacher seats that night. When we arrived in Cleveland and got out of our car, it was like instant electricity in the city. The magic in the air was indescribable and is still one of the greatest nights of my life. Late in the game, Jim Thome hit one of the longest home runs I've ever seen in person. It sailed over our heads like a missile and we could hear the ball zinging through the air. It pretty much sealed the win and will always rank up there with my wedding and the birth of my son as the greatest moments of my life. *—Randy Myers, Norwalk*

My son (my one and only child) was born July 26, 1995, during that magical season. The playoffs that year were a challenge in keeping quiet at home as game 1 of the ALDS vs. Boston and the ALCS games in Seattle went deep into the night. During Game 6 of the ALCS, after Kenny Lofton scored from second on the wild pitch, I went to my son's bedroom and lifted him gently and quietly out of his crib.

I brought him into the family room and held him until the game was over. I had waited so long for the Indians to make the World Series and I was determined Alex was going to be there with me when it happened. Somehow I managed to not wake him (or my wife). *—David Carson, Fishers, Indiana*

I couldn't believe that I had to work the night of the Indians' first playoff game of my lifetime. It was Game 1 of the 1995 ALDS against Boston, October 3, and my friend and I were medical students on call and taking care of patients at UH. We took good care of the patients, but in between would go to any empty room we could find and turn on the TV. In our experience it was the type of game that OF COURSE any Cleveland team would lose, so when Pena hit the winning home run we both screamed! I'm sure we would have woken up all the patients had they not all been screaming too. *—Dan Polster, Solon*

I remember the final game at the old stadium . . . I have a large family so we had to split up for the game. I remember my Mom who is a die-hard fan wanted us all together for the final out and when we were walking to their seats I see Bob Hope! My Mom has season tickets still to this day—she truly made me love baseball! *—Alice Nahodil, Akron*

THE END OF INNOCENCE

Lofton Flies Away from the Tribe, then Comes Home

Tom Hamilton was excited just to be on the flight.

It was late in spring training of 1997. Dick Jacobs had sent his private jet for John Hart, Dan O'Dowd, Mike Hargrove, Herb Score and Hamilton. They were flying to meet with some of Jacobs' best friends—and Cleveland powerbrokers—at the Pier House Resort. That was a luxury hotel owned by Jacobs in Key West.

Hamilton had been on these flights before. His job was to shake hands, talk Tribe and have dinner with the friends of Jacobs.

But this flight was different.

"As we took off, I realized the Indians were in the middle of making a big trade," said Hamilton.

Make that a *huge* trade. A *shocking* trade. Possibly a *franchise-shaking* trade.

"Grover had out a pen and a pad," said Hamilton. "He was taking Kenny Lofton out of the top of the lineup, and he was adding David Justice and Marquis Grissom into the lineup. He was making out different batting orders."

Hamilton knew that Lofton was heading into his free-agent season. But he didn't think Lofton would be traded. After all, the Indians went with Albert Belle for all of 1996, knowing he was likely to leave after the season. At one point, Hamilton saw Hargrove looking at one of his lineups and saying: "If we can't keep Kenny, I'm OK with this."

There was discussion about Justice, who had played only 40 games in 1996 because of a shoulder injury. Was he healthy? Could he replace Belle in left field? They talked about how Grissom was a Gold

Glove-caliber center fielder. He didn't compare to Lofton as a hitter, but he might have been a superior defender in center.

"As we landed, I was told, '*No one say a word about this!*' " recalled Hamilton.

That night, Hamilton noticed that Hart and O'Dowd spent very little time with the guests at dinner. They'd leave the table, taking phone calls. Then come back. Then leave again.

And again.

And again.

And Hamilton was one of the few people in the room who had a clue of what was going on, but couldn't even hint at what was happening.

"Not if I wanted to keep my job!" he said, laughing about it years later.

The discussions began months before it happened. Tribe General Manager John Hart was on the phone with John Schuerholz, who had the same job with the Atlanta Braves. They were talking about how you can offer a player like Albert Belle $40 million, and that is quickly rejected. Free agency keeps changing the game, they said.

Schuerholz asked about contract talks with Lofton, because Lofton could be a free agent at the end of the 1997 season.

The Indians had offered Lofton $44 million over five years, but Lofton's agents had rejected it. Lofton seemed destined to follow Belle's path to free agency.

Suddenly, the two men began talking a trade.

Were the Braves interested in Lofton?

Would the Indians consider replacing Belle in left field with Justice?

Hart also discussed Grissom, the Braves' center fielder.

The talks sort of stopped. Neither could believe they actually were discussing a deal of this magnitude. Here were the Braves, the team that had won more games in the 1990s than anyone else. Here were the Indians, who had won more games than anyone in the last three years.

Here were two teams that played in the 1995 World Series, and they were considering a deal that went to the heart of both clubs? The general managers pondered what they had discussed. And for the next seven weeks, nothing much was said about it.

But both men kept thinking about it. Over and over, they thought about it. General managers are like that. They make lineups, lists and payroll budgets in their heads. They keep looking for an edge.

By the spring of 1997, Lofton had already made three All-Star teams. He had won four Gold Gloves. Five times, he led the American League in stolen bases. He was a career .313 hitter.

And at 29, Lofton seemed to be in his prime.

Hart was angry at the quick dismissal by Lofton's agents. The contract would have made Lofton the highest-paid player in Tribe history. It was $4 million more than they offered Belle.

"We will not be held hostage to the Kenny Lofton Road Show," Hart told his staff.

Hart and Schuerholz were old friends. Hart knew Schuerholz was looking to dump Justice. The Braves needed to clear money to sign pitchers Tom Glavine and Greg Maddux. Hart kept thinking about Lofton being in the final year of his contract, and he wasn't sure how Lofton would react. Would he have the best year of his career to be worth even more money? Would he be angry because the Indians didn't meet his price? How would his pending free agency affect Lofton's performance in 1997?

At one point, Hart told Schuerholz, "I'll trade you Lofton for Justice and Marquis Grissom."

Schuerholz said he didn't think he could do something quite so big. There were a few weeks left in spring training. The Tribe had at least one scout at every Atlanta spring game, usually former big-league catcher Ted Simmons.

"Justice's [surgically repaired] shoulder is fine," Simmons told Hart. "He's swinging free and easy."

Hart offered the same deal to Schuerholz again.

"John, I don't think we can do it," said Schuerholz.

Not long after rejecting Hart's offer, Schuerholz saw Justice.

"I thought I might be traded to the Cubs," Justice said. "I never heard a word about the Indians. But Schuerholz told me, "I'd bet my house and my family that I won't trade you.'"

For the first time all spring, Justice thought he'd open the season in Atlanta.

In the final week of spring training, Hart received another call from the Braves.

"We're ready to go," said Schuerholz.

Hart wanted to check with O'Dowd, Hargrove and some others once more.

"I kept thinking if we traded Kenny, it would be the end of an era," Hart said. "He was the last one."

Lofton grew up with the Tribe along with Belle and Carlos Baerga. Those three were the motor that drove the 1995 Indians to the club's first World Series in 41 years.

Hart called Simmons.

"Grissom is a terrific player," Simmons said. "Justice is really hitting the ball. He's a man possessed."

In Key West, Jacobs hosted a meeting with Hart, O'Dowd and Hargrove. The consensus was that Lofton probably would not re-sign with the Indians, that he wanted "Albert Belle money."

Belle signed a $55 million deal for five years with Chicago White Sox. It was the richest contract in baseball at the start of the 1997 season.

"If you think it's a good deal, do it," Jacobs said. "Don't blink."

Then Jacobs talked about one of his rules of business: When you come to a fork in the road where you can make the safe choice or take a risk, take the road with the risk.

Why?

"If you did your homework, then the road with the risk can lead to the biggest gain," said Jacobs.

The shrewd businessman often said that was how he made some of his best real-estate transactions. That night, Hart talked on the phone three times with Schuerholz. The Braves general manager was having dinner and talking on his cell phone. Justice and Grissom were signed to long-term contracts. Both were good guys who would be comfortable in Cleveland.

The deal had risk, but the reward could be enormous. The Braves also wanted a prospect in the deal, and after some arguing, the Indians reluctantly added Alan Embree to the package. By 10 p.m., both sides had agreed on the trade that would be announced the next day.

Hart did not sleep that night. He paced. He made lists. He tried to read, but the words meant nothing. He had no idea what book he had in his hands. He got up and paced some more. He thought about the controversy of trading Baerga in mid-season in 1996. He thought about the agony of Belle. He thought about the final days of Eddie Murray, which ended in bitterness before he was traded to Baltimore. Now, he was going to trade Lofton.

"I just felt sad," Hart said. "I hated to see what had happened to this team that I wanted to keep together forever."

But Hart kept telling himself: "We can't have another Albert Belle. We can't just have this guy walk out of here."

Jacobs agreed.

Both teams kept the trade talks silent.

No players would be told. No agents. No one at all.

For the Indians, the only ones who knew about the talks were Hart, Hargrove, Assistant General Manager Dan O'Dowd and owner Dick Jacobs. Only two members of the Braves' front office knew of the talks—Schuerholz and Manager Bobby Cox.

And yes, Hamilton, who just happened to be along on the flight—and to watch the Tribe work one of its biggest trades in history.

When Kenny Lofton came to work at Winter Haven's Chain O' Lakes Park that morning, he had no hint that this would be a day he'd never forget. The Indians were playing the Toronto Blue Jays, and Lofton was planning to start in center field. Standing by his locker, he was showing off a new poster of himself to teammate Omar Vizquel. It was a picture of Lofton in a tuxedo, surrounded by other pictures of Lofton in a Tribe uniform. Lofton batting. Lofton stealing bases. Lofton making great catches.

"What do you think, Omar?" he asked. "Think the kids will like it?"

He meant the kids he helped mentor in Cleveland through a summer baseball program.

That poster still was on his mind when Hargrove approached him.

"Kenny, no need to get dressed," Hargrove said. "We need to go see John."

He meant Hart.

Lofton started thinking, "They don't tell you to see the general manager right before a game unless . . ."

Lofton's thoughts stopped there.

It was about 9 a.m. when Lofton arrived at Hart's cramped office in Winter Haven. He sat in a straight-back chair, the kind you'd see in a 1950s dining room. Hart's desk was old, almost ancient. It came with the little office in the tiny ballpark that the Tribe inherited in 1993. That was after the Boston Red Sox had moved to Fort Myers. No one wanted to train in Winter Haven, a forgotten town surrounded by orange trees and mostly sagging, sad houses in a rather depressed part of central Florida.

"I think the Red Sox signed Ted Williams to a contract on this very desk," Hart once said.

Across that same desk, Hart was about to talk trade to Lofton.

"Kenny, we've traded you to the Braves," Hart said.

Lofton didn't hear much else. His mind went blank. He couldn't speak.

He heard the words "business decision."

Later, Lofton would say: "I guess it's all just a business. The Indians are a business. The Braves are a business. They sent me from one business to another."

Lofton returned to the Tribe dressing room, feeling like the walking dead. He went over to his locker, sat down. He wanted to put on his uniform, the one that said "CLEVELAND" on the front and "LOFTON" on the back. But it wasn't his uniform anymore.

He sat and stared. He told a couple of teammates, "I've been traded to Atlanta." The next thing he knew, he was hugging everyone in the dressing room.

"I guess I should call someone," he said.

So he called his agents, and they were stunned. They never even heard a rumor of a possible trade.

The phone rang in the Tribe dressing room. It was Carlos Baerga from Port St. Lucie, where the Mets trained. He wished Lofton well.

The phone rang again. It was Eddie Murray, who was calling from Tempe, Ariz., where the Anaheim Angels trained.

Lofton faced several members of the media. Despite his contract issues, he never believed that the Indians would trade him. He insisted that he wasn't determined to become a free agent.

"It never came from my mouth," he said.

But it did from his agents. The press conference ended.

Lofton went into the dressing room.

In West Palm Beach, Atlanta Manager Bobby Cox delivered the news to Justice and Grissom.

They heard the same words as Lofton: "John wants to see you."

Only this was Braves GM John Schuerholz. "Remember when I told you that I'd bet my house and family you won't be traded? . . ." he said to Justice.

Justice couldn't remember anything else he was told, other than that the trade was to Cleveland.

"I thought . . . Cleveland . . . that's OK with me," he said.

Grissom was in shock. Like Lofton, he never expected to be traded. Unlike Lofton, he'd signed a long-term deal at what he considered to be bargain dollars in order to remain in Atlanta, which was his hometown. Grissom felt like weeping.

Six months later, one of these teams would be in the World Series. At the time the trade was made, few thought it would be the Tribe.

While Hart traded Lofton, he still missed Lofton. He also wanted to bring Lofton back in 1998. After losing in the Game 7 of the World Series, Hart had another meeting with O'Dowd and Hargrove. In the back of Hart's mind was Lofton.

He asked O'Dowd and Hargrove to list the team's greatest needs.

The first was a big-time starting pitcher.

The next was a leadoff hitter.

Hart, O'Dowd and Hargrove all had those two in order at the top of their lists.

"Marquis Grissom did a great job for us and he's one the finest human beings that I ever met in baseball," O'Dowd said at the meeting.

Left unsaid was that the Tribe missed Lofton's speed in the leadoff spot.

Grissom batted .262 with 12 homers, 66 RBI and a .317 on-base percentage. He also stole 22 bases. Lofton had spoiled the Tribe when it came to leadoff hitters.

With the Braves, Lofton batted .333, but he missed 35 games with a groin injury. He stole 27 bases, but was caught 20 times. He seemed moody to the Braves, and they had little interest in signing him. The 1997 All-Star Game was in Cleveland. Lofton made the National League team, and received a standing ovation from the Cleveland crowd when he appeared in the game. Some of the Braves executives and players believed Lofton missed Cleveland, and the All-Star made that very clear.

Lofton had a close relationship with O'Dowd. When free agency opened, O'Dowd called Lofton's agent and set up a time to talk with Lofton. About 10 minutes into the conversation, O'Dowd realized that the reports about Lofton missing Cleveland were true. He wanted to come back. O'Dowd told that to Hart and Hargrove.

Hargrove was on vacation in Hawaii when GM John Hart called.

"Grover, what do you think about us signing Kenny?" Hart asked.

"John, don't tease me," said the manager. "Please, go do it!"

Hart did some homework and discovered the only team with a serious interest in Lofton was Milwaukee. He was convinced that the Indians would be far more attractive to Lofton than the Brewers. He also had another idea. Since the Brewers were looking for a center fielder, why not trade them Grissom? Sandy Alomar and Jim Thome called Hart and told him to pursue Lofton—that Lofton "wanted to come home."

Lofton's market value dropped dramatically. Instead of the $44 million that the Tribe had offered him after the 1996 season, the new price was $24 million for three years with a fourth-year team option. Lofton agreed to come to Cleveland for that contract. Grissom was making $5 million a year. The Tribe told Milwaukee, "Look, we'll trade you Grissom. You get a center fielder for $5 million—and you'll save almost $3 million compared to signing Lofton."

The Tribe shipped Grissom and Jeff Juden to Milwaukee for some marginal pitching prospects: Ben McDonald, Ron Villone and Mike Fetters. The point of the deal was to take Grissom's $5 million off the payroll and make room for Lofton.

"Even after Kenny was traded [to Atlanta], in the back of my mind, I thought if everything broke just right, we'd get him back," Hargrove said in the spring of 1998.

"The only reason we traded Kenny was economics," said Hart. "We loved him as a player and person. That offer [$44 million for five years, rejected by Lofton in the spring of 1997] was the biggest offer we made to any of our players. We never lumped Kenny in with the guys on the team who supposedly had problems here. We traded him only when it was obvious he didn't want to sign with us."

With the Braves, Lofton tried to be the clubhouse DJ—a role he had with the Tribe. But many of the players didn't like his taste in music. Too loud. He also was sullen with the media.

"Kenny found out that the grass was not always greener somewhere else," said Hargrove.

Lofton averaged 31 steals while hitting .280 from 1998 to 2001. He wasn't quite the impact player as before, but was still a factor at the top of the Tribe lineup.

Lofton even returned again in the middle of the 2007 season, playing for a Tribe team that won 96 games.

"When Kenny came back for the last time, a lot of the younger players couldn't understand why he got a standing ovation when he came to bat," said Hamilton. "I don't mean just the first game back, but lots of people stood and applauded every time he came to bat in 2007. The fans always appreciated the players from that era."

Mark Shapiro remembered how his small deal to bring back Lofton in 2007 was greeted with wild enthusiasm.

"Every time he came to bat for us at home, it was a 'Holy Cow' moment because of how the fans reacted," said Shapiro. "Fans acted as if it was one of the greatest moves that we had ever made. They so loved the players from the 1990s."

About 10 minutes after Lofton signed the contract to return to the Tribe for the 1998 season, he was sitting in Hart's office. His cellphone rang. It was Carlos Baerga, just calling to talk. He had no idea Lofton was coming back to Cleveland. Baerga had been traded to the Mets during the 1996 season. He told Lofton to tell Hart, "Get me back."

That's because for so many of those Tribe players in the 1990s, Cleveland was the best place for them to be—and they never realized it fully until they had left.

Belle Blows Out of Town

For Albert Belle, it was never better than 1995.

But after the season, Belle was justifiably upset when passed over for the MVP award in favor of Mo Vaughn. That was just the start of the year of outrage for Albert.

The Tribe tried to sign him, offering Belle an extension worth $40 million for five years. Belle wanted at least $10 million a year. The Indians refused. Belle entered the final season of his contract feeling disrespected.

The $10 million would have made him the highest-paid player in the game, and he believed he was worth it. Remember, he was coming off a season for the ages—hitting 50 homers, 52 doubles with 126 RBI in 143 games. Belle was always a man who measured his worth by the numbers, be it in the box score or on his paycheck.

He made $5.7 million in his final year with the Indians.

Things began to happen.

Some bad things, some sad things.

Virtually all of them were unnecessary.

Early in the 1996 season, he hit Sports Illustrated photographer Tony Tomsic with a ball. Bill Colson of Sports Illustrated wrote that Tomsic took some photos of Belle, who was stretching before a game at Jacobs Field. Photographers are allowed to take photos of players in pre-game warmups, but Belle became upset and heaved a ball at Tomsic, hitting the photographer in the hand.

Later in 1996, Belle crashed into Milwaukee second baseman Fernando Vina and drew a suspension that later was reduced from five games to two.

Belle was being booed everywhere.

"Albert's human, some of these things bothered him," Hargrove said at the time. "He is not the ogre that he has been made out to be. He is not a bad person. But when you talk to Albert, he only hears what he wants to hear."

In New York, fans threw balls and garbage at him. In Chicago, three guys dressed in bibs and diapers waved rattles and screamed at Belle in left field.

Belle was upset when the Tribe cut Eddie Murray's contract from $3 million to $2 million, despite Murray batting .323 with 21 homers in 1995. Belle was right about that. It was a dumb move by the Tribe, alienating several players, as Murray was one of the leaders in the clubhouse. Belle saw the team selling out every night at home, yet it seemed to be squeezing the cash when it came to Murray and others.

That summer, Carlos Baerga was traded. Murray was traded. The magic and fun of 1995 was gone, and there was a sense Belle would disappear soon—right after the season.

Everyone seemed so tired.

The Indians were weary of Belle's self-destructive behavior.

Belle was sick of what he deemed a lack of respect from the Tribe, along with being made an unfair target by the media.

Through it all, Belle did what Belle always did.

He hit. And hit. And hit.

Belle finished the 1996 season with 48 homers and 148 RBI, and batted .311.

"I didn't think Albert would leave," said Hamilton. "I guess I was naive. We were winning. Chicago was going the other direction. Remember, this was back when nearly everyone wanted to play in Cleveland."

After the Tribe was knocked out of the 1996 playoffs in the first round by Baltimore, the Indians began rebuilding and Belle was not in the blueprint.

"Albert was a lightning rod for the franchise," General Manager John Hart said after Belle left.

But the Indians were just burned out by Belle at the end.

* * *

Chicago.

That was the stunner when Belle signed with another team.

The assumption was that Belle was headed elsewhere, but the White Sox? He absolutely deplored the White Sox. They were the team that checked his bat in 1994, and the team that led to his seven-game suspension for using a corked bat.

At the press conference in Chicago, Belle was asked about the corked-bat situation.

"A situation occurred late in the season when I bumped my head on the roof of the dugout and I developed amnesia," he said. "I can't remember back that far."

"Great answer," bellowed Jerry Reinsdorf, the White Sox owner.

Belle was guaranteed $50 million over five years.

He also received a sixth year worth $10 million, with $5 million guaranteed.

That brought the final contract to $55 million, the largest ever given a player at that point in baseball history.

He also had a "no trade" clause.

Even more stunning was a clause in the contract ensuring that Belle would be among the top three highest-paid players in baseball. If Chicago refused to give him a raise so he remained in the top three, Belle could void the contract and become a free agent.

The Indians had absolutely no interest in matching that deal, especially with the clause about remaining in the top three when it came to salary.

The White Sox also made an interesting (but unrealistic) sales pitch to Belle. They drove him around town where Michael Jordan, Dennis Rodman and Frank Thomas were featured on huge billboards. Reinsdorf also owned the Bulls, who were in the midst of their championship stampede during the Jordan Era.

"I treated Albert like I did Michael Jordan," Reinsdorf said at that press conference.

Belle believed Cleveland never fully appreciated him, at least when it came to commercial endorsements. His personality and unwillingness to do things like show up for the news conference to introduce his own candy bar didn't exactly enhance his marketability. But it was also true that Chicago was a much larger city with more endorsement opportunities. Reinsdorf talked about Belle being the White Sox version of Jordan.

"This is a chance for a fresh start," Belle said at his press conference. "It's a chance to put the past behind me . . . My reputation will change over time . . . I like where the White Sox are headed. They are determined to win a championship."

Belle felt that way because the White Sox met his price.

"It is unfortunate how things worked out [in Cleveland]," Belle said. "The fans stuck by me in tough times. I won't forget that. But it's time to look forward and to move on."

At the press conference, Belle said twice, "It's not about the money."

Of course, it was about the money.

Mark Shapiro offered an insight into the mindset of some players. Shapiro has a unique perspective. He has been in the front office as a general manager and then team president, but he also is the son of Ron Shapiro, one of baseball's leading agents.

"For a lot of the players, one of the markers they use for a level of respect is their contracts," said Shapiro. "They think, 'What is a statistical measurement for how I'm valued compared to other players?' The contract and salary is a way for some guys to equate that, and a lot of the time, the agents want them to equate it that way."

In other words, respect comes from making more than the other guy—at least, for some players.

Shapiro made another good point about how some players can't wait to become free agents "because they haven't been able to make a lot of decisions in their lives."

Shapiro mentioned that a player can't determine what team drafts him. Or what level in the minors he will play. Or when he will be promoted to the majors. Or who will be his manager. Or even where he will bat in the lineup or play in the field.

When the chance comes to be a free agent, a player can pick a situation based on his priorities.

"Albert is a very competitive guy, and being the highest-paid player was very important to him," said Shapiro.

After leaving the Indians, Belle would never play in the postseason again.

In fact, his career would last only four more years. He never played on another team with a winning record.

Belle never became baseball's version of Michael Jordan in Chicago.

He lasted only two years with the White Sox. When several players passed him in salary, Belle used the option to negate his contract and become a free agent.

In 1998, he had a monster season with 49 homers and 152 RBI, batting .328 for the White Sox. But their record was only 80-82, and they declined to give Belle a raise. The White Sox had to raise his $10 million salary to $11.5 million annually, according to terms of the contract, to keep him among the top three players in salary.

So Belle entered free agency with the goal of becoming baseball's highest-paid player—again.

And he did, as Baltimore gave him a 5-year, $65 million deal.

In 1999, he hammered 37 homers with 117 RBI, batting .297 for the Orioles, who were 78-84. But something was happening with Belle. His hip was bothering him.

A lot.

Remember that Belle seldom complained about injuries. He never sat out games. So when he said he was hurting, the pain was serious.

In 2000, Belle limped through much of the season. He still hit 23 homers with 103 RBI, batting .281.

More revealing, he batted only .248 with five homers in his final 64 games.

He missed 20 games in September with a sore hip. The next March, the Orioles issued a statement that Belle was "totally disabled and unable to perform as a Major League baseball player."

He had a degenerative hip condition.

Belle came to spring training in 2001, but his hip prevented him from playing. He quietly retired at the age of 34. He was paid the final three years of his contract, even though he didn't play. Baltimore was reimbursed about 70 percent of those three seasons because the contract was insured. So Belle was paid $85 million for playing only four years after he left the Tribe.

His stats were staggering.

From 1991 to 2000, he led everyone in baseball in RBI (1,199) and total bases (3,207) while being fourth in home runs (373).

His manager in that final year with the Orioles was Mike Hargrove.

"I liked Albert and I appreciate how he produced," said Hargrove. "I knew that he would be there every day. And he was prepared. He was good for 45-50 homers and 140-150 RBI [in Belle's prime]."

Hargrove paused.

"I feel sorry for Albert" because his career was cut short, said Hargrove. "He was a great player."

Hamilton said Belle "could have owned the town."

Belle's anger and departure prevented that from happening.

"But to this day, some people will tell you that Albert was their favorite player," said Hamilton. "He represented Big Bad Cleveland. The town was the subject to all the jokes and had a bit of an inferiority complex. But not Albert. He didn't take crap from anyone. Cleveland had a player who could just dominate the other team, and they loved him for that."

1996: The Loss of Innocence

Tom Hamilton calls it "the year reality hit for the new Tribe."

The new Indians began in 1994, the year they moved into the new stadium. It was the year they were in playoff contention when a baseball labor dispute wiped out the final 49 regular-season games and the postseason.

Then came 1995, which was one big celebration for anyone who cared about the team in Wahoo red, white and blue. Losing in the 1995 World Series didn't feel so bad because . . . hey, they actually made it to the World Series.

First time in 41 years.

"And no one was really going to complain about that," said Hamilton. "Besides, I think most of us figured we'd be back in 1996 . . . and win it this time."

The Tribe had a 100-44 record in 1995, and most experts believed they'd win 100 games again.

On the surface, it seemed more of the same for the Tribe.

The final record was 99-62. They moved into first place in the Central Division on April 13 and they won it by 14½ games.

They led the American league in hitting and pitching, highest batting average, lowest earned-run average. They set a franchise record for runs scored. They won 19 games in their last at bat. Every home game was sold out, and the final attendance was a franchise record of 3,318,174.

"That 1996 team still had great talent, but something had changed," said Hamilton. "It wasn't as much fun. Just getting to the postseason wasn't enough. We knew we should win the Central Division. It's like we were playing six months of baseball just to start the playoffs."

But there was more.

For a while, no matter what John Hart did, it was the right move. The 1995 season made Hart even more determined, more driven and more obsessed than ever with putting together a team that could win the World Series. He also wanted to keep the profit margin up. Remember that owner Dick Jacobs preferred to make at least 8 percent every season once they moved into the new stadium.

In 1995, Eddie Murray batted .323 with 21 homers and 82 RBI in 113 games. His OPS—a stat not used back then—was .891, close to All-Star level. After the season, Murray was a free agent. He had earned $3 million with the Tribe in 1995, and he figured he was due some type of raise.

Yes, Murray would be 40 in 1996, but the man still batted .323. He was one of the team leaders, a player who could command some respect from the likes of Albert Belle, Kenny Lofton, Carlos Baerga, Manny Ramirez and Jim Thome—the Tribe's young emerging stars.

But Hart offered Murray a one-year, $2 million deal.

So he wanted to cut Murray's salary from $3 million to $2 million after one of the greatest years in franchise history, a season when the ballpark was packed every night and it was obvious ownership was cashing in.

Hart's stance was that Murray could no longer play first base . . . he played there 26 times in 1994 and 18 times in 1995. And if Murray didn't like the offer, he could shop for a better deal elsewhere. After all, he was a free agent. Who was stopping him from leaving?

Murray ended up signing for the $2 million, because it was the best offer.

"But Eddie was mad about it, and so were the other players," said Hamilton. "The players looked at it as, 'We went to the World Series. Eddie had a great year. He means so much to the team . . . and they are cutting his salary? That's not right.' And Eddie was very upset. He showed up in spring training angry about it."

Belle was heading into his free-agent season. He believed the Tribe treated Murray with a lack of respect, and figured the front office would do the same for him. There also was a racial element. Belle considered Murray one his role models. If the front office treated a black star like this, how would they deal with him?

There is no reason to assume any racism behind Hart's decision.

For him, the color was green. He believed there was little reason to pay Murray $3 million or more when no other team was willing to do so. He had done the research and knew there was little interest in Murray from other teams, because few teams wanted a 40-year-old designated hitter.

Hart just wanted to make what he thought was the wisest deal for the team.

"It really wasn't about the money with Eddie," said Hamilton. "It was principle. The players thought Eddie deserved to be treated better, and this became a problem later on."

Murray told the Tribe that if they planned to cut his salary because he was just a designated hitter, then they could forget about him playing any first base. That didn't seem like a major issue, but Mike Hargrove liked the option of Murray playing first base at least once a week.

"Later in the season, that became an issue," said Hamilton. "We signed Julio Franco to play first base, and he got hurt. They asked Eddie to play first base."

Murray refused.

He said since they thought he was strictly a designated hitter and since they had cut his pay, that's what he'd do—be a DH.

Usually, that position would be viewed as selfish by teammates, but not in this case. Most supported Murray. Hargrove was in a horrible position, because it wasn't his idea to cut Murray's salary. He never would have done it. He knew the value of Murray's leadership. As a former player, Hargrove knew that a veteran could go to another team for less money—and that's fine. It's the player's decision.

But when you cut the pay of a future Hall of Famer after a team went to the World Series, that creates a problem.

After the 1995 season, Hart decided not to re-sign first baseman Paul Sorrento.

It was sort of a strange move, because Sorrento had 25 homers and 79 RBI in 323 at-bats. He was a platoon player, facing mostly right-handers. But Sorrento hit for power. His batting average was only .235, but the OPS was .847.

"Paul was a great guy to have on the team," said Hamilton. "Like

Eddie Murray, he was key to the team chemistry. Paul got along with everyone—white, black, Latinos, you name it. You could drop him in the middle of Ethiopia, and in a few weeks, he'd have some close friends. On a team with a lot of egos and strong-willed people, Paul was very underrated. And for gosh sakes, he batted eighth in 1995 and hit 25 homers. Think about that, the eighth hitter has 25 homers!"

Hart acquired Sorrento in one of his best trades, sending pitchers Oscar Munoz and Curt Leskanic to the Twins. Sorrento was stuck in Class AAA as the Twins had a star in Kent Hrbek playing first. That's why Minnesota traded him.

In 1995, Sorrento made $1.1 million.

Money was not the issue. Sorrento received no interest from the Tribe, and the Mariners signed him to a $1 million contract in 1996 with a team option of $1.5 million for 1997. He was 30 years old.

"John Hart was looking for a first baseman who'd make more contact and was a better all-around hitter," said Hamilton. "Paul didn't play that well in the 1995 postseason [7-of-34, .206, 1 RBI]. Not sure if that had anything to do with it."

Hart told reporters after the 1995 season that "power doesn't always win in the playoffs."

The Tribe was 1-4 in the postseason against left-handed starters, and that may have led to Hart deciding to dump Sorrento.

To replace Sorrento, the Indians signed Julio Franco to a two-year, $5.3 million deal.

Franco spent the 1995 season playing in Japan. He was 37 years old. To be fair to Hart, Franco also was a career .301 hitter and in excellent physical condition.

"It wasn't a bad move [at least on paper]," said Hamilton. "But I think Paul added so much in terms of chemistry. You need 'glue-guys,' players happy to be out of the spotlight and glad to support the team and the manager—and they also can produce when they play. Paul and Eddie Murray were two of those guys."

Murray and other Tribe players noticed how Sorrento was cast aside by the front office. They also saw how Franco's 1996 salary ($2.4 million) was more than what the Tribe offered Murray after cutting his salary. They saw how Sorrento signed with Seattle for the same $1 million that he made with the Tribe. Some players were thinking, "Eddie and Paul helped us get to the World Series, and they bring in

Franco from Japan and pay him even more money. Something is not right."

Yes, it wasn't long after the team's parade down Euclid Avenue following the World Series that money became an issue.

Not only were the decisions made on Sorrento and Murray questioned by some of the core players, the Tribe's major free-agent acquisition was pitcher Jack McDowell.

"We needed another starting pitcher," said Hamilton. "The question was where to find one, especially because the front office wanted to find a guy who could be an ace."

The 1995 starting rotation was Charles Nagy, Dennis Martinez, Orel Hershiser, Mark Clark and several others who were used as the fifth starter.

"I know they got down to Kevin Brown and McDowell, trying to decide who'd be the best," said Hamilton. "It was hard to argue with signing McDowell. He pitched for the White Sox. We saw him all the time, and he was tough. Really tough. He seemed to always find a way to beat you, no matter if it was 2-1 or 5-4."

In 1995, McDowell was with the Yankees and was 15-10 with a 3.93 ERA. He had a miserable postseason, a 9.00 ERA in two games as the Yankees were knocked out of the first round of the playoffs by Seattle.

"Jack made his first career relief appearance in that Game 5 against the Mariners," said Hamilton. "He was the loser. Jack told me that after the game, [Yankees owner] George Steinbrenner was going through the locker room, shaking hands with the players. He came to Jack and said, 'Thanks for what you did for us this year, and good luck next year wherever you end up pitching.' Right there, Jack knew he was done with the Yankees."

Looking back, it's hard to see any real warning signs that McDowell was fading.

The Tribe's 1996 media guide mentioned how McDowell had won more games than any other American League pitcher from 1990 to 1995, but the media guide also mentioned: "Left his last two starts of the season after five innings due to a strained muscle in his upper right back. He did not pitch in the regular season after September 21 . . . injury bothered him since August."

Even in September, he was 4-0 with a 3.00 ERA.

Now, it's a good guess there was more to this strained back problem than the Indians knew.

But at the time, McDowell was 30 years old. He had never been on the disabled list. He had twice won 20 games (in 1992 and 1993) for the White Sox.

Even in the 1995 season, he started slow (6-5, 4.56 ERA) but was 9-5 with a 3.32 ERA after the All-Star break. The only red flag was that the Yankees had no interest in keeping him as a free agent.

The other option was Kevin Brown, who had a 10-9 record and 3.60 ERA with Baltimore in 1995. In 1994, he was 7-9 with a 4.82 ERA.

Yes, Kevin Brown had won 21 games in 1992. But he was a year older than McDowell and had not been as effective lately.

And in 1995, Brown spent some time on the disabled list with a finger injury.

Both pitchers were represented by the hardball agent Scott Boras.

"There was some internal debate, but in the end, they went with McDowell," said Hamilton. "Contracts may have played into it a bit, but they seemed to favor Jack at that point."

Everything from age to stats gave the edge to McDowell.

The Indians signed McDowell to a two-year, $10.3 million deal.

Brown signed with Florida for $13 million over three years.

And yes, that's the same Kevin Brown that the Tribe faced in the 1997 World Series, when McDowell was on the disabled list with a bad arm.

It's hard to fault the Indians on the decision. At the time of the signing, it was praised by nearly everyone as a strong move to give the Tribe a pitcher who not only should help them return to the post-season, but to the World Series.

"Not long after we got Jack, you could tell he wasn't the same guy," said Hamilton.

McDowell had a 2.04 ERA in April, but it soared to 5.19 in May and stayed high for the rest of the year.

His final record was 13-9 with a 5.11 ERA.

It's very possible McDowell pitched the entire season with an arm problem.

"He made 30 starts," said Hamilton. "He wasn't very happy here. He was sort of suspicious of people. Even in his best days with the White

Sox, he was never Mr. Warm and Fuzzy. I have a hard time criticizing the move. It just didn't work out."

Here's a look at the 1996 Tribe opening-day payroll for the key players:

1. Albert Belle, $5.7 million.
2. Jack McDowell, $4.8 million.
3. Carlos Baerga, $4.8 million.
4. Dennis Martinez, $3.8 million.
5. Kenny Lofton, $3.6 million.
6. Charles Nagy, $3.5 million.
7. Omar Vizquel, $3.0 million.
8. Sandy Alomar, $2.6 million.
9. Julio Franco, $2.4 million.
10. Eddie Murray, $2.0 million.
11. Jose Mesa, $1.9 million.
12. Orel Hershiser, $1.7 million.
13. Jim Thome, $1.6 million.
14. Manny Ramirez, $1.1 million.

A few things jump out:

1. Thome and Ramirez were early in their careers, both having arrived to stay in the majors in 1994. They had only two years of experience, so big money was not coming their way immediately.

2. McDowell immediately became the second-highest paid player on the team. If he won 15 to 20 games and was a factor in the playoffs, there would be no complaints. But just like Tribe fans, the veteran Tribe players expected production from a man with that kind of contract.

3. Franco was making more than Murray and Hershiser, and nearly as much as Alomar. He had replaced the popular (and cheaper) Sorrento. Franco didn't endure the tough times of the early 1990s, nor did he play a role in the good times of 1995. He came from Japan. There was some resentment in the dressing room over his signing.

Now, it's time to be fair to Hart, because it's so easy to second-guess when looking back more than 15 years in the rear view mirror.

In the spring of 1996, Hart talked about wanting to build a team "that wins a division title in something like three of the next four years. I want us in the postseason consistently for the rest of this decade."

This interview was done in the small press room at the Tribe's old Winter Haven spring training quarters.

"Teams turn over," he said, talking about the 1993 Blue Jays, who went to the World Series but had only four players left on the roster at the opening of the 1996 season. Free agency and contract demands forced trades, along with the need to replace older players.

"My challenge is to keep this team from falling off the face of the earth," said Hart.

In the spring of 1996, the only player headed to free agency was Belle.

But Hart was worried about Murray turning 40 and losing his bat speed. He was worried about Dennis Martinez, who would turn 41 that season. And Orel Hershiser would be 37.

His three major free-agent signings in 1994–95 paid off, as Martinez, Murray and Hershiser gave the team the experience needed to reach the World Series. But they were getting old, and it seemed they had already defied the laws of aging.

Hart also was unhappy that Baerga had shown up heavy. He was making very little progress signing Lofton and Belle to extensions. He felt the pressure of getting the team back to the World Series to keep the fans content. They had already sold out the entire 1996 season before the first day of spring training.

"Part of the reason the fans are crazy about us and we sold out so fast was that they feel they know the players," said Hart. "The core of the club has been around for quite a while, and it's going to stay."

Remember, he said this in the spring of 1996.

A lot changed by playoff time.

"The easy thing to do was nothing," Hart said several times during the 1996 season, usually after he did something.

Something really big.

Like trading Murray back to the Orioles (his original team) on July 21. The Indians picked up pitcher Kent Mercker, who threw only 11⅔ innings for the Tribe. At this point, dealing Murray made sense, because he was unhappy and an unhappy Eddie Murray can be a problem—especially when he refused to play first base. Of course, Hart's short-sighted view of Murray's contract situation led to the grim mood of the veteran.

On July 29, he traded Baerga to the Mets for Jeff Kent and Jose Vizcaino. Baerga was batting only .267 with 10 homers in 100 games. He had made 15 errors at second base, and his range seemed to shrink more each month.

The following spent time on the disabled list at different times during the season: Dennis Martinez, Franco and McDowell. Martinez was 9-6 with a 4.50 ERA and simply couldn't stay healthy. At 41, he was finally done.

Then there was Albert Belle.

Belle came into the season even more angry than normal.

He was upset because Mo Vaughn was voted the MVP award. Belle believed he had superior stats:

Belle batted .317 with 52 doubles, 50 homers and 126 RBI in a 144-game season. No other major-leaguer has ever had 50 homers and 50 doubles in a season.

Vaughn batted .300 with 28 doubles, 39 homers, 126 RBI. The Indians had a better regular-season record than Boston, and then knocked the Red Sox out of the playoffs.

Belle couldn't understand it. He had a better year on a better team. It is true that MVP voting is finished before the end of the regular season, so the playoffs had no impact. But Belle knew Vaughn had a pleasant, media-friendly personality. He also played on the East Coast, where there were more voters. And Belle figured some writers were voting against him because he had been so hostile to them.

In some cases, that was true. It was personal. Belle could act like a jerk, and Vaughn was more mature in his dealings with the media. And Vaughn had a big year. So many writers put Vaughn first and Belle second on their ballot.

In spring training, Belle was fined $50,000 going back to an incident in the 1995 World Series when he cussed out reporter Hannah Storm in the dugout.

On April 6, 1996, Belle threw a baseball at Sports Illustrated photographer Tony Tomsic. The photographer was hit, but not injured. Belle said he didn't mean to hit anyone with the ball. He was summoned to New York to meet with American League President Gene Budig, and ordered to receive counseling.

On May 31, 1996, the Indians were in Milwaukee playing the Brewers. Early in the game, Belle was on first base and a ground ball was hit to second baseman Fernando Vina. He tagged out Belle, then threw to first base for a double play.

That was in the third inning.

In the eighth inning, Belle was hit in the shoulder by a pitch.

Once again, he was on first base and when a ground ball was hit to Vina. Once again, Vina went to tag out Belle and try for a double play. But this time, Belle decked the 5-foot-9 Vina with a forearm to the neck. Vina's head snapped back and he ended up flat on his back. It was a vicious blow, but Vina was in the baseline.

That's why the umpires didn't eject Belle.

In the ninth inning, Belle batted again. He was hit by a pitch (in the shoulder again), this time by reliever Terry Burrows, who threw two inside pitches before finally plunking Belle.

At this point, Belle figured he was still behind. He had been hit by two pitches, but knocked down only one second baseman.

So in the bottom of the ninth, Belle told Tribe pitcher Julian Tavarez to even the score.

The first pitch from Tavarez went behind the back of the Brewers' Mike Matheny. He rushed the mound. Both dugouts emptied. Some punches were thrown. It was a mess. The Indians won the game, 10-4.

After the game, Belle told reporters, "The first time, I could have crushed [Vina]. The second time, he was open game. He could have thrown to the shortstop [covering second base] and I'd have slid into second."

Belle then added, "I was upset because I shouldn't have been hit the first time in a 9-3 game. If he wants to hit me, fine, then I'll hit the second baseman. If they want to hit me again, then our pitcher is going to even things out."

Oh, boy.

Anyway, Belle was summoned once again to New York to face American League President Gene Budig.

Belle's point was that Vina was in the baseline. And after he hit Vina, he was not ejected. He wasn't even ejected after the fight in the ninth inning.

Budig first ordered a five-game suspension, then reduced it to two games.

Hart accompanied Belle to New York for all of these meetings with

Budig, and joked about needing to rent an apartment in Manhattan if this kept up.

"But I do know the Indians were just getting tired of all the stuff around Albert," said Hamilton. "He was a great player, but so much was going on—especially that last season."

In games in New York, fans threw baseballs and mini-bats at him. A June 14 game was stopped twice to pick up things on the field that had been heaved at Belle at Yankee Stadium. He was booed everywhere.

And through it all, he kept hitting.

Late in the 1996 season, Belle thought the Tribe's clubhouse was too hot. He turned down the thermostat on the wall. A few innings later, someone had turned it up again. He turned it down, and someone again changed it. A raging Belle grabbed his bat and belted the thermostat, breaking it.

Some of his teammates put a sign in Belle's locker reading: 8 MR. FREEZE.

No. 8 was Belle's number . . . and some would say it's how cold he wanted the clubhouse.

Belle also had an incident when he smashed a teammate's CDs when he didn't like the music in the clubhouse.

But he kept hitting.

When Orel Hershiser called a players-only meeting in the outfield, everyone came together . . . except Belle, who stood about 100 feet away, swinging a bat.

And through it all, he kept hitting.

When the season was over, Belle had been fined three different times, suspended once and batted .311 with 48 homers and 148 RBI.

In the spring of 1996, Belle had turned down a five-year, $40 million offer to stay with the Tribe. He was determined to become the highest-paid player in baseball, and figured it would not happen in Cleveland.

Looking back, Hamilton wonders, "How did that team ever win 99 games?"

The Tribe won more regular-season games than anyone else in baseball with two key starters—Martinez and McDowell—combining for 22-15 record and a 4.88 ERA. Kenny Lofton (.317, 75 steals) also won his fourth Gold Glove in center. A scowling, growling Belle put up Hall of Fame numbers. But Baerga and Murray had major declines and were traded.

More importantly, the team attitude had soured.

The Tribe was still talented, and you'd expect them to win 90 games. That's especially true after going to the World Series, which led to the team's focus shifting more to getting paid and personal stats than a return to the World Series.

"It's like we lost our innocence," said Hamilton.

But Mike Hargrove somehow kept the ship from capsizing during the regular season.

"Grover would tell me how people have no idea how hard it is to win a division title," said Hamilton. "I'd say, 'Grover, we have a 15-game lead.' He'd tell me that there was a lot going on under the surface. There was this sense that we couldn't keep that 1995 team together, things were changing."

Hamilton still thought the Tribe would return to the World Series.

"Why not? We still won 99 games," he said.

The best-of-5 playoff system was set up strangely, with the team having the worst record hosting the first two games. In the case of the Tribe, that was at Baltimore.

The remaining three games (if needed) would play be played in Cleveland.

"What kind of reward is that for having the best record?" asked Hamilton.

Furthermore, Baltimore's Robbie Alomar had spit on umpire John Hirschbeck during a September 27 game when they argued at home plate. He should have been suspended for the playoffs, but Alomar appealed and his case was put on hold until after the postseason.

"So Robbie got to play," said Hamilton. "And Robbie was a great, great player. There were games where you wondered, how do you ever get him out? I was surprised by the spitting incident, because I'd never heard anything bad about Robbie. He was always considered a good guy, never a problem for anyone. When he played for us [1999–2001], he was a terrific person."

In 1995, this wouldn't have mattered. Nothing mattered. That team was together. That team was determined to make it to the World Series. That team had so much fun reaching the postseason. Nothing would stop them. Not Robbie Alomar. Not opening on the road. Not anything.

"This team, it seemed like a six-month wait just to start the playoffs," said Hamilton. "We knew we'd win the Central. The only measure of success was to win the World Series."

Then came the first game in Baltimore. Bottom of the first inning. First batter for the Orioles was Brady Anderson, who homered. It was the fourth pitch of the game from Charles Nagy.

Anderson had hit 50 homers that year, at the age of 32. He had only 72, total, before that season in his career.

As Hamilton said, "Brady hit it out, and it was like Baltimore was saying—'Look out!'—they weren't going to back down. They had just manhandled us."

The Indians lost that game, 10-4. Nagy gave up seven runs. B.J. Surhoff hit two homers.

"It was just a bad game," said Hamilton. "I was thinking about how the Orioles now had Eddie [Murray], and he really had them focused on beating us. After that first game, I didn't feel very good about the series."

During the regular season, the Tribe and Orioles played 12 times. The Indians were 7-5 vs. Baltimore.

In nine of those games, a team scored at least nine runs.

The Tribe hit .336 vs. Baltimore, and Baltimore batted .312 vs. the Tribe.

So a 10-4 final score was not a shock.

Nor was the 7-4 final score in Game 2. These two teams could hit. But the Orioles won again. Reliever Eric Plunk was the loser in Hershiser's start.

"Suddenly, we come home, we're down 0-2 and the season could be over in one game," said Hamilton. "That was so hard to believe."

In Game 3, the Tribe won 9-4. Jack McDowell stumbled through five innings, allowing four runs. But the Tribe was hitting. Albert Belle hammered a grand slam in the seventh to break open the game.

"Albert's home run brought the fans back into it," said Hamilton. "I thought, well, maybe we can still win this thing."

When the 1996 playoffs ended, 44,000 people were so silent, it seemed as if Jacobs Field had been turned into Cleveland's largest cemetery. It was the same stadium that shook with cheers and chants of "AL-BERT" only 18 hours before. And the same stadium that had been hosting baseball parties since it opened in 1994, the same stadium that had never been the sight of a real disappointment until the Indians lost 4-3 in 12 innings to Baltimore, ending the Tribe's season.

When Hamilton left the stadium, it was nearly empty. There were a few white hot-dog wrappers fluttering in the wind like miniature surrender flags.

"I was devastated," said Hamilton. "I never thought that team would lose in the first round of the playoffs. I was like the fans . . . totally shocked, completely depressed. The playoffs ended in four games, still hard for me to believe."

The same went for the players.

The usually rocking dressing room was a baseball tomb. Grown men still wearing their uniforms shook their heads while staring at nothing.

"It feels as if someone just stepped on my heart," said Omar Vizquel, right after the game.

The reason for recalling how it was after the Tribe was wiped out of the 1996 playoffs is to accent what Hamilton called the "reality" that came to the Tribe that season. No longer would it be easy. Often, it would be a trial.

After that game, Vizquel talked about how Baltimore's Roberto Alomar came to home plate with the tying run on second base in the ninth inning.

"We had two strikes on him and two outs," he said. "Jose [Mesa] was pitching with a [3-2] lead. Ninety percent of the time, we win."

Not this time.

"Two strikes on Robbie Alomar," Vizquel repeated. "Jose threw a pitch. It was strike three, down the middle. They called it a ball. I couldn't believe it. He was struck out, but they called it a ball. You'd think that the umpires were mad at us instead of at him."

He meant that the fallout from Robbie Alomar's spitting incident nearly led to an umpire boycott. He thought of how the umpires were outraged by Alomar's presence on the field, believing Alomar should have been immediately suspended. Vizquel thought they would keep Alomar on a short leash and give him a big strike zone, because Alomar should not have been in uniform (at least according to the umpires).

Yet he caught a break from the umpires. He beat the Indians.

"He stuck his bat out and dropped that single into left-center," Vizquel said. "He was fooled on the pitch, but he got a hit, anyway."

That made the score 3-3. That led to three extra innings of agony, and Alomar winning it all with his 400-foot homer.

Nothing lucky about that hit.

"It was like it was just not meant to be for us," said Vizquel.

Once upon a time, all the breaks seemed to go the Tribe's way.

But after that 1996 loss to Baltimore, Jim Thome sat in front of his locker, staring at his right hand.

"Broken," he said. "A stress fracture [of the hamate bone]."

Thome hammered 38 homers in that 1996 season.

"I hurt it in the first game in Baltimore," he said. "I fouled a pitch straight back, and that was it."

What kind of luck is that?

Thome swings at a pitch . . . fouls it off . . . and breaks a bone in his hand?

He played two more games and by the end of the series, he could barely grip a bat. He sat out the first 11 innings of Game 4. So instead of having Thome at third base in the most important game of the season, there was Jeff Kent. Kent was 0-for-3 and was shaky at third, although his glove at least didn't cost the team a run.

"You have no idea how frustrating it was for me to just sit and watch," Thome said. "Nothing I could do."

It was that way for the Indians. No matter what they did, it wasn't enough. Somehow, they found a way to strike out 23 Oriole hitters—and still lost. They found a way to lose even with Cal Ripken (of all people) pulling a boneheaded move and being thrown out by Manny Ramirez (of all people). They lost even though four Oriole infielders couldn't catch one crucial pop up.

They received a courageous, six-inning, 12-strikeout performance from Charles Nagy—but lost.

This is what 99 victories gets a team? You win a marathon by two miles, and then they tell you to run a sprint. You stub your toe and stumble. The race is over.

You end up with this key matchup with the winning run on second base in the bottom of the ninth inning—Jesse Orosco vs. Jose Vizcaino.

How can it come down to that? But it did. And Orosco retired Vizcaino (playing second base for the traded Carlos Baerga) and Kenny Lofton.

The Indians were inspired when Sandy Alomar drove in two runs with a clutch hit, yet younger brother Robbie came along to steal thunder from Sandy's bat. That weekend, Robbie was still dealing with spitting on an umpire ("a terrible thing my brother did," Sandy said during the series, still stressing that he loved his brother).

Robbie homered in the 12th off Mesa, who was working in his fourth inning. The bullpen was pretty much empty except for young Chad Ogea, and Hargrove was sticking with his best reliever.

Yes, just as Mesa couldn't close the deal in 1997.

After the game, Robbie Alomar talked about being booed, and said, "It's like being Albert Belle going to other cities."

And Belle would be heading elsewhere . . . for good . . . as this was his last game with the Tribe. He was 3-of-15 with two homers in the playoffs.

That game lasted 12 innings, 4 hours and 41 minutes.

It also set up even more changes, and set the stage for one of the best surprises in Tribe history—the 1997 team.

Hart and Hargrove, the Tribe's Odd Couple

John Hart would wake up in the middle of the night, turn on the light and make a list.

Trade possibilities.

Available free agents.

Payroll projections.

Possible promotions from the farm system.

The lists never ended. The man slept, but not more than five hours most nights.

"John is a guy in perpetual motion," Hargrove said in a 1995 interview. "With him, everything is go . . . Go . . . GO! It's do . . . Do . . . DO! He concentrates on the team for 20 hours a day."

Hargrove paused, then explained: "If I tried to keep John's pace, I would just get overloaded. I usually work 12-14 hours a day, but I like to get away from baseball for a few hours each day. If I don't, I'm not as productive."

This interview was done before the Tribe won anything in 1995. The year before, the Tribe was 66-47 and one game out of the Central Division lead when the 1994 baseball strike ended the season. In fact, Hargrove entered the season in the final year of his contract. Hart didn't want to discuss Hargrove's future beyond 1994. There was a sense that Hart, who had managed in the minors, had significant doubts about Hargrove's ability to transform the team into a contender.

But in July of 1994 when the Tribe was battling the White Sox for first place, Hart signed Hargrove to a guaranteed contract for the 1995 and 1996 seasons, with a team option for 1997.

"I knew Mike was good with a young team, but I wanted to see what he'd do with a contender," Hart said not long after giving Hargrove the new contract.

There was a part of Hart that liked to keep Hargrove a bit on edge, not feeling too secure.

He considered that motivation.

Hargrove thought it was a bit of needless intimidation, that dealing with the stress and second-guessing that comes with managing 162 games a year was more than enough pressure.

"They are different people," said Hamilton.

So true.

You can start with how they looked. Hart was a workout fanatic. In shape. Eat right. Wear expensive suits when needed, or sport shirts that seemed to fit perfectly.

Hargrove battled weight problems near the end of his baseball career, and that continued as a manager. No one would ever say Hargrove was a sloppy dresser, but he wasn't nearly as consumed with clothes as Hart.

After some losses, Hart looked as if his house had just burned down. He was angry, devastated and expecting the worst.

"You can ask anyone who knows me," said Hart. "We'd have a 10-game lead in September and I was a nervous wreck, waiting for the other shoe to drop. And even after we won, I was worried about our players getting into trouble in the [nightclubs] in the Flats. I always could find something to worry about."

So Hamilton is right. These were two very, very different people.

The Tribe broadcaster talked about how "Sharon [Hargrove's wife] and the five kids were always No. 1 with Mike. John was married and had a daughter. He thinks the world of his family. But to John, baseball was 24 hours a day, 365 days a year. Mike loved his job but knew baseball had its place. I really thought they were great checks and balances for each other."

But at times, they also drove each other nearly insane.

Hart loved to talk, especially about baseball.

And he enjoyed brainstorming. He'd spend an hour on an idea that seemed to have little basis in reality, simply because he liked the intellectual exercise of pondering what appeared to most people to be imponderable.

Hargrove would sit in meetings where Hart would pull out his lists . . . and there were so many lists . . . and the manager would think, "I can't try all these things."

And he'd think, "Why are we even talking about this idea—no way it can happen."

And he'd think, "Johnny Mac [John McNamara] always told me that I had to get along with the general manager. So be patient."

And Hargrove would, at times, bite down on his lower lip when the meetings took strange turns. But he endured.

It took him years to understand that Hart was hoping that in his list of perhaps 10 ideas, one or two would be worthy of being used by the manager.

After all, part of what made the Tribe a contender in the 1990s was the creativity of the front office in areas such as long-term contracts for young players and trading veterans such as Joe Carter for top prospects.

Hargrove also had times when he thought Hart was micromanaging him, that the general manager didn't trust him.

That was especially true early in their relationship, in the 1992–94 seasons.

Hart often said, "I like spirited debates."

Hargrove considered some of them more like criticisms. Hargrove knew that Hart had managed in the minors. And that Hart had managed the Indians for 19 games at the end of the 1989 season. And Hart sure sounded as if he thought he could manage the Indians in the middle 1990s, or at least that's how Hargrove felt during some of their meetings.

One of Hart's management styles was to challenge the people who worked for him, to create an argument to see how convinced the person was of his point of view. Hart would do that even if he agreed with Hargrove, just to make sure Hargrove was positive of what he planned to do. Hargrove would grow weary of the back-and-forth conversations. After a while, they seemed confrontational for no apparent reason.

As Hargrove said early in 1995, "John needed to see that I was just as intense in my own way as John was . . . and I needed to be confident enough to tell John, 'That's really not a good idea.' "

"Communication is the key," said Hart. "The three key people are the owner, the general manager and the manager. They have to be connected. I wanted my manager to know what was going on, so that's why I had Mike included in everything all the way up to the ownership level. Mike sat in meetings that he probably would rather have skipped because they had to do with economics and things like that. But I wanted him to know the economic challenges that we were facing. When there is a lack of communication, and the owner/general manager/manager don't know what's going on—things can get sideways real fast. I could walk into the clubhouse and manager's office as a former baseball guy and understand what was happening on the field. Mike sat in the owner's meetings, and he knew he was part of the process when we talked about the big-picture things."

Over the years, some Tribe fans have forgotten that Hargrove was an excellent player, a .290 hitter in 12 big-league seasons. Maybe they have seen old video of Hargrove at the bat. He was the "Human Rain Delay," stepping out of the box after every pitch, tugging on his batting gloves, adjusting his helmet and engaging in other nervous habits before stepping back up to the plate.

But it was more than that.

Hargrove was an extremely selective hitter. Four times in his career, he drew at least 101 walks. He usually worked deep into counts. He fouled off a lot of pitches. His career on-base percentage was .396.

In some ways, he was like that as a manager.

He was careful about what he said, measuring each word. He was the same way in meetings with the front office. All ideas—like all pitches—aren't anywhere close to being considered equal.

No matter if you're talking politics or baseball, Hargrove was a steady, conservative Texan. He believed that at times, "less was more." He didn't quite say it that way, but a few well-chosen words can deliver greater impact than a long, emotion-fueled speech.

Hart was so passionate about baseball, and he would have loved to have had Hargrove's playing career. But three seasons and making it as far as Class AA was the peak.

When Hargrove joined the Tribe coaching staff in 1990, he already was a name to Tribe fans. Most believed he would end up as the manager—and that he should end up as the manager. That was especially true because he spent four years in the minors, coaching and managing at each level.

Hart was a nobody to Tribe fans.

Assistant General Manager Dan O'Dowd never even played pro ball. And like Hart, his name had no value in baseball circles because there was no major-league playing career attached to it when he arrived in Cleveland.

O'Dowd was like Hart . . . wired . . . relentless.

"John and Danny were very proactive," said Hamilton. "They were aggressive, and in a good way. They thought out of the baseball box, and they had to do that to be a success with the Indians. You couldn't do things the same way as most other teams. And they were more emotional than Mike."

Hamilton believes Hart and O'Dowd "brought out the best in Mike, but Mike did the same for them . . . There were times when Mike would say, 'I know you want to react [with a player move], but you've got to sit back and let this play out for a while . . . it's a long season.' " Hamilton paused, then added, "Grover could pull Danny and John off the ledge if he felt they were over-reacting to a losing streak or something like that . . . But they also could push Grover when they thought he was just being too patient."

Hart said that he had seen some general managers who were almost afraid to confront their manager, but Hart promised himself, "I'll never let my team run away" because his grip on the situation was too loose.

In 1994, Hargrove was content to let Manny Ramirez open the season in the minors. Ramirez was 21 at the end of spring training. He had played only 40 games in Class AAA. Yes, he batted .317 with 14 homers in 145 at-bats. But Ramirez was so inexperienced in the field and on the bases. He also had a tendency to try to pull too many pitches.

But Hart said Manny's time was right now.

Hart insisted he never told Hargrove or any manager "who to play or where they bat in the order," but Hart did pick the final roster. He made the trades. And you can be sure he had lots of suggestions about who should play.

As Hart once said, "I'm pretty flexible, but there are times when a general manager has to tell his manager, 'This is how it will be . . .' "

And there were times when Hargrove saved Hart from making an emotion-driven move that could have been very damaging to the team.

It was Hart who suggested that the Hargrove put a failed starter named Jose Mesa into the bullpen.

"In spring training [of 1995], I remember John saying how Mesa could be a closer," recalled Mark Shapiro. "He said closers came from strange places. But he wanted a guy with a power arm, and that was Mesa."

In 1993, Mesa was 10-12 with a 4.92 ERA as a starter for the Tribe.

In 1994, Mesa was put in the bullpen (7-5, 3.82 ERA), but was 2 of 6 in save situations. He didn't appear to have the composure to handle the pressure of the ninth inning.

"After Steve Olin died [in the 1993 boating accident], we went through so many closers," said Hamilton. "We were desperate to find someone."

In 1994, no reliever had more than five saves. Those who tried to close were Jeff Russell, Steve Farr, Eric Plunk and Paul Shuey.

One of the most amazing aspects of the 1995 season was how Mesa saved 46 of 48 games. He had a 1.13 ERA. And this was right in the middle of the Steroid Era. In 1995, the average American League pitcher had a 4.71 ERA.

Hart consistently found strong arms and put them in bullpen. Besides Mesa, other examples were Danys Baez, Eric Plunk, Steve Karsay and Paul Shuey.

"People still don't quite understand what we did in Cleveland," said Hart. "We had to strip the franchise down to bare bones—trade guys like Brook Jacoby, Greg Swindell and Joe Carter. We couldn't keep winning 72 games or whatever. A lot of clubs can't do that—strip it bare—because they are in larger markets and there are great expectations. But Cleveland could because we had a few years before moving into the new stadium. Strip it clean, get as many good prospects as possible and give them time to develop."

That's easier on the front office than the manager.

Young players make so many mistakes. Young players often make the manager and coaching staff look bad because it seems as if they don't know the basics. Well, they don't—and part of the reason is they have been rushed to the majors by the front office, which wants the young guys to play.

For example, Manny Ramirez and Albert Belle were not ready to play the outfield in the big leagues when the Tribe promoted them to Cleveland. But they could hit. And they hit so much, they didn't pay a lot of attention to the coaches who tried to help them defensively.

"Mike was a manager who was very secure in his own skin," said Hart. "He was the perfect manager for a young club because he was a player's guy."

And once the team bloomed in the middle 1990s, Hargrove was viewed as a manager with a lot of talent.

If the team won, it was because Hart had acquired the players and because the players were terrific.

If the team lost, it was because Hargrove didn't maximize the talent.

Consider that Hart was twice named the Sporting News Executive of the Year (1994 and 1995), but Hargrove never was voted Manager of the Year.

During the 1995 season, Detroit Manager Sparky Anderson told Hargrove, "Kid, I want you to know that I appreciate the job you are doing. You're a good manager. We all see that. But you also need to understand that you'll never get the credit you deserve because your ball club is so good . . . You really won't get the credit for being a good manager until you are gone."

Anderson was speaking from his own experience managing the Big Red Machine of the 1970s in Cincinnati.

The other reasons more positive press went to Hart was that Hart is a natural salesman and promoter.

During one playoff series, Hart rode his motorcycle on to the field during batting practice of a day off between games.

"The guys still joke about that when I see them," said Hargrove.

Hargrove knew that the best managers didn't take credit for success—they gave it to the players. He had played for some managers who were self-promoters. Hargrove knew players resented managers who took that approach.

He vowed never to be that kind of manager, so he remained low-key.

"Some of those teams were not easy to manage because of all the egos," said Hamilton. "Mike never was given enough credit for the job he did as manager. There were so many times when it seemed the thing could crash and burn, but it never did until the 1999 playoffs. John and Mike had a very long run together."

They won five consecutive Central Division titles (1995–1999), and made two trips to the World Series (1995 and 1997). Their record together was 721-591 (.550), and they were the most successful general manager/manager combination in Tribe history in terms of reaching the postseason.

"I thought our relationship was mis-characterized," said Hargrove. "John and I disagreed on a lot of things, but never to the point where we shouted or were mad at each other for weeks on end and didn't talk. There was friction at times, perhaps more than there sometimes needed to be. But it was never bad friction. Most of the time, it was healthy. John is an emotional guy, not the most patient guy in the world."

Hargrove generally is subdued, and his patience often paid off.

"Grover let us be ourselves," said Kenny Lofton. "We were a different bunch, a special group. We had swagger. Other teams didn't like us. We were strong personalities, and Grover knew how to deal with us."

Omar Vizquel expressed the same opinion, and told the story of how catcher Tony Pena would go to the mound and sometimes sort of whack Mesa in the chest with a catcher's mitt.

"One time, Pena hit him in the face and we were thinking, 'What's that guy doing?' " said Vizquel. "But Mike knew that sometimes you had to let the players take care of things between themselves."

And Pena was one of the most respected veterans on the team, while Mesa had concentration problems on the mound.

"We had our own special chemistry," said Vizquel. "We had some really fun guys, and some very intense guys. Some people may have looked at us like the Bad News Bears, but we loved to play."

Hargrove said one of his main jobs was to "have a calming impact on a team where so many people were highly charged."

He said that several times a year, "I had guys in my office and I was trying to talk them down off [the emotional] edge."

One of Hart's comments about his manager was that Hargrove "could walk into a clubhouse that was in total disarray and walk out the other side about 15 minutes later—and everyone had calmed down and was starting to get along."

Hargrove talked about how the best teams had "veterans who help the players police themselves."

The Indians had that with Eddie Murray, Orel Hershiser and Sandy

Alomar. There were others. But in the 1994–95 seasons when the Tribe was learning how to win, those three stood out.

"Mike understood those teams so well," said Mark Shapiro. "He knew when to get involved with something, and when to let it be. He took a unique group and found a way to have them play together. Part of it was that he never panicked . . . I mean, NEVER. He managed that way because it's consistent with who he is as a person. He had a lot of experience and wisdom from being a very good player for a long time. There was some craziness around the team back then with all the personalities, but his calmness was exactly what we needed."

The only knock on Hargrove's managerial record in Cleveland was his failure to win a World Series.

"Let's think about 1995, losing to the Braves," said Shapiro. "Atlanta had [Greg] Maddux, [Tom] Glavine and John Smoltz in the rotation. That's three Hall of Famers."

In 1997, Hargrove may have done his best managerial job with the Tribe. That team had lost Albert Belle (free agency) and Lofton (trade). It had a modest 86-75 record. Yet, it reached the World Series. Florida was the superior team that year, owning a 92-70 record. But the Indians could have won it in seven games had Mesa held a ninth-inning lead.

Hart and Hargrove say they have never watched a complete tape of that game—too painful.

"When you get in the playoffs and World Series, it's a crapshoot," said Hamilton. "Bobby Cox won one World Series. All those great pitchers, and he won only one. Earl Weaver . . . another great manager with all those great pitchers . . . he won only one World Series. To hold that against Mike is ridiculous."

Hart thinks back to the 1990s and remembers "the festive atmosphere, the horns honking after games and how our guys just BURST on the scene. I never took it for granted, and Mike was part of that."

Hargrove said fans often come up to him "and say thanks for all the good times in the 1990s. We had so much fun."

Hargrove smiles and then says, "I had even more fun than you did!"

Jaret Wright: One Special Season

"It's hard to believe."

Those words were spoken by Jaret Wright when he visited Progressive Field in 2013.

Wright could have been talking about 1997, when he went from pitching the first game ever at Akron's Canal Park to starting the last game of the season in Game 7 of the World Series.

That was when Wright was 21 years old.

But this Jaret Wright was 37, and he was thinking about something else.

"My last game was here," he said.

Wright was remembering April 29, 2007.

"I was pitching for the Orioles," he said. "I lasted only a few innings."

The Tribe was headed to the playoffs that 2007 season. Wright allowed three runs in three innings.

"The day after that game in Cleveland, I called Dr. [Lewis] Yocum," Wright said. "He had done both of my shoulder surgeries. I wanted to know if there was anything else he could do."

No, said the doctor.

"There was nothing left in my shoulder to operate on," he said.

Wright shook his head and smiled.

He doesn't want anyone's sympathy for a career that ended at the age of 31, a career that never came close to its enormous promise of 1997.

Yes, hard to believe, because Jaret Wright seemed indestructible in 1997.

"I never felt nervous back then," he said. "I was throwing 95 . . . even 100 miles an hour. I'd just aim for the middle of the plate and watch the ball move. I'd even look back at the scoreboard and see how hard I threw."

He laughed, almost as if he were talking about someone else.

"The first time I came to Cleveland was in 1994," he said. "I had just been drafted [No. 10 in the first round] and the Indians had just signed me. I was there with my parents. We were in one of the suites, and they put my name up on the scoreboard during the game. It blew me away, I thought that was so cool."

Jay Robertson was the scouting director who pushed for Wright to be the Tribe's pick. On the conference call after Wright was drafted, Robertson predicted Wright would throw "harder than Tom Seaver, harder than Roger Clemens . . . maybe harder than anyone . . . ever."

Wright felt that way.

"I figured if I could throw hard enough, no one could hit it," he said.

Wright is the son of Clyde Wright, a former major-league pitcher who had a career 100-111 record with a 3.50 ERA. In 1970, he was a 22-game winner for the Angels.

His son grew up in Anaheim, and loved to surf in the Pacific Ocean. He also played football for Katella High, where he was a star linebacker. In baseball, he was being clocked at 94 mph by scouts as a junior. Scouts love young pitchers who light up the radar gun. It makes it easy to draft them high. You can teach a pitcher to throw a curve. You can convince him that he needs a change-up. But you can't teach someone to throw 94 mph at the age of 17. That's God-given. That's pure physical talent. And yes, that's a multi-million dollar arm.

And Wright had it.

Even better, his father had taught him an effective overhand curveball that broke more than a foot down along with darting away from right-handed batters.

The scouts who saw Seaver and Clemens in high school had flashbacks when watching Wright. He was featured in a small story in Sports Illustrated as one of the best high school pitchers in the country. As a senior, Wright was 6-foot-2 and 220 pounds. He had a 7-2 record with a 2.98 ERA, including 100 strikeouts in 75 innings.

Robertson said he had never seen a pitcher with Wright's ability. The Indians had never paid more than a $650,000 bonus for an amateur player.

Wright signed for $1.2 million, plus another $80,000 if he wanted to attend college.

It's fascinating to look back at the top of the 1994 draft. Here are the top 10 picks:

1. Paul Wilson, Mets.
2. Ben Grieve, A's.
3. Dustin Hermanson, Padres.
4. Antone Williamson, Brewers.
5. Josh Booty, Marlins.
6. McKay Christensen, Angels.
7. Doug Million, Rockies.
8. Todd Walker, Twins.
9. C.J. Nitkowski, Reds.
10. Wright, Indians.

The best players in that first round were selected not long after Wright—Nomar Garciaparra (No. 12 to the Red Sox) and Paul Konerko (No. 13 to the Dodgers).

While the Indians would have loved to have picked Garciaparra or Konerko over Wright, no one in the draft could have delivered the immediate results that Wright did for the Tribe in 1997.

At the start of 1997, the Tribe had no idea that Wright would soon be in Cleveland.

In 1996, he was 7-4 with a 2.50 ERA at Class A Kinston. He missed two months with a broken jaw. He was at a Class A All-Star Game when he walked into a player taking a practice swing with a bat. He needed surgery, but recovered in time to pitch in the final month of the season.

Wright was 3-3 with a 3.67 ERA in eight starts for Class AA Akron to open 1997. He was averaging 10 strikeouts per nine innings, and the Tribe moved him up to Class AAA Buffalo. Wright was 4-1 with a 1.80 ERA in seven starts.

"Jaret had dominant stuff," said Mark Shapiro. "I was minor-league director at this time, and John [Hart] was in love with Jaret. It was more than his stuff. He was fearless, absolutely fearless. He thought he could beat anyone. Being the son of a big-leaguer took away some of the awe factor. Jaret wasn't polished, and he could just out-stuff people. Pure talent. One of the things I was doing was trying to get John to be patient with Jaret."

Hart was never afraid to rush a player who had tremendous physical gifts. He agreed with Charlie Manuel in the spring of 2001, when CC Sabathia was promoted to the majors without even pitching in Class AAA.

Manny Ramirez roared through the farm system in slightly less than three seasons to make it to Cleveland.

Wright had only 342 minor league innings when he came to Cleveland. That was June 24, 1997, at what was then an always sold-out Jacobs Field. He beat Minnesota, 10-5.

"Back then, I never was nervous," he said. "I was ready for anything."

He believed the big leagues were his destiny, part of his birthright. His fastball was consistently in the 95-99 mph range. He had an angry slider that sliced the outside corner against right-handed hitters.

"I felt like I could just blow people away," he recalled.

"He has no fear," Omar Vizquel often said of Wright that season.

The Indians didn't worry much about the future in 1997. They were desperately trying to return to the World Series—or at least, the playoffs. The starting rotation was a disaster after Charlie Nagy (15-11, 4.28 ERA) and Orel Hershiser (14-6, 4.47). And both of those guys seemed to be working the corners, not as sharp as in the past.

After Nagy and Hershiser, no one else won more than eight games. Chad Ogea was 8-9 with a 4.99 ERA and Wright was 8-3, 4.38.

They had Jack McDowell (3-3, 5.09) with his cranky elbow and sour disposition. There was John Smiley (2-4, 5.54) who broke his arm while warming up. That's right, Smiley's arm shattered throwing in the bullpen.

"Jaret had a very violent [pitching] motion," said Shapiro. "It would have been nice to take our time, smooth out his motion. But he was just overpowering people. He was ready in terms of talent—and we needed him. You needed to be there in 1997 to feel the sense of urgency that we did."

So the Indians turned to Wright and his atomic arm that seemed to make a fastball explode on the way to home plate.

Pitch counts?

The Indians paid attention, but most teams didn't use 100 as a warning sign as they do today.

Wright started 16 games for the Tribe that season, and threw at least 106 pitches in seven of those starts. He heaved the ball to the plate 134 times in a 6-3 victory over Oakland in July.

"I didn't care about pitch counts," he said. "I never wanted to come out of a game. We were in the pennant race. My arm never bothered me."

Wright paused, thinking back to 1997.

"When I didn't know what to do, I'd just rear back and throw harder," said Wright. "I had sort of a violent motion. I remember Charlie Nagy telling me that I could hurt my arm throwing like that. Charlie talked about dealing with his elbow problems . . . I was like, 'Hey, that's never going to happen to me.' "

He paused again.

"I was cocky," he said. "I felt invincible."

Why not? The Tribe was 12-4 in the 16 games that he started. He was 7-0 when pitching after a Tribe loss. By the end of the 1997 regular season, Wright had emerged as the Tribe's best starter. This was the peak of the Steroids Era. The average American League team had a 4.56 ERA.

The Indians opened the 1997 playoffs against the Yankees. Wright started Game 2 in New York and beat the Yankees, allowing three runs in six innings.

"Really, I never was nervous back then," he said. "It's hard to explain, but it was just a feeling that I had."

When Wright faced the media in New York before his first playoff start in Yankee Stadium, he said: "There's a lot going on. People are yelling at you—and I don't even know these people."

And he said it with the tone of a self-assured 21-year-old who could care less about those New Yorkers.

"What? Am I supposed to act like I'm scared to death?" he told the reporters in that packed media room. "That's just not me."

Hargrove compared Wright to a young Roger Clemens.

Now, that sounds ridiculous.

But if you saw Jaret Wright in 1997, it seemed possible.

Everything seemed possible back then.

He beat the Yankees twice in that series.

"I never felt surprised to be there," Wright said at the time.

He meant the majors. The playoffs. And yes, the World Series.

Wright won Game 5 of the Yankee series, sending the Tribe into the ALCS against Baltimore.

He pitched only once against the Orioles, shelled for five runs in three innings.

But in the World Series, he won Game 4 and held Florida in check.

When it came to Game 7, Manager Mike Hargrove had to decide between Wright and Nagy.

"Grover told me that one of the toughest things he had to do was tell Charlie that he wasn't starting Game 7," said Hamilton. "That was Charlie's game to pitch. He was the leader of the staff. Grover thought the world of Charlie, and Charlie had been such a warrior for all those years."

Nagy had one excellent start in the postseason—7⅓ scoreless innings against Baltimore.

But in his other three starts, he gave up 13 earned runs in 15⅓ innings. His only start in the World Series produced five runs allowed in six innings.

Wright held Florida to three runs in six innings in Game 4. That was his third postseason victory. No one second-guessed Hargrove's decision. Wright was the team's best and hottest pitcher at that point.

"Grover called me the night before and said I was starting," said Wright. "He wanted to know I how I felt."

Wright said he felt good.

"Back then, I always felt good," he recalled. "I didn't stay up worrying or anything, I just went to sleep."

Before the game, Wright told the reporters in the media room: "When you dream, you don't dream about pitching in the playoffs or in the first round. It's always the World Series. You dream about the World Series."

Wright allowed one run in 6⅓ innings in a game the Tribe lost 3-2 in the bottom of the 11th—Nagy taking the loss.

"Given the magnitude of the game, it was one of the greatest performances that I have ever seen," said Hamilton.

That was Jaret Wright's 21st major-league start. Including the playoffs, he threw at least 106 pitches in 10 of those starts.

But at that point, who was counting? The goal was to do whatever it took to win the World Series.

"Also, I don't know how much pitch counts factored into what happened with Jaret," said Shapiro. "He had a violent . . . and I mean VIOLENT . . . delivery. It put so much stress on his arm. Could we have changed it? I don't know. But in 1997, no one was talking about changing anything about Jaret's mechanics. He was pitching so well. But we did know that his delivery—more than the pitch counts—put stress on his arm."

After the 1997 season, John Hart faced a huge decision.

Assistant General Manager Dan O'Dowd "found out that Montreal wanted to trade Pedro Martinez," said Hamilton.

The Expos had a list with the names of three pitchers, in this order:

1. Jaret Wright.
2. Carl Pavano.
3. Bartolo Colon.

"The Indians could have gotten Pedro if they gave up Wright and Colon," said Hamilton. "But put yourself back after the 1997 World Series. How could you trade Jaret Wright?"

Remember, he was the next Roger Clemens. The next Tom Seaver. Even Bob Feller was impressed by Wright.

Martinez was a year away from free agency, and his price tag would be high.

But the real holdup was Wright.

"The Indians tried to build a package around Colon and others," said Hamilton. "But the Expos really wanted Wright. After that, they turned to Boston for Pavano."

In 1997, Colon was 4-7 with a 5.65 ERA. He had arm troubles in 1996, and pitched only 77 innings that year in the minors. So Wright was a far more attractive prospect.

"If you look back, two things happened that hurt the Indians," said Hamilton. "First, they didn't trade for Martinez because at that point, it was almost impossible to give up Wright. Second, Wright failed to turn into an ace."

* * *

In 1998, Wright was 12-10 with a 4.72 ERA.

Occasionally, his shoulder ached. Hitters also began to not swing at his high, rising fastball. His walks piled up.

He was crushed for seven runs in two innings, starting against the Angels in his hometown of Anaheim. He still had some sensational starts, but others were disasters.

The playoffs went from a dreamlike 3-0 record in 1997 to 0-2 with a 9.82 ERA in the 1998 postseason.

By 1999, he lost confidence in and velocity on his fastball. He was 8-10 with a 6.06 ERA. He was on the disabled list twice with shoulder and back issues.

He hit two batters in the head, one with a curveball. He was suspended for five games for throwing at batters.

"At that point, I was a mess," said Wright. "I was hurting physically. My control was shot. I didn't want to hit anyone in the head. I had wanted to come inside like I always did, but I'm telling you—there were games when I didn't know where the ball was going."

In 1999, he walked 5.2 per nine innings, compared to 3.5 in 1997. He hit seven batters in 133 innings, not excessive. But he was labeled a headhunter.

"Suddenly, I knew how Charlie [Nagy] felt when he said you can't pitch like you know you should because your arm doesn't feel right," said Wright. "It's so frustrating. You can't get healthy."

Wright had shoulder surgery in 2000.

"You get scared," he said. "I was a right-handed pitcher. It was not like I could learn to pitch with my left arm. A position player, he can come back from more injuries because he doesn't depend as much on one part of his body like a pitcher does. Maybe an outfielder can move to first base or DH. But a pitcher has to be able to throw."

He had elbow surgery in the spring of 2001.

He had a second shoulder surgery in the fall of 2001.

Remember how Wright said he "never felt nervous" when first coming to Cleveland?

"Now, I was nervous every time I was coming back from surgery," he said. "I was wondering if I'd ever pitch again—or how would I be able to pitch?"

In 2002, Wright was 2-3 with a 15.71 ERA for the Tribe. They didn't offer him a contract for 2003.

"I then went to San Diego," he said. "I was like the last guy in the bullpen, the mop-up guy. It was humbling. I'd sit out there and wonder what had happened to me . . . and if I'd ever pitch again. Getting hurt is so hard. There is depression. The team is playing, and you're not. As a kid, you are taught to play through pain."

In August 2003, he was claimed off waivers by Atlanta.

"My arm felt good and I really learned how to pitch," he said. Pitching coach Leo Mazzone "taught me to pound the outside corner at the knees. I was a different kind of pitcher, not throwing as hard. But I loved to pitch again."

Wright was 15-8 with a 3.28 ERA for the Braves in 2004.

That winter, he signed a 3-year, $21 million deal with the Yankees. The arm problems returned.

"I never was the same after that," he said.

In Wright's 1997 season, he threw 216 innings beginning with that game at Akron and ending in the World Series.

All that at the age of 21.

The next year, it was 203⅔ innings . . . at the age of 22.

That wouldn't happen now in the age of coddling pitchers.

"I never think about the innings I threw," he said. "I wanted to pitch all the time. I felt great."

But wasn't the heavy workload behind his injury problems?

"I don't think it's why I got hurt," he said. "Who knows why you hurt your arm? Some guys, they count all their pitches and keep the innings low—and they still get hurt."

Wright looks back in wonder at 1997.

"It was an amazing time," said Wright. "The city loved us. We'd walk into a restaurant and people would stand up and clap."

Members of the great Tribe teams of the 1990s seldom had to buy a dinner or a drink. Some of his teammates told him to cut back on the nightlife.

Wright admitted, "I made some bad decisions back then. What did I know? I was 21."

And he thought it would last forever.

"The good thing about struggling is it humbles you and you learn from it," he said. "I still wish we could have won Game 7. That's my only regret with the Indians. It would have meant so much to the city."

When Wright retired at the age of 31, "it was a relief," he said. "I was so tired of getting my butt kicked. It was so frustrating. I remember Charlie Nagy telling me that if you play a while, you will get hurt. If you play long enough, it seems everything hurts. That's how I was at the end."

Wright is very upbeat, a father of four children under the age of 9. He made about $30 million in baseball, so money is not an issue.

"I play in a coed softball team with my wife," he said. "I play with the kids. I surf. I play golf. There is a void [from not playing]. But I'm grateful I got to pitch. I loved being with the Indians, I really did."

Herb Score's Quick Goodbye

Nearly every year during the All-Star break, Herb Score would take his wife Nancy to see their financial advisor.

"Herb would go over his investments and talk a little about retirement," said Nancy.

After they'd leave, Herb usually said something like, "I guess I have to keep working for another year."

But this time, it was different. It was the All-Star break of 1997. Nancy and Herb had been married for 40 years.

"We were told that we could retire and pretty much have the same standard of living," said Nancy. "Herb didn't say much when we were in the office."

They returned to the car, and then Herb looked at her and said, "I guess that's it, I'm going to retire."

Nancy laughed as she told the story in 2014. There was no discussion. "You'd have to know Herb," she said. "Once he made his mind up, that was it. His feeling was once we were ready to retire financially, we'd retire."

Then Herb told her not to tell anyone.

"He didn't want people to make a big deal about it," she said. "I was sworn to secrecy."

Score went back to doing the games on radio as if nothing was different.

"I had no clue what was going on," said Tom Hamilton.

They had been paired up since 1990.

"Herb is a very private person," said Hamilton. "We got along great. But Herb was not going to tell you much about his personal life unless he wanted you to know."

So while Nancy knew her husband's plans in July of 1997, virtually no one else did.

After the 1996 season, the Baltimore Orioles approached Hamilton about becoming their lead radio broadcaster, replacing Jon Miller.

"As flattering as that was, I really didn't want to leave Cleveland," said Hamilton. "And Jon Miller was an icon in Baltimore. It's not smart to replace an icon."

The Orioles had to receive permission from the Indians to interview Hamilton. After talking to Baltimore, the Tribe front office held a meeting with Hamilton.

"They said they had no idea how long Herb wanted to keep doing the games," said Hamilton. "I told them that the last thing I wanted was any sense that I was trying to force Herb out."

The two sides talked for a while, then the Indians said, "We know how you feel about Herb. We feel the same way. Here's our idea. We will pay you like a No. 1 broadcaster. You just keep working with Herb as you have always done. It can be for another year, another 10 years. Whatever Herb wants to do, but we want to give you a contract extension right now."

Hamilton nearly jumped out of his seat. "I was ecstatic!"

It was the perfect solution. He would be paid like a No. 1 broadcaster. And he would become the No. 1 broadcaster whenever Score retired. But it was up to Score to decide how long he wanted to continue.

Hamilton signed the extension.

"I can never thank the Indians enough for how they have treated me," said Hamilton. "At this point in my career, Wendy and I had four kids. The money in Baltimore would have really helped. But we didn't want to leave Cleveland. I was ready to spend the next 10 years working with Herb."

It was early August of 1997. Hamilton can't remember the exact date.

"I just remember it was a home game," he said. "Between innings, we'd take off our headsets and shoot the breeze a bit, nothing very important."

Suddenly, Score said, "Oh, Tom, I almost forgot. I want to tell you that I'm quitting at the end of the year."

Hamilton just stared at Score. Immediately, he knew that his partner wasn't kidding. He had never joked about retirement. He never even talked about retirement, except in some vague terms.

Once in a while, Score would say he planned to retire "and do nothing . . . I'm very good at doing nothing."

But Hamilton never had serious conversations about it with Score.

"Herb, we gotta talk about this," said Hamilton.

Behind Hamilton, the engineer said, "Ten seconds to air time."

Score smiled and put his headset back on.

"I was doing play-by-play," said Hamilton. "We're back to doing the game and Herb is getting the biggest charge out of dropping this on me in the middle of the game. I couldn't wait for the inning to be over."

When the inning ended, Hamilton took off his headset and said, "Herb, what are you talking about?"

"It's time," he said. "This is going to be it."

"But Herb . . . " said Hamilton.

"I just talked to Dennis [Executive Vice President Dennis Lehman] earlier in the day, and I wanted you to know," said Score.

As the game went on, they kept having a discussion between innings.

"I was trying to talk him out of it," said Hamilton. "I kept asking him why."

Score told Hamilton about his trip to the financial advisor.

"He said that if I wanted to, I could quit and still have the same lifestyle," said Score. "The moment he said that, I knew I was done."

Then Score made Hamilton promise not to tell anyone.

A few days later, the Indians came to Hamilton and said, "Herb doesn't know this, but we plan to honor him later in the season."

And the Indians made Hamilton promise not to tell Score.

"So I was keeping secrets from everyone," Hamilton said, laughing. "Herb eventually found out. There was a press conference for him. But he really didn't want to do it."

Or as Nancy Score said, "When Herb said he was done with something, he was done."

"Herb was one of those people who looked at life through the windshield, not the rearview mirror," said Hamilton. "He never spent time thinking about what could have been, or going over things from the past. He hated to talk about his career or the old days. He was never a guy to ask 'Why me?' about anything."

Hamilton said part of the reason was Score's strong Catholic faith.

"We used to go to Mass together every Sunday morning on the road," said Hamilton. "One of the first times, he told me to meet him in the lobby at 7:20. I think I got there at 7:21. He was gone."

Later, Hamilton saw Score and asked, "Herb, did you forget about me?"

Score said, "Nobody was there at 7:20."

From that point, Hamilton was always at least five minutes early when meeting Score.

"We once went to a Mass and I looked around and everyone else was Vietnamese," said Hamilton. "I mentioned that to Herb, and he said, 'It's Catholic. We're here. It still counts!' "

Score always went to church in a suit and tie.

"Didn't matter if it was 95 degrees, that's how Herb dressed not just for church—but any time he went out on the road," said Hamilton.

Hamilton said Score's attitude was that all games were important, that there should be no difference for a broadcaster between a regular-season and a playoff game.

"Herb took pride in staying on an even keel," said Hamilton.

But in their eight years together, there was one exception. The Indians were playing in Baltimore. It was Game 6 of the 1997 American League Championship Series.

"It's the top of the 11th inning," said Hamilton. "There were two outs, the score was 0-0. Tony Fernandez was the batter, and he hit a homer."

Then Hamilton was stunned to see Score become so excited, he jumped out of his chair.

"Never in eight years did I see Herb do that," he said.

Then Score proclaimed, "And the Indians are going back to the World Series!"

Hamilton stared at him. Suddenly, Score remembered that the game was in Baltimore. It wasn't over. The Orioles still had to bat in the bottom of the 11th inning.

So Score added: "Maybe."

That's right, "The Indians are going back to the World Series . . . Maybe!"

The perfect call from a man who had watched so much bad Cleveland baseball for so long, a man who knew all that could go wrong.

"After Herb said 'Maybe,' he sat back down and continued to do the game as always," said Hamilton.

Score's final game was Game 7 of the 1997 World Series, a game the Tribe lost 3-2 to Florida in 11 innings.

Edgar Renteria singled off Charles Nagy to drive in the winning run.

Score simply said, "Line drive. Base hit. The game is over."

So were the dreams of a World Series parade in Cleveland, something Score never had a chance to see despite doing the games for 34 years.

"And so that is the season for 1997," he said. "And there's very little else we can say except to tell you it's been a pleasure. I would like to thank all the fans for their kindness over the years. You've been very good to me. And we hope that whoever sits in this chair next, you'll be as kind to them as you have been to me."

Score paused, then said, "Tom will be back with the post-game show."

Hamilton said The Plain Dealer had a writer and a photographer in the booth to cover Score's final game.

"The photographer said that he must be coming back, right?" said Hamilton.

Hamilton told the man, "Oh, no. He's gone."

Hamilton next saw Score on the team bus.

"People were sobbing, just sobbing," said Hamilton.

Not just because it was Score's last game, but because the Indians were so close to winning the World Series.

"I looked over at Herb and he said, 'Well, that's that,'" said Hamilton. "And that was it for Herb."

Score dealt with a lot of health problems in his retirement, including a series of very severe strokes. He died in 2008 at the age of 75.

Score did his first Tribe game when he was 30, his last when he was 64.

Dick Jacobs Knew When to Buy . . . and Sell

Tom Hamilton believes that most fans never fully understood the essence of Dick Jacobs.

"At the end of the day, he was always a businessman," explained Hamilton. "Emotion never entered into the equation with Dick. He didn't make his money in sports. He wasn't a huge sports fan growing up. His way of doing business was to 'take the emotion out of it.' That's how he viewed it. And he believed that your biggest mistakes were when you made decisions based on emotion."

Hamilton then told this story about the man who owned the Tribe from November of 1986 through the end of the 1999 baseball season. It was 1996 and Hamilton was walking through the newly opened South Park Mall in the Cleveland suburb of Strongsville. It was a shopping palace, and Jacobs owned and developed the property. Hamilton was raving about all the new stores, the layout—everything state of the art when it came to massive indoor shopping centers.

Hamilton was asked by Jacobs to be the master of ceremonies at an event at the mall.

"I wasn't about to turn him down," said Hamilton, laughing.

As they walked through the mall, Jacobs stopped and told Hamilton, "Take a good look around."

Hamilton did.

Jacobs then said, "You'll never see another one of these again."

A startled Hamilton asked, "What do you mean?"

"These are done," said Jacobs. "Malls like this, they're not going to be built any more. There's a new wave coming down the road, and it's not anything like this."

Hamilton started to say that there will always be shopping malls . . . but stopped.

This was Dick Jacobs talking business. And when he talked business and business trends, everyone should listen. And when the man who was one of the pioneers of mega-shopping mall development says that the day of those malls would soon be over, it was time to pay attention.

That's because Jacobs never said anything to bring attention to himself. He preferred to listen more than talk, and only those closest to him would hear opinions like the one that Jacobs expressed to Hamilton.

"He had the ability to see what was coming 10 years down the road," said Hamilton. "When was the last time a big shopping mall opened? Now, it's the outdoor malls, not indoor."

Jacobs knew that back in 1996, if not earlier. He sold South Park Mall in 2002.

Hamilton said he forgot about that conversation until the new breed of outdoor malls such as Crocker Park and Legacy Village opened up in the Cleveland area. Jacobs didn't tell Hamilton what was coming next, but Hamilton saw it several years later.

Hamilton had another revealing story from that day at the mall with Jacobs. There was a man running for a state office. Jacobs saw him and told Hamilton, "I don't want that guy anywhere near the microphone. He wasn't invited, and I don't want him saying a word."

Hamilton said he agreed.

"And Tom," said Jacobs. "If he somehow gets to the microphone and speaks, you're fired."

Jacobs said it with a smile, but Hamilton knew Jacobs meant every syllable.

"The man never got near the microphone," said Hamilton. "I had four kids and I loved my job."

Some of those who knew Jacobs said if there was a motto to be put on his tombstone, it should be: BUY LOW, SELL HIGH.

Jacobs grew up in the Goodyear Heights neighborhood of Akron. He often told friends about "smelling the rubber burning" from the nearby tire plants. His father worked at one of them. In a 1995 interview, he talked about cutting lawns for money. He talked about working at Swenson's, a local hamburger joint where carhops still sprint to customers pulling into the parking lot.

"Within a few weeks, I knew the good tippers from the bad ones," he said.

Jacobs made a joke about his "big feet." He talked about how he stepped in front of the other carhops to rush to the cars that would supply the best tips.

One of the reasons he became a brilliant businessman was figuring out where the money would come from—and getting to it first.

"I could spot a big Caddy coming two blocks away," he said. "I'd tell the other guys, 'This one is mine.' "

By 1986, Jacobs and his brother David owned 42 shopping malls across the country. They also owned 18 Wendy's restaurants. He capitalized on people moving to the suburbs by putting up malls in their neighborhoods so they wouldn't have to go into the city to shop.

Later, when so many businessmen were following his example, Jacobs began buying up land in downtown areas and developing office buildings. In the early 1980s, he saw many cities—including Cleveland—heading for a revitalization in their somewhat blighted downtown areas.

One of those depressed properties was the Cleveland Indians.

By the time Jacobs became involved in negotiating for the team, the franchise was owned by a dead man. To be specific, it was the estate of F.J. "Steve" O'Neill.

O'Neill made his money in the trucking industry, and he purchased the team in 1978. He died in 1983. The franchise then went to his estate, and part of the proceeds from the sale was to go to Catholic Charities. His nephew, Patrick O'Neill, was put in charge of finding a buyer. Patrick O'Neill had not been involved with the Tribe before the death of his uncle.

Patrick O'Neill is one of the unsung heroes because he was a novice in this high-level business. He turned down lucrative offers from groups looking to move the franchise elsewhere. The frustration and pressure was weighing on O'Neill, who wondered if he'd ever be able to find the "right buyer" worthy of his uncle's legacy.

"My goal was always to make sure the Indians would stay in Cleveland," O'Neill said in a 1986 interview.

Jacobs also had a goal. Yes, it began with keeping the team in Cleveland. But he also wanted to make a great buy.

"When you talked to people on the inside—people who really knew Dick and how he did business—you learned that he very much wanted to win, but he was also out to make a profit," said Hamilton. "To him, winning games was fun, but he didn't want to lose money in the process."

More than once, Jacobs told associates: "I'm not going to lose money to win."

As Hamilton said, "He was a businessman first. Yes, he wanted the team to win. But he was even more competitive on the business side. The right deal really got his competitive juices flowing."

When Dick Jacobs approached Pat O'Neill, he had one question: "Is this team for sale? No messing around."

Pat O'Neill had spent more than two years sorting through potential buyers. Some in the Cleveland business community wondered if he really wanted to sell the team. Others thought he was a bit paralyzed because he felt such an enormous responsibility to find the right buyer—that his fear of making a mistake caused him to turn down everyone.

Pat O'Neill did want to sell. He was emotionally worn down by the burden of searching for a buyer.

Jacobs stressed his Cleveland-area roots, his real-estate experience and his plan to convince the politicians to build a new ballpark. He talked about how the ballpark was the key to any success in the future for the Indians. Jacobs was prepared to invest in the Tribe, and yes, to lose money for several years. But his eye was on the big payoff—the new ballpark, the winning team and the incredible rise in the value of the franchise.

Pat O'Neill correctly believed that Jacobs would do everything possible to keep the team in Cleveland. It would be a public-relations nightmare for Jacobs to move the baseball team out of his hometown. Yes, Jacobs was a bottom-line guy, but he was not utterly heartless.

Jacobs talked about the kind of deal needed so he could put his plan into action.

When the sale was announced, the price was reported as $40 million.

In reality, it wasn't close to that.

Here's how it broke down:

1. Jacobs paid about $18 million in cash.

2. He assumed the $3 million loan that the O'Neill estate had given the franchise to keep it running the previous two years.

3. He also paid back the $14 million in loans the franchise had from various banks, some of these loans dating back to several ownerships before O'Neill bought the team in 1978.

"Part of the reason that I bought the Indians is that I didn't want them to end up in St. Petersburg or somewhere else," Jacobs said in a 1995 interview. "In the past, some of the owners didn't have the money to run the team. Others had it, but didn't feel comfortable making the investment."

Jacobs structured his deal with waiting several years for the new ballpark in mind. He was willing to carry the debt and take the losses at the old Stadium. He would find the right men to build a winning team on the field. Those three became Hank Peters, John Hart and Dan O'Dowd in the front office. In the meantime, he'd pressure the area politicians to get a new stadium built.

While the eventual bottom line was the real scorecard for Jacobs, never underestimate how he saved baseball for Cleveland. Very few businessmen had the clout and the vision to make what became Jacobs Field a reality. His business acumen also helped him lead the front office.

"I was close to [Assistant General Manager] Dan O'Dowd," said Hamilton. "Dan said when he came to the Indians [in 1988], it was worse than an expansion team. They had a horrible situation at the old stadium with [Browns owner] Art Modell getting all the money from the suites. The concessions contracts were so terrible for the Indians, it was a joke in baseball circles. They had no chance to compete with the lease agreement with Modell. Until they got their own ballpark, they were held hostage."

It took nearly seven years for Jacobs to turn a profit on the Tribe.

In various interviews, he estimated that he lost about $20 million in that span. It's hard to know if that is accurate, but it's possible as the Tribe played at the old Stadium from 1987 to 1993.

But we do know how the bottom line looked after that. When Jacobs decided to turn his franchise into a public company and sell stock, he had to make the financial documents available.

Here's what was revealed:

1993: The Indians made a $3.9 million profit. That was the final year at the old Stadium. Attendance rose from 1.2 million in 1992 to 2.2 million in 1993 as fans came for one last look at the old ballpark. The team also received $3 million as part of an expansion fee from the Colorado Rockies and Florida Marlins.

1994: The team lost $500,000 in the first year at the new stadium. That's because the baseball strike ended the season after the Indians played 113 games, wiping out the final 49.

1995: The team made a profit of $6.7 million.

1996: The team made a $10.2 million profit.

1997: The team made a $22.6 million profit.

1998: The team made a $13.6 million profit.

1999: This was not made public, but estimates are that the team made at least $10 million in the last year that Jacobs owned the team.

So in the last five years that Jacobs owned the team, they made at least $56 million. And that came after the initial loss of $20 million from 1987 to 1992.

The fans also received a lot of victories, home runs and fireworks for their bucks.

But consider that in 1996, the team made $10.2 million. The Indians also declined to make Albert Belle the highest-paid player on the team, allowing him to sign with the White Sox as a free agent. In the spring of 1997, they traded Kenny Lofton after he turned down a contract extension. Rather than lose Lofton (like Belle) to free agency, he was shipped to Atlanta.

And in 1997, the Tribe went to the World Series, and made another $22.6 million.

While the Indians had some top five payrolls during this era, the goal was to make at least an 8 percent profit, according to those who dealt with Jacobs in the Tribe front office. So General Manager John Hart was careful not to chase high-priced free agents from other teams. The biggest contracts usually went to their own players.

Then Jacobs began to sell stock in the team, a deal that would eventually net him another $48 million in profit.

None of this is meant to diminish what Jacobs accomplished. But it is to add some perspective to his ownership.

When the Tribe moved into the new ballpark in 1994, the only franchises that had built new stadiums in the 1990s were the White Sox (1991) and Baltimore (1992). This was the perfect time for Jacobs as the main revenue sources for teams were ticket sales, luxury boxes and suites. By 2005, most teams had new ballparks and cable television was the prime source of income.

In a 1992 interview with The Plain Dealer's Stephen Phillips, Jacobs said: "I want a contender, a positive cash flow and a fair return on our investment."

That's what he promised, and that's what he delivered.

Jacobs was more than a guy who kept both eyes on the bottom line. He was a very gifted manager of people.

"Dick Jacobs had a way of making people feel comfortable," said Hamilton. "He invited Wendy [Hamilton's wife] and me to dinner during spring training in Winter Haven. We went out to this 5-star chalet-type restaurant in the country. He had the team vice presidents there and the manager—all the top people with the team. This was in 1993. I was just 'the other guy' doing the games with Herb Score. But he sat there and talked to Wendy and me for a long time as if we were equals. He wasn't one of these guys telling everyone his business—or how successful he was. He was careful never to say anything to get himself in trouble. He was very interested in other people."

Mark Shapiro said Jacobs "was an incredible listener."

Shapiro said Jacobs had the ability "not to need to talk . . . and there is incredible power in that. He didn't talk unless he had something meaningful to say. It gave him a presence and real strength."

He loved to bring his baseball people together when a big decision, such as a trade or a major contract offer, was to be made.

The group was small: General Manager John Hart, his assistant Dan O'Dowd and Manager Mike Hargrove. After O'Dowd left, Shapiro moved into that spot for those meetings.

"He let you do your job," said Hargrove. "He wanted us to stay on budget. He wanted to know why we were making the decisions that we were making. But he didn't claim to be an expert [in baseball]."

Hart told the story of a long discussion when the Indians were interested in acquiring Bret Saberhagen, a pitcher with Kansas City. Hart and Hargrove spent a lot of time discussing his ability. Jacobs was listening, but also reading about Saberhagen in the Kansas City media guide.

Then Hart noticed that Jacobs was counting . . . he reached the number five.

"What's that?" asked Hart.

"The number of times that he's been on the disabled list," said Jacobs.

Hart and Hargrove were aware of that, but Jacobs mentioning it made them reconsider it.

Did Jacobs veto the pursuit of Saberhagen?

No.

But he also issued a warning, indicating the risk bothered him.

They wisely didn't sign Saberhagen, who had several more injuries in his career.

Hamilton said it took a few years for Jacobs to get to know him.

"I was always 'Herb's partner,' " said Hamilton. "I even used to introduce myself to Mr. Jacobs that way. I got to know him better in spring training. He used to fly John Hart, Danny [O'Dowd], Mike Hargrove, Herb and myself down to his hotel in Key West to meet some of his friends from Cleveland—and some real movers and shakers in town. He'd send his private plane to Winter Haven to pick us up. One time, we're on his phenomenal private jet. I was looking at the woodwork, thinking it was better than anything I'd ever seen in any house.

"As we're flying along, fog set in. We couldn't land in Key West. We were circling around and circling around. We were in the air for two hours, and running out of fuel. John was on the phone with Dick, telling him that we had a game the next day and maybe we should head back. Instead, Dick had us land in Fort Myers to refuel. He kept telling John that the fog would clear. He also wanted our baseball people to meet his friends. He got a kick out of that, having his friends meet Herb, John, Mike and the rest. I just got to tag along."

In fact, Jacobs would have his Cleveland friends in Key West for a week. They would fly up to Winter Haven for a game, then fly back to Key West. All on his private jet. They never stayed overnight in Winter Haven. He much preferred his Pier House Hotel on Duval Street in Key

West to anything near the Tribe's antiquated spring-training headquarters.

"After a few years, I still introduced myself to Dick as 'Herb's partner,'" said Hamilton. "Dick knew who I was, but it became a joke between us. He was always great to me."

Over and over, you hear that from nearly everyone with the Indians who worked for Jacobs—he was a good boss.

"Dick was incredibly loyal and incredibly generous to those who worked for him," said Shapiro. "He was an old-school business guy. He valued loyalty. He rewarded those who worked hard for him."

Jacobs had only two general managers in his 12½ seasons: Hank Peters and John Hart. Hargrove was hired as manager in the middle of 1991, and Jacobs resisted thoughts of firing Hargrove when Hart became impatient with his manager. His two assistant general managers were O'Dowd and Shapiro. He believed in continuity, and that made him very popular with his key baseball employees.

After the Tribe lost in the seventh game of the 1997 World Series, it seemed Jacobs sensed it was time to sell.

The team was at its peak with that $22.6 million profit. Jacobs also saw new trends coming in baseball, trends that he didn't like.

More and more cities were building ballparks for their franchises. Cable television became a bigger source of revenue. Cleveland's television market was limited. Detroit was about 150 miles away, the same with Pittsburgh. To the south about 250 miles was Cincinnati.

That made three different major-league teams within a four-hour drive of Cleveland. That also meant a limited geographic area for cable television. To Jacobs, that meant it would be hard to grow revenue from cable television.

Meanwhile, the Indians were in the midst of the 455-game sellout streak. There was no more money to be made from the ballpark, no more tickets to be sold.

He also saw rising salaries and massive free-agent contracts. He knew more and more stars would leave Cleveland—unless he wanted to enter into deficit spending.

That wasn't going to happen.

As Shapiro said, "Dick didn't engage in much sentimentality when it came to baseball. He'd say it is a good thing for the community. He enjoyed owning the Indians, but it was a business to him."

And from a pure business perspective, it was time to sell.

He planned it carefully—and secretly.

In June of 1998, he put the team's stock up for sale.

In July of 1998, he became one of the possible owners of the expansion Browns. He would drop out a few months later. Why enter the process? Because Jacobs wanted to see how the NFL handled the sale of a franchise.

On May 14, 1999, Jacobs announced the Indians were for sale. He hired the investment bank Goldman Sachs to run the sale, the same company that did it for the NFL when the Browns were on the market. And they used the same secret-bid process. The Dolans never talked to Jacobs until their bid was accepted. Nor did they know what anyone else offered.

The Dolan family purchased the team for an announced price of $323 million. Current Tribe CEO Paul Dolan said the cash price of the team was about $260 million. There were other elements of the sale that brought it to $323 million.

But let's go with Dolan's figure of $260 million in cash paid to Jacobs.

Remember, the actual cash that he paid for the team was about $18 million. All of these mega-deals are complicated.

And the stock deal netted him another $48 million.

It's hard to know about all the year-to-year profits, but they were huge.

It's conservative to estimate that he made about $350 million off the Indians in his 12½ years of ownership.

When Jacobs sold the team, he was 74 years old.

"He saved baseball for Cleveland," said Hamilton. "Herb used to tell me about the other owners before Dick Jacobs. He said no other owner came close to what he did for baseball in Cleveland. Herb would say, 'Tom, there were times when we didn't know how we'd make the next payroll. Everything was done on the cheap, cutting all the corners. We had no chance, no plan, until Dick Jacobs arrived.' "

Jacobs bought the team with the intention of keeping it in Cleveland, finding a way to get a new stadium built, then putting together a consistent winner.

And yes, make a profit, too.

And when he left, he had done all that. He left at just the right time.

"Yes, he was a businessman first," said Hamilton. "But the way he ran his business was very good for the Indians and their fans."

Players

[FANS WRITE IN]

Midway through Game 1 of the 1997 ALDS at Yankee Stadium, our child was born. My wife and I both thought we were having a girl, but lo and behold, we had a son. We never really settled on a name for a boy, but I suggested we had to name our son after an Indians player since he was born during a Tribe playoff game. My wife remembered that the only name she liked was Jaret, so that was the name we chose, giving me a new favorite Tribe memory. *—Bruce Gerber, Worthington*

A couple of days after the Tribe lost Game 7 to the Marlins in 1997, I was in Cleveland Hopkins Airport. I was 14 years old, sorely disappointed but still proud of my Tribe. The airport was pretty empty, but when I got to my gate, wearing my Indians cap, I noticed a young man in a suit sitting at the next gate by himself, reading the paper or a magazine. It was rookie phenom, playoff hero and Game 7 starter Jaret Wright. I couldn't believe my eyes: Here's a guy who just pitched lights out in Game 7 of the World Series, was this close to being a rookie World Series MVP, just sitting in the airport waiting to take a regular ol' flight. I didn't want to disturb him, so I didn't go over, but after a few minutes I saw a small family and a few others go over and get autographs, so after they quietly moved on, I decided I wouldn't get such an opportunity again. I walked over, congratulated him, and asked him for his autograph on my hat. He kindly obliged by signing "Jaret Wright 27" on the underside of the bill, and then went back to his reading. To this day, it's still odd to think of him just sitting there by himself, a few days removed from nearly winning the World Series MVP as a rookie. *—Ezzie Goldish, University Heights*

I have many memories from going to Indians games with my dad as a kid. Being 8 or 9 years old, all I saw were the Indians winning. I went to two World Series games, one All-Star Game and numerous Divisional and Championship series games through the '90s. One memory is in 1997, being at the All-Star Game in Cleveland and seeing Kenny Lofton as an Atlanta Brave. Eventually Kenny came over and started to sign autographs. I told Kenny as loud as I could how much we missed him in Cleveland, and I remember him looking back up at me from signing and going, "I miss you guys too." *—Doug Selvey, Wapakoneta*

My high school years were 1994–97 so these teams were who I grew up watching. I used to love getting autographs in the players' parking lot after home games. Kenny Lofton was the best. He had a crowd of people waiting for him to sign after every game. He would borrow a black sharpie from someone at the front of the line and made sure to sign their item for them. Then, he would ask to use that pen to sign autographs. He would sign and chat with fans all the way down the fence. When he was done he would find the person who the pen belonged to, thank them and wave to the crowd. Kenny was a class act. *—Ryan Sweeney, Macedonia*

Before Jim Thome's last game as an Indian, Tribe players were waiting to greet fans as they came to the turnstiles. I was with my 10-year-old son and I was like a little kid when I saw that Thome would be greeting us. With free agency looming, the groups in front of us begged Thome not to leave Cleveland and I could tell it was making Thome uncomfortable. Thome greeted my son with a smile, handed him a comic book and shook his little hand. He quickly moved to my hand and, as we shook hands, I looked him in the eye and said, "Jim, no matter what happens in the off-season, I wish you nothing but the best. You and those great teams brought so much joy and I thank you for that. I hope it was as much fun for you as it was for me." Thome squeezed my arm, put his other hand on my shoulder and with a smile on his face, said "It has been a LOT of fun hasn't it?" I like to think in that brief moment he and I were reflecting on those great teams and fans and knew we were saying goodbye to it. *—Eric Furniss, Marion*

Like many other fans, Jim Thome was my favorite Tribe player. I became a Jim Thome fan during one game when I was watching him play for our Canton-Akron AA team. It was a family day out to the ball game. My younger brother, Travis, decided to go hang out behind the home run fence to see if he could catch a home run. Sure enough, Jim Thome hits one out and Travis catches it. The next time Thome is in the on-deck circle, my mom yells to him, "Hey Jim! My son caught your home run ball! Would you sign it for him?" Jim continued to look straight ahead at the field, but shook his head yes. We thought he would forget. But as the game ended, the teams shook hands and Jim turned to look for us in the stands and came over and signed the ball. Great guy and an even better player! *—Chris Middleton, Alliance*

My parents took me to the 1996 Wahoo Winterfest, where my 4-year-old self was in heaven. There I was, near all my favorite players. From what I recall (and my parents have confirmed years later), we were walking upstairs and I could look down and see all the players. My favorite player, Jim Thome, was signing autographs down below, so what did I do? I yelled, "Hey, Jim Thome!" and frantically waved. Jim waved back and smiled, calling back, "Hey, buddy." He didn't have to acknowledge a kid yelling his name, but he did. Talk about making a lasting memory. *—Daniel Mitchell, Ashland*

My favorite player was Jim Thome. I wore out more than my fair share of Thome T-shirts over the years. So naturally, when my family visited Winter Haven in 2001, I had one mission: meet the man himself. After the game wrapped up, I slowly made my way down to the railing on the first base line. After waiting in line, it was our turn. I was so nervous that I almost hid when we reached the front. Jim gave me a smile and waved me forward. He took a picture with my younger sister and I before signing the foul balls we had caught during the game. It was (and still is) the most excited I've ever been to meet a player. Every moment of that day will forever be burned into my memory. *—Dale Armbruster, Parma*

My favorite player on the Tribe (and my all-time favorite player to this current day) was Sandy Alomar Jr. Through one-sided, emotionally charged trades (sound familiar, Cleveland?), I had accumulated over 100 different baseball cards featuring Sandy. I had paid no attention to the laughter of my friends as they pointed out lopsided card values according to Beckett Baseball. *—Bill Beaufait, Montgomery*

My favorite Indians player of that era was Sandy Alomar. He was the picture of class and humility, and I loved his on-field leadership. In the early '90s, during the off-season, I went to a Cavaliers game at the Richfield Coliseum and who do I see within shouting distance? Sandy Alomar. I had some baseballs in my car, so I ran out into the parking lot, got a ball and came back into the Coliseum (security let you re-enter in those days!). I whistled loudly and yelled Alomar's name. He looked at me as I held up the ball and pen. With a big smile on his face, he yells back, "You gotta base-a-ball?" He clapped his hands together and encouraged my throw. Sandy caught the ball, signed it, then threw it back to me. The autographed ball has sat on my desk for over 20 years. As I look back, that is the best encounter I've ever had with a professional athlete. He was gracious, appreciative and willing to do something nice for a fan.
—Ron Corpora, Hudson

I was 8 years old in the '95 season. My dad took me and my brother to The Jake to watch a game. I don't remember much about what happened inside the stadium, but I vividly remember what happened after. We walked over to the players' parking lot and were hopeful we could snag some autographs from some players. After about an hour or so of waiting, players started filing out. Kenny Lofton and Jose Mesa both signed our hats and a few balls that we had brought. However, my brother and I weren't quite satisfied. We both wanted an autograph from Sandy Alomar. Only problem was that Sandy was hurt a lot that season and didn't play that day. We yelled to a few players who were leaving to see if he was coming out. They explained, yes, but he would be late as he was with the trainers. The crowd dwindled from 100 fans, to 50, to about a dozen left hopeful to score a signature from the Tribe's backstop. Finally, Sandy emerged from the clubhouse and walked straight to his silver Porsche. The remaining 12 people cheered, yelled, begged and pleaded for his attention. He didn't look up. Heartbreak. He was leaving. He drove up to the gate spoke to the guard, and he waved the remaining crowd to come over. We approached the car. Sandy smiled and said, "I will sign everyone here an autograph, just don't touch the Porsche." He kept his word. He signed autographs for the next 15 minutes while sitting in his convertible. He was tired, probably frustrated with his injury and he could have went home but didn't. He made two little boys Tribe fans for life that night. Coolest night ever.
—Matthew Loczi, Cleveland

Having been a Tribe fan since the early 1960s, I took great, make that immense, pleasure in the successes in the 1990s. While my husband, two sons and I were watching Omar and Robbie Alomar execute yet another spectacular double play, I specifically remember telling my two sons (who were 11 and 7 in 1996) to watch every play by Omar and Robbie Alomar and commit them to their memory. In your lifetime you may never see another infield combination as breathtaking and awesome as they were. *—Cindy Frase, Akron*

I remember attending batting practice before a mid '90s Tribe game. Enrique Wilson, then a rookie infielder, was shagging fly balls in the outfield with several others, when Omar Vizquel showed up and decided to have some fun. Every time Wilson tried to catch a fly ball, Vizquel would trip him. It was like watching a couple of young boys goofing around, rather than millionaire athletes. It was one of the things I loved about Omar Vizquel and the Tribe of that era. He was extremely gifted, but he also radiated joy when he played baseball. *—Craig Swarts, Columbus*

Omar was always my favorite. I switched from center field to shortstop because of him. I've met hundreds of "famous" people, but hanging with Omar after batting practice once before a home game was a major highlight of my life and the only time I was ever star-struck. My jaw was somewhere in the dirt near home plate. He remains my own personal Babe Ruth. *—Geoff Grant, Hempstead, North Carolina*

I remember attending a game in 1996 with my family. The game was originally scheduled as a Sunday afternoon game but was changed to a Sunday night game to be the ESPN Game of the Week. It was actually the second game of a day-night doubleheader. Since we had already had planned on going to Cleveland that day, and had no baseball game to go to until 8:05 p.m., we decided to make a day of it in Cleveland. We visited both the Rock and Roll Hall of Fame and the Great Lakes Science Center. After visiting the halls, the first game wasn't over so we decided to go down to the lake at Edgewater Park. While walking along the rocks all of a sudden my son came down yelling that Omar Vizquel had driven up in his yellow Porsche and gotten out to get some ice cream cones for his family in his car. We immediately ran back and were able to talk with Omar and get autographs from him. My wife couldn't believe her eyes as Omar was shirtless. What a thrill it was for all of us as who would have thought we would meet Omar Vizquel in between games of a doubleheader outside the park. What a day to be without a camera. *—Rich Herrmann, Galion*

I was waiting outside the players' parking lot one day before a night game hoping to get some autographs. I happened to see a bright yellow Porsche pull into the BP station across the street. It was Omar Vizquel. Along with about 10 other fans, I went over to the gas station. There was Omar getting ready to pump gas. One of the gas station employees came out to tell us to leave him alone. But with a big smile, Omar said it was OK, and told one of the fans, "You pump and I'll sign." He signed and took pictures with everybody. *—Bill Hubish, North Olmsted*

I am a lifelong Indians fan, but had never gone to spring training. I finally went in 1994. The Tribe had played its last game at the old stadium and was stocked with new, exciting players. We visited training camp during the week before games started. There were only about a dozen fans at the camp. We got to meet Kenny Lofton, Carlos Baerga and Charles Nagy. All of the players were friendly and posed with our 10-month-old for pictures. Charles Nagy was exceptionally friendly and played with him and our other children. It was a special visit for me and my family. We went to a couple more spring trainings since, but never felt the closeness we did during that visit in 1994. *—Mike Nowak, Cleveland Heights*

In 1995, I was 8 years old. My older brother Ben was 10. The hottest thing in our household was none other than Albert Belle. Obviously, in the midst of his historical 50-50 season, we idolized the man that summer (among other Tribe legends). We all played baseball. I was an infielder and a pretty good hitter. Ben could not hit the broad side of a barn; he was a very gifted pitcher, but his swing was ugly and laborious. So we hatched a plan. Ben's birthday is in August, and we conspired to get him something that would help with his hitting issues ... a Louisville Slugger wooden bat with the wood grain handle and the all-black barrel, just like Albert swung. Much to Ben's (and my) excitement, he did indeed receive the black barreled Louisville Slugger for his birthday that year. Much to his dismay, he continued to do his best Mario Mendoza impression every time he stepped up to the plate. *—Alex Painter, Richmond, Indiana*

It was 1995, I was 8 years old, and it was the most incredible season I can remember. Albert Belle was crushing everything. The Indians couldn't lose. My parents did their best to get me to like other players due to Albert's less than impressive on-and-off the field antics, but I could not be persuaded. I had to see every single at-bat. I will never forget him hitting those grand slams. I thought it was the greatest thing that ever happened. I remember being devastated when Albert left for the White Sox. My youthful mind did not know how to process and understand that baseball was a business. I remember telling my parents that I would play for the Indians for any amount of money, and that I would never want to go play for another city, no matter how much money they offered me. *—Doug Smythe, Washington, DC*

I was born in 1991, so I discovered baseball at the perfect time as a child in Greater Cleveland. Choosing my favorite player was easy. I loved Manny. It seemed as if he hit a home run every at bat. There was nothing more captivating to an impressionable young boy. He was a god. *—Kyle Gillihan, Brunswick*

I'll never forget Opening Day 1993, but it had nothing to do with what went on inside the lines. Days before the opener, the team, the town and all of baseball were rocked by the tragedy on Little Lake Nellie that took the lives of Steve Olin and Tim Crews and destroyed what was left of Bob Ojeda's career. So we were all there for Opening Day, 80,000 plus. After the team was introduced, including a heavily-bandaged Ojeda, the widows of the two fallen Tribesmen were introduced. After a moment of silence—which was awe-inspiring in itself because how often do 80,000 remain silent?—Grover presented Olin's and Crews' jerseys to their widows. Was there a dry eye in the place? Probably so, but not mine or anyone around me. I have long forgotten the game and the final score, but I will never forget that moment. *—Vince Granieri, Cincinnati*

I attended countless games in the '90s, traveling from Youngstown to Cleveland three to four times a month to watch the Tribe. However, some of my fondest personal memories come from my trips to Toronto, Ontario. My family and I made three trips to watch the Tribe in '95, '97 and '99. We stayed at The Westin Harbour Castle, where the players stay. It was such a thrill as a teenager to see my heroes roaming the lobby, interacting with fans. I have to admit, riding in an elevator with Ramirez and Thome was a little intimidating . . . yet awesome! After one game I noticed Albert Belle in the lobby by himself reading a magazine. He had a stern look on his face (it wasn't a great day at the plate). However, I approached him anyway for an autograph. To my surprise he was very cordial and signed a ball for me and said no problem. I still have that ball on display nearly 20 years later. *—Dennis Biviano, Raleigh, North Carolina*

We were at Wrigley Field in the late '90s watching the Tribe play the Cubs. We ran into John Hart in front of the stadium and had a cordial conversation with him. As Dick Jacobs exited a vehicle and approached us, some Chicago fan ran up to him and tried to sell him some tickets to the game. *—Raymond Francel, North Ridgeville*

I saw Jim Thome signing autographs when I was 5 or 6. I leaned over the railing and yelled, "Hey, Jim Thome!" He stopped signing, looked up, waved, and called back, "Hey, buddy!" I got to meet my hero that day. *—Daniel Mitchell, Loudonville*

I'll never forget being down in the east bank of the Flats after the Indians won the 1995 AL pennant, dancing to "This Is How We Do It" in the Beach Club with Manny Ramirez and Julian Tavarez. The excitement and atmosphere was electric! *—Mike Weber, Mentor*

My aunt is a huge Omar Vizquel fan. In the late '90s, she was diagnosed with breast cancer. I wanted to do something to pick up her spirits so I asked a close friend that knew Omar very well if she could get an autograph. We ended up getting back signed photos made out to her. To say she was ecstatic is an understatement and it absolutely lifted her spirits during her battle. And what do you know, she beat that cancer and still loves Omar to this day! *—Chris Moore, Chesapeake, Virginia*

REBUILDING

Tom Hamilton, An Old-Fashioned Radio Man

"When you grow up on a farm, you're always talking to yourself," said Tom Hamilton.

Think about 150 acres in rural Wisconsin and about 50 cows. Think about getting up in the morning when it was still night—or at least, very dark—to milk the cows.

Now think about wanting something else beyond the farm, besides the cows.

Think about dreaming of one day doing games on the radio from big cities in faraway places.

That's what a young Tom Hamilton did.

"When I was in the eighth grade, we moved into Waterloo [Wis.]," said Hamilton. "It was only a town of 2,000 about a half-hour from Madison, but I was glad to be in the eighth grade and off the farm."

Frank Hamilton had taken a job with the Perry Printing Company. The pay was steady, and the burden of dealing with everything from temperamental cows to fluctuating milk prices was lifted.

"And I was just so glad to be in a town so I could play with my friends," said Hamilton. "On the farm, most of the time I didn't see anyone but my three brothers and sister. You spent half the time hating each other."

Hamilton laughed as he told the story, but you know there was some truth in it. Farm kids know about isolation. They know about how the town kids often look down upon them. They know that for all the idyllic portrayals of farm life in movies and on television, it's a grueling, 7-day-a-week, 24-hour existence. When you have cows, you can never take a day off. They have to be fed. They have to be milked. If it is winter and they are inside, their stalls have to be cleaned.

Cows and chores.

Every day.

"At night, I'd listen to the old Milwaukee Braves games with Earl Gillespie on the radio," said Hamilton. "They had some great teams with Eddie Mathews, Hank Aaron, Warren Spahn and Lew Burdette. Milwaukee was about an hour away, but it was unimaginable. Back then, there were something like nine games on television. It was basically the Saturday Game of the Week."

Several times, Hamilton talked about how doing games on the radio "seemed so beyond me."

Yet, he mentioned how in the back of his mind, he'd listen to those games and think . . . maybe, just maybe . . .

"When I was in high school, I would pick up WGN on the radio and listen to Vince Lloyd and Lou Boudreau doing the Cubs," he said. "And I listened to Eddie Doucette doing the Milwaukee Bucks—that was when they had Kareem Abdul-Jabbar and he was known as Lew Alcindor. I loved to listen to games on the radio."

Hamilton played several sports in high school, but he knew that "sports would be no Camelot to me, so I went to Brown."

He paused.

"Not the Ivy League school," he said. "Brown College in Minneapolis."

It's a school known for its broadcasting program.

Hamilton started so low in broadcasting, that eventually making it to Appleton, Wis., was a major move.

He began in Shell Lake, Wis. Then WTTN in Watertown, Wis.

"I did everything," he said. "I was a disc jockey. I did the news. I did sports. I did high school games."

In Appleton, he was all sports. There were high school games, Lawrence University games and "Green Bay was only a half-hour away, so I got to do a few reports each week on the Packers."

He also did the Class A Appleton Foxes baseball team in the summer, "but we only carried 25 games."

At this point, Hamilton realized that there were 26 major-league baseball teams. This was the late 1970s. You put two guys in the booth, and that meant only 52 jobs.

It's much harder to make the majors as a broadcaster than it is as a player. Not only are there fewer jobs, but the broadcasters often stay on their job for decades.

"I thought it would be easier to get a job in a city where they had a major Division I college team," said Hamilton. "You could do basketball and football games, and also do weekday sports at a local station. That seemed like a dream job to me."

The dream almost happened . . .

"I was in Appleton, and I heard that a station in Lincoln was looking for someone to do Nebraska football and basketball," said Hamilton. "It seemed like my dream job. This is when the Cornhuskers were a powerhouse in football. This was big-time college sports."

The station manager told Hamilton to come to Lincoln for an interview, but that he had to drive.

It was a 10-hour drive, but at that point, Hamilton would have crawled from Appleton to Lincoln with a dairy cow on his back.

"I remember going to that interview thinking that I would get that job," said Hamilton.

The general manager was all smiles when he met Hamilton and shook his hand, "Tom, you can't believe the great news."

Hamilton was thinking, "Are they going to hire me without even an interview? Wow!"

Then the general manager said, "We just hired Ray Scott to do the Nebraska football games."

Hamilton loved Ray Scott. He listened to the broadcasting legend doing the Green Bay Packers games.

Hamilton just stared at the man thinking, "This may be great news for you, but what about me? I drove all this way and . . . "

The general manager said, "We apologize, but this just happened yesterday. Ray just called . . . and can you believe it, I'm talking to Ray Scott on the phone! And Ray says he's interested in the job at our station . . . "

Looking back, Hamilton said, "The guy was like a little kid who just got everything he wanted on Christmas morning. Meanwhile, I'm ready to cry. I mean, I grew up LOVING Ray Scott . . . now I HATED Ray Scott because he just took my job!"

The general manager said, "I do have some good news. Ray only wants to do the football, so we will hire you to do the basketball."

Hamilton said, "How can I make a living just doing basketball games?"

The general manager said, "You can be a sales representative for the station."

"But I can't sell anything," said Hamilton.

So Hamilton hit the road back to Appleton, exactly 599 miles.

"Longest drive of my life," said Hamilton. "I was getting up at 3:30 in the morning to go to the station in Appleton. I was working 10-12 hours a day at the station, then bartending at night to make a few extra bucks. I had been there for five years [1977–81], and I wasn't even making $20,000 with the two jobs."

As he watched the broken white lines on the highway and the trucks speed past, he wondered where his life was going.

"Most of my friends were making more money," he said. "Most of them were married and starting families. They seemed to be getting somewhere."

Hamilton thought of all the other jobs that he had applied for, how none of them even led to something as promising as Lincoln. His job history was a bunch of small dots on the Wisconsin map: Shell Lake, Watertown and Appleton.

"At some point, you ask yourself if you're going to quit," he said. "I thought about it, but I just loved radio so much! I couldn't quit."

Not long after that long drive from Lincoln to Appleton, Hamilton sent out more tapes and letters. He received job interviews in Columbus, Ohio, and Milwaukee.

"In Columbus, they wanted someone to do the Clippers on WBNS," he said. "It was Class AAA baseball, and I didn't have enough experience. But I also had an interview at WISN in Milwaukee, and I got to do Wisconsin football."

His partner would be Earl Gillespie.

As much as he loved listening to Ray Scott call the Packers games, Hamilton idolized Gillespie calling the old Milwaukee Braves. Gillespie did the Braves from 1953 to 1963. He also was a Milwaukee television sports anchor, and did college sports. He was known for yelling "HOLY COW!" when a member of the Braves hit a homer.

"Earl was a wonderful man," said Hamilton. "We went out to lunch one day and this waitress was telling him about a fish that she caught. Earl also hosted an outdoors show. She was talking about the fish, and he was asking her lots of questions about her fishing trip. They talked like old friends, and Earl made her feel like a million bucks and the most important person in the world that day."

The first few years in Milwaukee went well. Hamilton did the morning sports and Wisconsin football. One winter, he was hired to do the University of Colorado basketball, and flew back and forth for the games while still keeping his job at WISN in Milwaukee.

But in 1984, his station laid off several people—including Hamilton.

"They told me how it wasn't my fault, all the things they tell you," said Hamilton. "But I started to wonder, is someone trying to tell me something?"

Hamilton needed a job, any job.

"I did some part-time radio work in Milwaukee," he said. "But that didn't pay enough. I was hired by the Northwestern Mutual Life Insurance Company. Their home office was in Milwaukee, and I did voice-overs for commercials and videos about buying term life insurance. I hated it. I mean, I HATED every minute of it."

In 1986, Hamilton received a call from WBNS in Columbus.

"I couldn't believe it," he said. "Here I was, laid off and doing radio part-time—and they called ME! They said they remembered me from the last time that I interviewed for a job there. They asked me to come in for an interview."

Hamilton was hired to do morning-drive sports and Ohio State football pre-game, halftime and post-game shows.

"I was interested in doing the Clippers, but they had Terry Smith doing the games," said Hamilton. "Terry also did Ohio State football. I told the station that I'd go down to Clippers home games and help Terry, just give him a break for a few innings. I told them that I'd do it for free."

The station liked the idea, especially the FREE part. Smith was all for it, because he was calling the entire game.

"I did two innings most games," he said. "I was getting up at 3:30 to do the morning drive, and getting home late after the Clippers game.

In the back of my mind, I was thinking about using those two innings to put together an audition tape to try and get a baseball job somewhere."

Most broadcasters who aren't former players and come from small markets are very driven to reach the majors. They make a lot of moves. They deal with rejection. They are paid very little. They work terrible hours.

"Even in Columbus, I was working 80-hour weeks in football season," said Hamilton. "Columbus was really good for me. I met my wife there. Wendy was doing the morning news at the same station."

After the 1989 baseball season, Hamilton read a story in The Plain Dealer that Paul Olden was leaving his job as Herb Score's partner doing the Tribe games on the radio.

"I didn't do anything about it," he said. "Wendy was pregnant with our son Nick. I was immersed in Ohio State football. I wasn't even the main guy doing the Clippers games."

During the Christmas season, Hamilton saw another story about the Tribe radio job. Supposedly, they were down to four candidates. Hamilton was telling Wendy how he could have competed with those guys, because none had major-league experience.

"Why don't you apply?" said Wendy.

"It's too late," he said.

"You don't know," she said. "They haven't hired anyone yet."

"I probably won't get it," he said.

"You don't know that, either," she said. "Let them make that decision. Don't discount yourself. Let's go make an audition tape."

So Wendy and Tom Hamilton went to an early Mass and then spent about 10 hours on Christmas Day at the radio station going through his Columbus Clippers tapes. Remember, he did only two innings for home games.

At this point, the Indians were on WWWE (now called WTAM). Hamilton's station (WBNS) was the flagship for Ohio State football. The Buckeyes were on WWWE, and WBNS carried the Tribe and Browns games (WWWE being the flagship station).

Now the story becomes a bit complicated. The essence is that a program director at WBNS knew the key executives at WWWE, David

George and Bob Tayak. He called them and asked if they'd listen to Hamilton's tape.

The executives said they had previewed more than 200 tapes and were down to the final four.

"Just give the guy a listen," said the program director.

As a favor, WWWE agreed to listen to the tape.

"I got a call from them saying their final four was now a final five," said Hamilton. "I don't think Herb ever listened to my tape, but [team President] Hank Peters did. And they said Hank 'liked what he heard.' He had final approval over the announcers."

Hamilton was hired.

"They offered me $40,000, and that was less than I was making in Columbus," he said. "Wendy also was working in Columbus, but she was going to quit after we had Nick. But I couldn't turn down a chance to do major-league baseball. It's what I dreamed of doing when listening to Earl Gillespie on the farm."

Hamilton paused.

"Without Wendy, I never would have gotten this job," he said. "I was starting to think that maybe I wasn't good enough to get a baseball job. She was the one who kept encouraging me, and then she helped me put the tape and my resume together."

Hamilton's first season was 1990.

He became the lead broadcaster starting in the 1998 season.

"Now, it's 25 years later and it's hard to believe because it went by so fast," said Hamilton.

Hamilton is much like Joe Tait, the legendary Cleveland broadcaster. Tait was the first voice of the Cavs from their inception in 1970 through 2011, except two seasons during the ownership of Ted Stepien. He also did the Tribe on the radio (1973–79) and then on television (1980–87).

Tait grew up on an Illinois farm and worked in several small markets before his break came in Cleveland.

Tait admires Hamilton, calling him a "true radio guy." By that, Tait means Hamilton knows the first job is to describe the action, give some color to the game by talking about the ballpark, the uniforms, the weather and just being the "eyes" of the fans at the game. Tait also believes that a broadcaster must keep reviewing and recapping the game, because listeners tune in and out.

"I've done Big Ten basketball on television for more than 20 years," said Hamilton. "When Ohio State asked me to do their games, I jumped at the chance. I like college basketball. I also figured I better get something else in case baseball didn't work out long-term. So I have experience doing television, but I really prefer baseball on the radio. Radio is true play-by-play. On TV, you are there to set up the analyst. Radio is still the primary medium for baseball. It's six months, virtually every day. I still love it."

1997: The Best and the Worst Season

In 2014, John Hart had dinner with Mike Hargrove.

This may seem strange to some fans, because Hart fired Hargrove as the Tribe's manager after the 1999 season. It was extremely painful for Hargrove, who is the only manager in franchise history to lead the team to a pair of appearances in the World Series.

But after many years, the two men still get along. They also have the common experience of the Tribe of the 1990s.

During the dinner, the subject of Game 7 in 1997 came up.

"To this day, I have never watched a tape of that game," said Hargrove.

"You know, neither have I," said Hart.

And the two men didn't speak much more about it.

The hard part is that in many ways, both were at their best in 1997. Hart rebuilt the roster. Hargrove juggled so many new players, pulling the team together when it meant the most—during the playoffs.

While it was the year in the 1990s that the Indians came the closest to winning a World Series, it also was when Hargrove was nearly fired in the middle of the season.

"Looking back, that may have been my most satisfying season," said Hargrove. "I really enjoyed managing that team."

Here was the Tribe's 1995 opening-day lineup:

- Kenny Lofton CF
- Omar Vizquel SS
- Carlos Baerga 2B

- Albert Belle LF
- Eddie Murray DH
- Jim Thome 3B
- Manny Ramirez RF
- Paul Sorrento 1B
- Tony Pena C
- Dennis Martinez P

Now, compare that the with the opening-day lineup for 1997:

- Marquis Grissom CF
- Omar Vizquel SS
- Jim Thome 1B
- Matt Williams 3B
- David Justice LF
- Manny Ramirez RF
- Julio Franco 2B
- Kevin Mitchell DH
- Sandy Alomar C
- Charles Nagy P

It's astounding how much had changed for the Tribe between the end of 1995 and opening day of 1997.

Sandy Alomar was a member of the 1995 Tribe. Yes, Tony Pena started the opener in 1995, but he was the personal catcher for Dennis Martinez. The regular catcher in 1995 was Alomar, the same as in 1997.

But look at the two lineups.

Only Vizquel at short and Ramirez in right field had the same positions both seasons. Thome was on both teams, but he had moved from third to first base in 1997.

The Tribe had only four non-pitchers who were key members of the Tribe in both 1995 and 1997: Alomar, Thome, Ramirez and Vizquel.

They had only three members of the rotation on both teams: Orel Hershiser, Chad Ogea and Nagy.

And they had only four relievers on both teams: Jose Mesa, Eric Plunk, Paul Assenmacher and Paul Shuey.

So from the end of the 1995 season to opening day of 1997, only 11 of 25 players remained.

"Look at the two rosters," said Tom Hamilton. "They don't even come close in terms of talent. We had so many stars on that 1995 team. They destroyed people. In 1997, we had to fight for every win."

Economics and age led to many of the changes.

Belle left after 1996 as a free agent to become the highest-paid player in baseball with the Chicago White Sox.

Lofton turned down a contract extension. Rather than keep Lofton for the 1997 season and then allow him to become a free agent, Hart traded his center fielder and reliever Alan Embree to Atlanta for Justice and Grissom.

During the 1996 season, Hart feared a drop in production from Baerga and Murray. He traded Baerga to the Mets, Murray to the Orioles. Dennis Martinez, Tony Pena and Paul Sorrento were not signed once their contracts expired.

"To stay competitive, we had to make major changes to the roster," said Hart. "There was no choice."

The final game of 1997 was painful, but the rest of the season makes Mike Hargrove smile.

"They were such grinders," said Hargrove. "I appreciated that team more than any other I had in Cleveland because they earned every win. They earned it. In 1995, we had so much fun—but we out-talented everybody, at least with our bats."

Hargrove thought about Matt Williams. He was picked up from the Giants, dropped into the middle of the lineup.

What the Indians didn't know when they traded Julian Tavarez, Jeff Kent and Jose Vizcaino to San Francisco for Williams was that Williams would soon learn his wife was leaving him. In fact, Williams didn't even know until his wife showed up in Winter Haven during spring training to tell him. That shocked Williams and the gloom hung over him for much of the season. That's why Hargrove appreciated Williams so much in 1997.

Hargrove had to do a lot of juggling that season.

Hart had the idea of signing 38-year-old Julio Franco and trying to play him at second base. At this point in Franco's career, he was mostly a first baseman or designated hitter. He had been a shortstop in the 1980s.

How was Franco at second base?

Well, he played the field wearing a batting helmet. It's never a good sign when your second baseman is wearing a batting helmet.

The second-base experiment lasted 35 games.

Then Hargrove turned to 35-year-old Tony Fernandez. He had missed the entire 1996 season with a broken elbow. Fernandez was solid at second base, batting .286 with 11 homers and 44 RBI.

But the team of Belle/Baerga/Lofton had changed dramatically.

"When I think about it, 1997 was a great and a painful year," said Hart. "We went through so many changes. It seems like almost all year, we were wrestling with different things. We were so used to winning 95 to 100 games and running away with the division, that season was almost a shock. We had to fight our way in."

When Hamilton looks at the 1997 opening-day lineup, he shakes his head over some of the names.

"Kevin Mitchell was the DH?" he asked. "I had forgotten all about that. You didn't want to get on the wrong side of Kevin Mitchell. I remember when he knocked out Chad Curtis with one punch."

That was in late May. Curtis and Mitchell were arguing about what kind of music was being played in the clubhouse, and also something about the ping-pong table. Hargrove called what happened "a scuffle." Curtis ended up on the disabled list. But the players came to the Tribe with reputations of being "difficult," which is being kind. Making it even worse for Hargrove, neither guy could play anymore.

Mitchell's Tribe career consisted of a .153 batting average (9-of-59). He did hit four homers. He also was very heavy. The team released him on June 3.

Curtis was a .207 hitter (6-of-29). He was traded to the Yankees on June 9.

Jack McDowell was supposed to be the ace of the staff, but he was 3-3 with a 5.09 ERA and had arm problems most of the season.

Franco flopped at second base.

Jose Mesa was shaky as a closer. He had only 16 saves in the regular season. Mesa had faced some off-season legal problems and he wasn't acquitted until early April. He didn't seem like the same pitcher he was in 1995 and 1996. Hart brought in Mike Jackson, who propped up the bullpen with 15 saves.

Williams was tremendous in the field at third base, but very streaky at the plate. He also was battling the emotional blues because of his divorce. Williams still hit 32 homers and drove in 105 runs.

The Indians were 44-36 at the All-Star break, only 3½ games ahead of the White Sox.

There were rumors that Hart was ready to fire Hargrove, and that the decision was overruled by Dick Jacobs.

This is where it gets murky.

Hargrove feared he could be fired, but never was told that in 1997. Hargrove and everyone else close to the Tribe knew that Charlie Manuel was a Hart favorite. If Hart ever did fire Hargrove, the batting coach would be the replacement. Understand that Manuel was not lobbying for the job or undercutting Hargrove. But if Hart wanted to make a change, it would have been easy for him.

"I admit we wrestled with a lot of things," Hart said in 2014, looking back at that 1997 season. "But I was not changing the manager. If anything, I was being patient with the club knowing that it would take time because of all the changes. I was frustrated because I thought we should be a 95-win team, and we weren't going to get there. But I decided to stay the course and see if we could get this thing figured out."

Perhaps that is true, or perhaps that's how Hart now remembers it.

Hamilton said he is sure that "Mike was in real trouble" during the middle of the 1997 season.

As for the role of Jacobs, you can be sure that he was against firing Hargrove in the middle of the season. He absolutely hated making big changes in his baseball management team, assuming he believed the men were doing a good job. He hired Hank Peters to be the team president, and allowed Peters to bring in his front office. Once Peters retired, Hart moved up. Hargrove was already in place as manager. If Jacobs were to green-light any managerial change, it would be after the season.

"The biggest shock that season was the 'White Flag' trade," said Hart.

That happened on July 31, the final day before the trading deadline. That's when Hart was dealing for Jeff Juden and John Smiley. Neither pitcher helped the Tribe. In fact, Smiley came to the Tribe with a sore arm. He was 2-4 with a 5.54 ERA when he did pitch. And on Sept. 20, he broke his arm warming up.

"That's still incredible," said Hamilton. "Who ever heard of a guy who breaks his arm warming up in the bullpen before a start?"

So Hart's mid-season deals did little for the Tribe.

But the "White Flag" trade was a winner for Cleveland. That deal had the Chicago White Sox sending Wilson Alvarez, Danny Darwin and Roberto Hernandez to San Francisco for six players. It was mostly a salary dump.

At the time of the trade, the White Sox were 3 games behind the Tribe. Alvarez (9-8, 3.03) and Darwin (4-8, 4.13) were in the rotation. Hernandez was the team's star closer with 27 saves.

The response in the Tribe clubhouse was, "Wow, the White Sox just quit!"

A fun story was "Jim Thome High Socks Night." That was on Aug. 27, when the entire team wore old-fashioned high socks with the uniform pants to celebrate Thome's 27th birthday. The players talked about it being a good-luck charm, and some of the players kept the high-socks look for the rest of the year.

But the Tribe was only 19-14 with the high socks in place.

In Hart's never-ending quest for more pitching, he made a small deal on July 31.

Hart's special assistant was Ted Simmons, who had been an outstanding catcher in the National League. Hart had sent Simmons on scouting missions to find pitchers.

"Ted had just watched Jeff Juden pitch," said Hart. "It was only a few hours before the trading deadline. Ted was telling me that Juden looked good, and we should try to get him."

Hart said, "Come on, Jeff Juden is just a guy."

Simmons said, "He was throwing the ball pretty well."

Hart said, "Jeff Juden? You want us to get Jeff Juden?"

At that point, the 6-foot-7, 245-pound Juden was 11-5 with a 4.22 ERA for Montreal. He was known as an underachiever and for being rather lazy when it came to conditioning.

But he also had won 11 games for the Expos by the end of July.

Simmons said, "John, why not Juden? Who else do we have?"

At the end of July, the Indians were 54-48 and leading Milwaukee in the Central Division by 2½ games.

"At that point, I was hungry to make a deal," Hart admitted.

He called Jim Beattie, the general manager of the Expos.

"I was thinking about Jeff Juden," Hart said.

He also couldn't believe he uttered those words . . . a few hours earlier, he didn't think they could possibly come from his lips.

"Juden?" asked a surprised Beattie.

"It's getting close to the midnight deadline," said Hart. "You want to make a deal?"

"Sure," said Beattie. "So you want Juden."

"Right," said Hart.

"I like that little lefty Kline," said Beattie.

Hart also liked the 24-year-old Steve Kline, but he didn't seem destined to help the Indians get back into the playoffs in 1997.

They made the deal: Steve Kline for Jeff Juden.

Juden showed up and looked out of shape.

Hart tells this story that happened the day after the deal.

"John, why did you ever send me Juden?" asked Hargrove.

"Well," admitted Hart. "I really don't know."

Juden was 0-1 with a 5.46 ERA in eight games for the Tribe. He was known mostly for answering reporter's questions with grunts and taking a guitar with him everywhere.

As for Kline, he pitched for 10 more years in the majors as a lefty reliever. His ERA was a productive 3.51.

One of Hargrove's favorite people on the 1997 team was Marquis Grissom, who took over for Lofton in center field and at the top of the batting order.

"He was a wonderful guy," said Hargrove. "And we had no idea what he was going through that season."

Grissom was the 14th of 15 children. He had bought each of his siblings a house, and he either helped them pay off a car or he bought them one. It wasn't wild spending. The purchases were practical, giving each a good chance in life.

But in 1997, his 47-year-old sister Mary was dying of AIDS.

On off days, he flew to Atlanta to spend time with her. Always friendly with teammates, the media and the coaching staff, Grissom kept this burden a secret. It didn't come out until the final days of the World Series.

"Some days I only had five or six hours to stay with her, get back on the plane and come back, but I went," Grissom told the Associated Press in 1998. "Didn't get a lot of sleep all last year. Didn't sleep at all."

Why not tell someone?

It was such a crazy season for Grissom. He batted .262 with 12 homers and 66 RBI. But he was replacing Lofton, who regularly hit .300 and led the league in stolen bases. Grissom did steal 22 bases. He played close to a Gold Glove-caliber center field, although not nearly as electric as Lofton—whose speed and leaping ability were made for ESPN "Web Gems" (which weren't around back then). Grissom was one of those center fielders who always seemed in the right position as he glided to a ball hit deep in the gap. He made tough plays look routine.

But he was in shock for much of the year. He didn't see the trade to Cleveland coming at the end of spring training. Rather than being with his sister in Atlanta and playing for the Braves in the National League, he was in the American League for the first time in his career. He didn't know most of the pitchers. He didn't have family in the city. Grissom grew up in Atlanta, so nothing felt right about the deal to Cleveland.

"Marquis told me that his dad named him that because he worked at a Ford plant where the made the Mercury Marquis," said Hamilton. "He was one of my favorite people. Always upbeat. He told me about buying his brothers and sisters cars and houses. He said, 'After I do it once, they are on their own.' I admired everything about him. None of us had a clue of what he was going through."

When people who were with the Indians in 1997 think back, they are amazed at all that happened.

Consider that Grissom struck out nine times in 23 at-bats in the American League Championship Series against Baltimore.

In Game 3, he lost a ball in the lights (and that hadn't happened to Grissom all year) that allowed the game to go into extra innings. The Indians would win, 2-1, in the 12th. You know how it happened? Grissom was on third. Vizquel was at bat. Hargrove gave the squeeze bunt sign. Grissom roared home. Vizquel—a truly great bunter—squared around to bunt.

"I have to get the bat on the ball, no matter what," Vizquel thought to himself.

But he didn't.

The ball went right past the bat of Vizquel . . . and right into the mitt of Baltimore catcher Lenny Webster. The pitch wasn't high. It wasn't in the dirt. It was right in Webster's glove. All he had to do was catch it and let Grissom slide right into him—out at home plate.

Webster dropped the ball.

Grissom was safe.

Game over.

Tribe wins.

They won in 12 innings with 21 of their batters striking out. They won on a botched play.

"When I missed the ball, I was ready to kill myself," Vizquel said. "Then I saw Marquis sliding into the plate, and then everyone was jumping up and down."

Grissom won Game 2 with a home run, a three-run shot in the top of the eighth. The Indians were behind 4-2. They had lost the opener, 3-0. They looked hopeless. Then Grissom with one swing, one whopping *whap* of a swing, brought the Tribe back to life.

Earlier in that game, Grissom was in the clubhouse, throwing up. After the game, he was sick and worn down from flying to Atlanta to be with his sister.

Then he scored on the crazy squeeze in Game 3.

Grissom struck out four times in four at-bats in Game 6—the one that sent the Tribe to the World Series.

The Tribe batted only .193 vs. the Orioles. Grissom ended up as the ALCS MVP. He then hit .360 in the World Series.

His sister died not long after the end of the World Series.

When Hart realized he had a chance to re-sign Lofton, he traded Grissom to Milwaukee before the 1998 season.

"He was a very big part of that team," said Hamilton. "Not many people remember that."

Yes, Grissom had a nice season, filling in for Lofton.

Yes, David Justice took over for Albert Belle and delivered 33 homers, 101 RBI while batting .329.

Yes, Manny Ramirez hit .328 with 26 homers and 88 RBI.

Yes, Thome produced 40 homers and 102 RBI.

Yes, Jaret Wright came up from the minors and was 8-3 with a 4.38 ERA for the Tribe down the stretch.

But the 1997 season belonged to Sandy Alomar.

"That year showed what I could do when I stayed healthy," said Alomar.

Most Tribe fans never fully appreciated how Alomar loved playing in Cleveland. While Belle left on his quest to be baseball's highest-paid player and Lofton was traded after he turned down a contract offer from the Tribe, Alomar was eager to extend his contract. His original contract ran through 1997. In spring training, he signed an extension for 1998 and 1999, with a team option for 2000.

"I never wanted to play anywhere else," said Alomar.

The 1997 season was incredible for the 30-year-old Alomar.

We can talk about the franchise-record 30-game hitting streak. That's right, a 30-game hitting streak for a catcher with crushed glass for knees. A 30-game hitting streak for a guy who had an infield hit about as often as Albert Belle smiled on the field.

But the 30-game hitting streak was only part of the story.

Many fans remember the 1997 All-Star Game. It was played in Cleveland. The MVP? Sandy Alomar. His two-run homer broke a 1-1 tie and gave the American League a 3-1 victory.

Or how about Game 4 in the first round of the playoffs against the Yankees? It was the bottom of the eighth inning. The Yankees had a 2-1 lead. Future Hall of Fame closer Mariano Rivera was on the mound. Alomar lined a home run over the right-field wall to tie the score at 2-2.

"I thought that was perhaps the biggest hit of the season," said Hamilton. "It came off Mariano Rivera. He never blows a save like that. We were down 2-1 [in the series]. Rivera takes the mound in a game like that, you figure the series was over."

But it wasn't.

After Alomar's homer tied the game, the Indians won it in the bottom of the ninth. That tied the series at 2-2. Then they won the final game, 4-3, to eliminate the Yankees.

Alomar drove in 19 runs in 18 postseason games. In the World Series, he hit .367 with 10 RBI.

But perhaps the stat that meant the most from 1997 is this: Counting the postseason, the Indians were 76-58 when Alomar started, 20-25 when he didn't.

Very few people know that Chad Ogea was supposed to be the MVP of the 1997 World Series.

He was 26 years old, a stocky 6-foot-2 and 220 pounds. Ogea had horrible knees, so painful it was hard for him to run. In that 1997 season, Ogea was 8-9 with a 4.99 ERA for the Tribe. He missed all of July and August with knee and elbow problems. He was considered the team's No. 4 starter.

But in September, Ogea was 3-1 with a 3.21 ERA. He was a control pitcher, a righty with a below-average fastball and a very tricky change-up. When it meant the most in 1997, he was at his best.

Ogea was 2-2 with a 2.32 ERA in the postseason.

In the World Series, Ogea was remarkable. He beat Kevin Brown in Game 2, allowing one run in 6⅔ innings.

Kevin Brown was Florida's ace, a guy with overpowering stuff. He had a 16-8 record with a 2.69 ERA in the regular season. But the Indians won that game, 6-1.

It was Brown and Ogea again in Game 6.

"We had lost Game 5 [8-7] at home," said Hart. "Now, we go to Miami. We're down 3-2. We wanted to win that Game 5 so bad . . . We had to deal with Brown in Game 6, and how can you expect Chad to beat him again? I doubt anyone gave us much of a chance. But Chad beat him . . . again. And I started to think, well, maybe we will win this thing . . . "

Ogea allowed one run in five innings, and he ripped two hits. He drove in two runs. He limped into second base on those cranky knees with a double. Those were the first hits for Ogea since high school.

The Indians were 4-1 winners, defeating Brown for the second time.

Ogea had a 2-0 record with a 1.54 ERA in the World Series. He had the two hits. He had out-pitched Kevin Brown.

So when the media vote was held during the middle innings of Game 7 with the Indians leading, Ogea was selected as the MVP of the World Series.

They were preparing the MVP trophy for Ogea, and that all changed in the ninth inning of Game 7.

That ninth inning of Game 7 changed everything.

Ogea didn't know that after the 1997 World Series, his knees would become so painful that he'd never pitch well again. He was 5-4 with a 5.61 ERA for the Tribe in 1998. In 1999, he was 6-12 with a 5.63 ERA for Philadelphia. That was his last big-league season—done at the age of 28. He pitched through 2001 in the minors, but couldn't stay healthy.

"Chad is a great guy," said Hamilton. "He owns a landscaping company in Louisiana. I loved to watch him pitch because he was fearless. He had that great change-up. No stage was too big for him, the pressure never bothered him. It's just a shame that his legs gave him so many problems. No matter what they say, he was the MVP of that 1997 World Series."

Yes, the ninth inning of Game 7 changed everything.

The Indians had a 2-1 lead.

That's when the NBC television crew was setting up in the Tribe locker room. Those who worked in the clubhouse put plastic on the lockers. Champagne was rolled in. Everything was set for the scene where the Indians were to celebrate their first World Series title since 1948.

"They called us out of the stands [in the ninth]," said Hart. "They wanted Dick and me to be in the clubhouse when the players came in after the game was over and we won."

But the game wasn't over.

"I'm not leaving," said Hart. "I'm very superstitious. I'm staying right here."

Hart was told that he had to go to the locker room. It was a demand of Major League Baseball.

"They kept telling me that we were the winning team," said Hart. "But we hadn't won anything yet. I kept telling them that."

Hart and Jacobs went to Mike Hargrove's office in the clubhouse.

"Herb Score was doing the ninth inning, so I was sent down to the clubhouse to do post-game interviews," said Hamilton.

Hamilton saw them wheel in the World Series championship trophy.

"This doesn't feel right," Hamilton said.

Tribe public relations director Bob DiBiasio said, "They do this every World Series. You have to be prepared."

Hamilton also was afraid of the jinx.

The score was 2-1.

The Indians had runners on first and third base with one out in the top of the ninth. Grissom was at bat.

A fly ball. A ground ball to the right spot. A passed ball. An error. A wild pitch.

There are so many ways to score a runner from third base with one out.

Grissom hit a ground ball to Marlins shortstop Edgar Renteria. The Indians thought he'd throw to second base to try to start an inning-ending double-play. But Renteria threw home, and the catcher easily tagged out Sandy Alomar. That run never scored as Brian Giles flied out to end the inning.

And it was 2-1 in the bottom of the ninth.

"I was nervous," said Hart. "But we turned the ball over Jose Mesa. He had saved so many games for us . . ."

Mesa gave up a base hit to Moises Alou to start the inning.

He fanned Bobby Bonilla.

The next batter was Charles Johnson. Mesa had a 1-ball, 2-strike count on Johnson. Sandy Alomar called for a fastball. Mesa shook him off. Alomar called for it again. Mesa refused a second time. Alomar then called for a slider, not feeling very good about it. But that was what Mesa insisted on throwing.

Johnson lashed a single to right field, sending Alou to third base.

Alou would score the tying run on a sacrifice fly.

"That made it 2-2 and we were going into the 10th inning," said Hamilton. "I was running out of the clubhouse and back up to the booth because I was supposed to do the 10th inning. And they were taking that World Series trophy out of there so fast . . ."

A sense of doom hung over the Tribe.

They lost it 3-2 in the bottom of the 11th.

The details are painful. Charles Nagy, who was not supposed to pitch, ended up pitching because the Tribe was running out of pitchers. Tony Fernandez missed a ground ball at second base. Renteria's winning base hit was a line drive that tipped off the glove of Nagy.

"I can still see that hit," said Hamilton. "The ball almost floated, it wasn't hit that hard. I thought Charlie might catch it. And it ended up in center field, and that was the ballgame."

The Indians trudged into the dressing room. The trophy was gone. The plastic was taken off the lockers. There was another media vote for World Series MVP, and Chad Ogea was voted out. The winner was Livan Hernandez.

After the winning run crossed the plate, Dick Jacobs shook Hart's hand.

"John, it was a great season, you gave it your best," said Jacobs.

Jacobs waited until all the players were in the clubhouse. He went to each player, shook their hands, thanked them and said, "Great season, I'm proud of you. We'll get them next year."

Then Jacobs left.

Hart talked to some players, but everyone was distraught—not much was said worth remembering.

"When I look back at that season, I think that we probably should not have beaten the Yankees in the first round," said Hart. "And we probably shouldn't have beaten Baltimore [in the second round]. They probably were better teams. But to this day, I know we were the better team in the World Series. We should have beaten Florida."

Only, the Indians didn't.

"I've always felt bad for Jose Mesa for getting the blame" for the loss in Game 7, said Orel Hershiser. "And I felt terrible for Charlie [Nagy]. I had an awful World Series."

Hershiser was 0-2 with an 11.70 ERA in two World Series starts.

"That October was the greatest postseason baseball that I ever saw," said Hamilton. "It seemed every game was so wacky, so dramatic. I know this will sound like sour grapes, but I always felt like Florida bought that team. After Game 6, I went to South Beach with some friends. I had never been there. Can you imagine what Cleveland would be like with Game 7 coming? In South Beach, no one had a clue what was going on. I went to church the next morning, and no one said a word about the game that night. It was the day of Game 7 . . . and it was like no one cared."

It sure wasn't like that in Cleveland.

Years later, fans still care deeply about what happened in that 1997 World Series.

After the 1997 World Series, John Hart had a problem. His team was oh-so-close to finally winning a World Series.

Hart thought about his last four Tribe teams up to that point: 1994, 1995, 1996 and 1997.

Of them all, the 1997 team had the least talent. It had the lowest winning percentage (.534) of those four teams.

Suddenly, Hart had only one goal—one thing left to do.

Win the World Series.

All the steps needed to reach that last mountain had been taken.

"How do I keep this going?" Hart asked himself.

The type of trades that made the Tribe into a powerhouse would no longer be made. Hart recalled the deal for Sandy Alomar and Carlos Baerga, made when Hank Peters was still the team president.

"After 1997, we'd never make a trade like that," he said. "We couldn't."

Hart meant that he couldn't trade an established star such as Joe Carter for top prospects such as Baerga and Alomar.

"Or we couldn't trade for Kenny Lofton and then wait for him to develop," said Hart. "We couldn't wait for anything. The park was selling out every night. There were high expectations. We had to keep trying to win it all now."

So if Hart made a major deal, it had to bring major talent that was major-league proven.

And he made some good ones, such as Kenny Lofton for Marquis Grissom and David Justice before the 1997 season. Or trading Matt Williams to Arizona (where he wanted to be traded) for Travis Fryman. Williams was in the middle of a divorce and his kids lived in Phoenix. Hart made an excellent move signing Robbie Alomar as a free agent.

But none of it was enough to win a championship.

"There was a sense of desperation to try and get back to the World Series and win it this time." said Hamilton. "And we started to make some trades that we never should have made."

Hamilton meant the concept of "feeding the beast."

By 1998, the Indians had created a monster of expectations and frustrations.

Two teams went to the World Series—1995 and 1997.

The 1996 team won 99 games, but lost in the first round of the playoffs.

"I looked at our farm system and we had all these young guys coming," said Hart.

He meant Brian Giles, Richie Sexson, Sean Casey, Bartolo Colon and others.

"I knew that a good group was coming in the next three years," said Hart. "Do we play them like we did with Thome, Kenny, Manny and those guys in the early 1990s? And can we wait a year or two? Or do we trade some of these young guys now so we can keep the run going? One of our strengths was identifying young guys with great talent and winning attitudes—and giving them a chance to play."

But they no longer were willing to wait.

So they began to make trades that Hart knew deep in his baseball soul were bad deals.

But maybe, just maybe, one of the trades could get them back to the World Series once more . . . with one more chance to finally win a title for Cleveland.

The Indians knew they needed a lefty reliever when facing the Yankees, and that could happen again as it did in the first round of the 1997 playoffs.

Hart liked Pittsburgh's Ricardo Rincon. The Pirates liked Giles, a player Hart knew had a chance to be a starting outfielder for up to 10 years. But he had re-signed Lofton. He had Ramirez and David Justice in the outfield. He could spare Giles.

Rincon was nothing special in the bullpen.

In the next 11 years after the trade was made on Nov. 18, 1998, Giles batted .292 (.906 OPS) with 248 homers. That was a deal the Tribe regretted for a decade. How do you trade an impact hitting prospect in the outfield for a lefty reliever?

Desperation, that's how.

Right before opening day of 1998, Hart knew he needed another starting pitcher. He targeted Dave Burba of the Reds.

The price?

Sean Casey. The first baseman was one of the favorites of the Tribe front office. They loved his attitude and leadership ability, along with the fact he was a career .348 hitter in his first three minor-league seasons.

Burba was 57-35 for the Tribe in five years, a solid starter with a 4.65 ERA.

Casey batted .305 over the next eight seasons.

On and on it went.

In the middle of 2000, the Indians traded Richie Sexson (who hit 31 homers for them in 1999) to Milwaukee for Bob Wickman, Jason Bere and Steve Woodward. Wickman became a good closer for several years. The other two pitchers failed.

Sexson hit 248 homers after leaving the Indians. Marco Scutaro, an eventual 10-year MLB regular who was in the Indians' minor-league system at the time, also was added to that deal as a player to be named later.

"We traded away so many good young players in that period after 1997," said Hamilton. "In the long run, it cost us."

Then came the trade that Hart didn't make after the 1997 World Series.

He was bidding against Boston for a chance to acquire Pedro Martinez from Montreal.

"They wanted Colon and Jaret Wright," said Hart. "Remember, this was right after the 1997 World Series. Jaret had pitched Game 7. People were comparing him to a young Roger Clemens."

Martinez had won the 1997 National League Cy Young Award. He was 17-8 with a 1.90 ERA. He also was heading toward free agency, meaning a trade also meant a new contract.

And Hart knew that Jacobs wanted his 8 percent profit margin. He knew that other teams were starting to increase their payrolls because more new ballparks were opening. He also believed Wright and Colon would be anchors in the starting rotation for years.

"I just couldn't make that deal," said Hart.

Boston did, sending Carl Pavano and Tony Armas Jr. to the Expos. The Red Sox then signed Martinez to a 6-year, $75 million deal. He continued to build on his Hall of Fame career.

"It really was never the same after 1997," said Hart. "We had some very good teams after that, teams that I thought could win a World Series. But we never got back."

In 1998, they lost in the second round to New York. In 1999, they won the first two games against Boston, then lost the next three (Martinez being the hero) and were eliminated in the first round.

Hargrove was fired after the 1999 playoffs despite having a 97-65 record in the regular season.

In 2001, the Tribe returned to the playoffs, and lost again in the first round.

Dick Jacobs sold the Tribe after the 1999 season. Hart left after 2000 to take over the Texas Rangers.

"We kept it going for a long time, when you think about it," said Hamilton. "It was an amazing run."

The 1997 Season

[FANS WRITE IN]

The year of 1997 was a magical year for me. In 1997, I experienced what I've since referred to as the Tribe Trifecta: I attended the home opener, the All-Star Game and the World Series, all in the same season. Like any Cleveland sports fan, one of those memories was thoroughly disappointing for me (a back-breaking Game 5 loss to the Marlins in the World Series). However, no one can ever take away my experience at the All-Star Game. *—Bill Beaufait, Montgomery*

I think there is one moment that gets overlooked. I was able to attend Game 5 of the 1997 Division Series against the Yankees. I have never heard that stadium louder than when Jaret Wright walked out to the mound for the start of that game. He then mowed down the Yankees and the Tribe advanced to play Baltimore. *—Dan Kaminski, Aurora*

The best Tribe game that I ever witnessed in person was with my brother. It was Game 5 of the 1997 ALDS against the Yankees. We had nosebleed seats and three-fourths of the way down the first-base line. I went to many games during that era, but none were as lively as this one. We witnessed two fights during the game between Yankees and Indians fans. We got to see Jaret Wright at his pinnacle (although we didn't know it at the time). We were all thinking during the game how a kid this young could be doing all of this. As the final popout was in the air, all that I can remember was a forever unnamed person screaming at the top of his lungs, "We're gonna do it!" As that popup came down, it was a scene right out of "Major League." Total strangers were hugging, high-fiving and jumping for joy. Being from Cleveland, I've never witnessed a championship, but I imagine this is what it must feel like, only multiplied by 100. *—David Boros, Drumore, Pennsylvania*

In October 1997, my in-laws took my wife and me to see "Stomp" at E.J. Thomas Hall in Akron. It just happened to be the same day as Game 6 of the American League Championship Series. It seemed the baseball gods were smiling on me, as the game started at 4 p.m. and "Stomp" did not start until 8 p.m. It seemed perfect. Or so I thought. The game went into extra innings. Distraught, I got in the car to go see "Stomp." We got to our seats, and noticed that someone 10 rows in front of us had a handheld TV. Remember, this was before smart phones. So everyone in our section was turning and reaching in hopes of seeing his small screen. When Tony Fernandez hit the home run, the crowd at E.J. Thomas erupted, and they erupted even more a few minutes later when the Indians won the game and the series. To top it off, "Stomp" delayed the start of their show until the game was over. When they finally came out for their opening piece, one of the performers was waving an Indians banner, and of course the crowd went wild. It was so loud, you could have sworn you were at the game. *—Doug Merideth, Akron*

My favorite memory of the 1990s teams was the 1997 Divisional Series against the Yankees. The series came to Cleveland with the Yankees up two games to one. When we got to the game, fan enthusiasm seemed low. The game started off badly. The Tribe trailed 2-1 for most of the game and the Yankees brought in Mariano Rivera in the eighth inning. He got two quick outs, then Sandy Alomar stepped up to the plate. I was sitting on the third-base side and remember him hitting a drive to right field. Indians nemesis Paul O'Neill went to the fence, jumped as high as he could and came down in a heap. I couldn't tell if he caught it until the fans behind the right-field fence started cheering. Soon, the entire stadium erupted. The Indians won the game in the ninth inning on a bad-hop single. Then, they won the series the next day. It was the first time they had won a playoff series at home. *—Michael Nowak, Cleveland Heights*

In 1958, I went to my first Indians game with my mom, which we won 4-1 against the White Sox and Minnie Minoso hit a home run. I was hooked but the 1990s were special times. I was at the game on Friday, September 8, 1995 against the Orioles when we the clinched the Division Championship. The celebration and the raising of the Division flag brought tears to my eyes as I had never experienced that before. The World Series and attending Game 4 really meant something I had never seen, my Indians in a World Series. Well, two years later in 1997, I attended not one but two World Series games. Attending the games with my two sons gave special meaning to me as my own father never took me to an Indians game. One piece of advice I gave the boys was "Cherish these moments, you never know when you will see this again." Boy was I right and, yes, the 1990s were and still are special to me. *—Len Gold, Solon*

Sitting in the bleachers, I'll never forget Brian Giles grabbing that final out right in front of me to beat the hated Yankees in Game 5 of the Division Series in 1997. No one knew the wild ride we had coming those next three weeks that followed, but on that night, nothing else mattered. Everyone stayed and just . . . cheered. I remember nobody leaving their seats and just roaring for a good 10 minutes after that final out. Strangers hugged and high-fived each other. It was a far cry from my childhood that had the videoboard at Municipal encouraging fans to bang the empty seat next to them to make noise alongside John Adams and his drum. It was an electric environment I'll never forget. Every time I've gone since, I've made a point to look out where I sat that night to mentally relive it. *—Mark Hazelwood, Norwalk*

I was 7 when Jose Mesa blew the save. Asleep, my dad walked into my room to tell me what happened. With my limited frame of reference, I assumed that Cleveland making it to the World Series was something that happened with some frequency, like my birthday or Christmas. "Won't we get there next year?" I asked. "We'll see," he said. I don't need to illustrate the following 15-or-so years, but enjoying the highs—and lows—of the Cleveland Indians with my dad will be something I will always cherish. And it'd be really cool if we actually won the thing, sooner or later. *—Alex Lubetkin, New York City*

My mom nixed me staying up for Game 7. Probably for the best. I remember walking down the stairs the morning after Game 7, looking at the cover of the Akron Beacon Journal, and crying my eyes out. That team won 86 games. They weren't glamorous. They had the worst record that year of any year in the late '90s. But they captured my heart. I will love that team forever. *—Anthony Gatti, Cleveland Heights*

October 26, 1997. I sat with my dad in our family room watching Game 7 of the World Series. I was only 14 years old. My dad had a habit of muting the game on television and listening to the radio broadcast. That night was no different. It was also Herb Score's final broadcast. I wanted to commemorate the occasion, so I recorded it in its entirety onto cassette tapes. All 11 innings. Eight full tapes. All Indians fans know the outcome. I've never listened to the tapes. *—Timothy Horak, Columbus*

For the only time in my life, I was SURE we were winning Game 7 because of what had transpired the previous month. So when they didn't, it hurt so badly that I cried myself to sleep for 45 minutes. I was 17 and didn't know any better. Time and perspective have enabled me to look at the fun times of that month. I still can't watch a clip of Edgar Renteria, though, without cringing a little. *—Graig Fravel, Columbus*

My favorite Indians memory of this era, of course, is of them winning the 1997 World Series in the decisive Game 7 against Florida. I will never forget how manager Mike Hargrove, going against instinct, chose NOT to put closer Jose Mesa in the game and the Indians won by a run—their first title since 1948. I remember opening the champagne bottles, people dancing in the street, the ticker-tape parade on Public Square. ... And then I wake up. Even 16 years later, it feels like someone punched me in the gut. *—Dan Polster, Solon*

I had just moved into an apartment in Palo Alto when the 1997 World Series began. I'll never forget Game 7. At the end of the eighth inning, with the Tribe leading by a run and three outs away from our first championship in far too long, my friend Chip called, his voice filled with excitement. He said, "Just calling to see if you're there." Nothing else needed to be said, and no one wanted to jinx anything. We both knew what was in the process of taking place. Hopefully, Chip and I would talk again and celebrate a few minutes later. Of course, we know what happened—that conversation, unfortunately, never took place. It had been a remarkable and memorable playoff run, but it ended, as has happened far too often in Cleveland sports history, with a painful and hard-to-accept disappointment. *—Jim Miller, Yonkers, New York*

I went to the 1997 All-Star game in Cleveland, for my brother won two tickets for the lottery giveaway. I remember the entire stadium going absolutely bananas when Sandy Alomar lined a homer into the bleachers. After the game, I ran into my high school buddy Toby Soots, who had a signed jersey and bat with him. He had caught the homer by Alomar and exchanged it for some gear. Awesome. *—Jared Gruttadauria, Hermosa Beach, California*

Looking Back

By Tom Hamilton

How quickly it went by.

That's what I keep thinking about the Indians of the 1990s.

It really went by so fast—and when you are in the midst of it, you think it will never end.

There were so many great teams with so many great players. I don't think most of us fully appreciated it at the time. It felt like the winning happened overnight, starting in 1995. Part of the reason was the 1994 strike. That team was in contention for the playoffs, and I believe they were going to make it. It would have been good for the players and the fans to experience a real race for the playoffs. I remember people saying Montreal would have won it all had there been no strike, but no one was playing better than the Indians right as the strike came. That team kept getting more and more confident, and there was a sense that they were knocking on the door.

But then came the strike on Aug. 11. We were one game behind the White Sox in the Central Division, and in place to get a wild-card spot in the playoffs. Kenny Lofton would have been the American League MVP that year, at least in my opinion. He was hitting .349 and stole 60 bases in 112 games. It was a great year, and it's lost in time because of the strike.

Instead of knocking on the door of the playoffs, it was slammed on Kenny and that 1994 team.

Then came 1995, and the Indians just kicked down the door.

When baseball came back in 1995, it seemed almost everyone was bitter about the strike—except the Indians and their fans. A lot of other teams went to spring training wondering what was going on, and how they'd play. But when the Indians reported to Winter Haven, their attitude was: "We got short-changed last year. Nobody realized how good we were. Now they'll see."

The Indians really peaked in 1995. Not only was that team so talented, but it was so unified. They hit the ground running. They couldn't wait to get to the park and play. While so much of baseball was stuck in the mud left over from the strike, the Indians were playing like nothing was going to stop them. The only question mark on that team was the closer. And once they figured out that Jose Mesa could close, there were no question marks.

Just think about those lineups:

- Kenny Lofton
- Omar Vizquel
- Carlos Baerga
- Albert Belle
- Eddie Murray
- Jim Thome
- Manny Ramirez
- Paul Sorrento
- Sandy Alomar

Think about it: Paul Sorrento batted eighth and hit 25 homers. Manny hit seventh. Sandy Alomar batted ninth. That team was 100-44.

When you left the ballpark after a loss that season, you said, "I can't believe they got beat!" It was like we expected them to go unbeaten—they were that good.

You always felt that no matter what the score or what had happened earlier in the game, they were going to find a way to come back.

The games were parties. The fans were in such a great mood. The national media would come to town and rave about the atmosphere in the ballpark.

They'd say, "This is the *loudest* park in baseball."

And it really was the loudest.

And you had a sense that the Indians weren't going to just beat the other team, they were out to devour the competition. In 1995, it was a playoff atmosphere for every game. It was something I've never seen anywhere else in all my years covering baseball, before or since.

We had 22,000 fans for batting practice. I'm talking about 22,000 to watch batting practice—and the stands were packed for the game. I remember some games in old Tiger Stadium when the Indians would come out to stretch before the game and 10,000 Tribe fans would give them a standing ovation. This was in Detroit! And it was before the game! The Tiger players would be looking around and wondering, "What just happened?" It was the same way in Chicago. People planned their vacations around watching the Tribe in nearby road cities, because it was so hard to get tickets for home games.

Now, all of this sounds so hard to believe.

But back then, it was life with the Tribe. It was like traveling with The Beatles when they were hot. There were times in Baltimore when we couldn't get through the lobby from the bus because so many fans were waiting for us. All these fans had flown in from Cleveland to watch us in Baltimore.

I doubt any of us really appreciated how unique this was—and how it probably would never be repeated. So many other teams and cities built new ballparks after we did, but no one else ever sold out for more than five years and went to the playoffs in their first five full seasons after the park opened.

Know what is amazing?

There is a generation of Tribe fans who grew up in the 1990s with those teams and figured, "We'll go to the playoffs every year." They weren't raised thinking that 70 wins was a decent season and 5,000 was the norm at the ballpark, like most Tribe fans. All they knew was the new ballpark, the sellouts and the winning—the perfect baseball storm.

That generation caught baseball lightning in a bottle and fell hard in love with the team.

Wendy and I had our third child in 1995 and our fourth in 1997. She'd tell me how she'd take the kids out in a stroller and walk around the neighborhood on some of those summer nights. She didn't need to have a radio with her. From block-to-block, she'd hear the game. Someone, somewhere always had it on. It seemed nearly everyone was flying a Tribe flag. So many had on Tribe T-shirts and caps and jerseys. It was like Cleveland had become one big college town.

Now looking back, losing the 1997 World Series was even more devastating than I realized at the time. It created a sense of desperation, a feeling that the window was closing on a chance to win a World Series. That led to some trades that the Indians normally would not have made—like giving up Brian Giles, Sean Casey and Richie Sexson for pitching. There was this foregone conclusion that we'd win the division, so how do we build a club to beat the Yankees and get back to the World Series?

In the early 1990s, it was, "Let's build the best team we can to win the division. Maybe that means giving a few kids a chance to play and living with their mistakes." But then it became, "We've got to win it all, and we've got to do it right now!"

During all those years, there were so many times when I'd be in Mike Hargrove's office and Grover would say something like, "One of the hardest things to do in pro sports is to win a division title. It's a six-month ordeal. There are so many things that can go wrong."

Grover felt the burden of winning a World Series. He knew that people took winning the Central and going to the playoffs for granted. He also knew that you only get so many shots at a World Series.

Now, I can look back and see what a crapshoot baseball can be in October. In 1997, we won only 86 games. I thought our teams in 1996, 1998 and 1999 were better. Maybe even the team in 2000, which missed the playoffs. In 2000, Gene Michael was scouting for the Yankees. He told me that "there's only one club that we don't want to face in the playoffs—that's the Indians. They are playing like the best team in the league right now."

But we missed the playoffs on the last day of the season.

We got hot at the right time in 1997, and we were cold at the wrong time in some of the other seasons. In 2000, we just missed the playoffs despite winning 90 games. We were only 44-42 at the All-Star break, and then finished 46-30. It just wasn't enough.

I think that all of us connected with the team thought that we'd get back to at least one more World Series after 1997—but it never happened.

Now I can look back and I remember what former Yankee Manager Joe Torre told me: "You guys have a great offense and you'll always make a run. But in the playoffs, it usually comes down to pitching."

We never had the typical No. 1 and No. 2 starters to match up with the best two starters on most other playoff teams. Joe Torre knew he had better pitching than we did. There were some games in October if we didn't get the big bang—the home run—we didn't score.

But just think about those teams and all the fun we had.

I've heard some fans say, "I just need to win one championship before I die!"

OK, so if we win a title, it's OK to die now? Who wants to base their life on that?

I know it's disappointing that we never won a World Series. I took it very hard in 1997. But I'll also take those six Octobers in seven years that we had from 1995 to 2001 and I'd love to relive all of that again. And I'd like to watch us build the team again like we did in the early 1990s as we moved into the new ballpark. It is about the journey, and those were great times. Remember how much fun we had during those summers, how the entire city was caught up in the Indians? That had a big impact in helping people nationally have a better view of Cleveland.

Yes, I miss those days.

But I also still love doing the games on the radio. I want fans to feel like they're at the ballpark when they listen. I still carry around a letter that I received from a fan years ago. It's in Braille, and it talks about how I'm the eyes of the fans who are listening. I'm there to paint the picture. Let them know how the weather is, where the wind is blowing, what the uniforms look like. It's not just a ground ball, it's a two-hopper, or it's a roller, or a really hard-hit shot. I still get excited going to the games. I think about what the great Herb Score said, how some nights you will see something you've never seen before—no matter how many games you have watched.

I know doing the games in the 1990s really helped me because fans still identify with that period. My goodness, they still wear the old jerseys from those days, that's how much those teams mean to them. What a great, great period that was for all of us!

Acknowledgements

The authors would like to thank Jacob Rosen and Mark Matthews for their great work with the fan emails and Jacob's keen eye on the manuscript. David Gray is a terrific publisher, and thanks for his patience with this project. His staff of Rob Lucas, Jane Lassar, Chris Andrikanich and Frank Lavallo are a tremendous support. Thanks to John Luttermoser for copyediting and Eric Broder for proofreading. Mark Shapiro and Curtis Danburg were a big help from the Indians.

For more information and samples from
other Terry Pluto books, visit:

www.TerryPluto.com

OTHER BOOKS OF INTEREST . . .

The Curse of Rocky Colavito

A Loving Look at a Thirty-Year Slump

Terry Pluto

A baseball classic. No sports fans suffered more miserable teams for more seasons than Indians fans of the 1960s, '70s, and '80s. Here's a fond and often humorous look back at "the bad old days" of the Tribe. The definitive book about the Indians of that generation, and a great piece of sports history writing.

"The year's funniest and most insightful baseball book."
– Chicago Tribune

Our Tribe

A Baseball Memoir

Terry Pluto

A son, a father, a baseball team. Sportswriter Terry Pluto's memoir tells about growing up and learning to understand a difficult father through their shared love of an often awful baseball team. Baseball can be an important bridge across generations, sometimes the only common ground. This story celebrates the connection.

"A beautiful, absolutely unforgettable memoir." – Booklist

Joe Tait: It's Been a Real Ball

Stories from a Hall-of-Fame Sports Broadcasting Career

Terry Pluto, Joe Tait

Legendary broadcaster Joe Tait is like an old family friend to three generations of Cleveland sports fans. This book celebrates the inspiring career of "the Voice of the Cleveland Cavaliers" with stories from Joe and dozens of fans, colleagues, and players. Hits the highlights of a long career and also uncovers some touching personal details.

"An easy, fun book to read and will surely bring back good memories for Cleveland sports fans who listened to Tait's trademark calls since 1970."
– 20SecondTimeout.com

Read samples at **www.grayco.com**